TYRANNY
FROM PLATO
TO TRUMP

TYRANNY FROM PLATO TO TRUMP

Fools, Sycophants, and Citizens

Andrew Fiala

ROWMAN & LITTLEFIELD
Lanham • Boulder • New York • London

Published by Rowman & Littlefield
An imprint of The Rowman & Littlefield Publishing Group, Inc.
4501 Forbes Boulevard, Suite 200, Lanham, Maryland 20706
www.rowman.com

86-90 Paul Street, London EC2A 4NE

British Library Cataloguing in Publication Information Available

Library of Congress Cataloging-in-Publication Data

Names: Fiala, Andrew, 1966– author.
Title: Tyranny from Plato to Trump : fools, sycophants, and citizens / Andrew
  Fiala.
Description: Lanham, Maryland : Rowman & Littlefield, 2022. | Includes
  bibliographical references and index.
Identifiers: LCCN 2021035440 (print) | LCCN 2021035441 (ebook) | ISBN
  9781538160480 (cloth) | ISBN 9781538160497 (epub)
Subjects: LCSH: Despotism. | Trump, Donald, 1946– | Political culture—
  United States.
Classification: LCC JC381 .F524 2022 (print) | LCC JC381 (ebook) | DDC
  321.9—dc23
LC record available at https://lccn.loc.gov/2021035440
LC ebook record available at https://lccn.loc.gov/2021035441

Philosophy is the midwife of wisdom.

—Plato, *Theatetus*

CONTENTS

PREFACE

> Tyrants would have cause to tremble if reason were to become the rule of duty.
>
> —Mary Wollstonecraft, *A Vindication of the Rights of Woman*[1]

We recently witnessed the failure of a would-be tyrant who attempted to subvert the rule of law and overturn the result of a democratic election. The American system was pushed toward a cliff. But constitutional guardrails slowed things down. Conscientious people pumped the brakes. And the system held. This was a lesson of tyranny averted. We should take stock and learn what worked—and what needs improvement—in our system and in our souls. And while the American crisis of 2020–2021 was frightening, a broader historical perspective helps. The threat of tyranny is common. But the cure is well known. It involves virtuous citizenship and a stable constitution.

The tyrant's rise and fall is an old story. Consider:

A plague descended on the nation as the tyrant ranted and raved, refusing to admit that he was the cause of the nation's ills. The tyrant lived in a fantasy world of his own creation. He refused to accept what was said by those who spoke truth to power. Instead, he listened only to those who flattered his ego and encouraged him in his delusion. The nation suffered profoundly under the tyrant and his plague. He tried to blame the plague on some other scapegoat. Members of the public were seduced by the tyrant and his sycophants to sacrifice everything on behalf of a lie. Violence erupted. When the awful truth was finally revealed, the chorus reached a tragic conclusion.

> Our lives are mere shadows.
> Happiness fades away to nothing.
> The tyrant's fall reminds us that
> No human creation lasts forever.
> Plague and trouble make victims of us all.

> (*Oedipus The Tyrant*, lines 1190ff)[2]

This is the story of Oedipus. It is also the story of Donald Trump. The players in this tragedy are found throughout history. They are the tyrant, his sycophants, and the moronic masses. The tyrant rages. The sycophants simper. The masses cheer and howl, fight and die. As the plague spreads, good things fall apart and decency suffers. This tragedy brings with it the risk of despair.

The good news is that the cure for this dis-ease is well known. It is, as Mary Wollstonecraft suggested, *reason*. Life in general must be made reasonable. This means we need a reasonable constitution as well as wise and virtuous citizens. Wisdom and virtue work together to prevent tyranny. Plato and Aristotle knew this, as did John Adams. Adams wrote in his diary when he was vice president of the United States, "Tyranny can scarcely be practiced upon a virtuous and wise people."[3]

But wisdom, virtue, and reason are often lacking. Wollstonecraft laments the fact that "tyranny, in whatever part of society it rears its brazen front, will ever undermine morality."[4] Tyranny is not only a political problem. It is also a moral and spiritual one. It afflicts our souls, as well as churches, businesses, and family life. Wollstonecraft's important contribution was to argue for the liberation of women in an era when women were oppressed by the tyranny of patriarchal families. Wollstonecraft was a contemporary of Thomas Jefferson and other thinkers of the eighteenth-century Enlightenment. Despite their claims to enlightenment, the heroes of this tradition suffered from moral blindness—as we all do. Jefferson's words inspired a revolution against the tyrant King George III. The words inscribed in the Jefferson Memorial state: "I have sworn upon the altar of god eternal hostility against every form of tyranny over the mind of man."[5] But Jefferson owned slaves, one of the most obvious forms of tyranny in the world.

We must all be careful of our blind spots. Reason aims to shed light by holding up a mirror. The remedy for tyranny is philosophical self-examination. This is an ongoing process, not a panacea. Each generation must seek to make progress on the path to enlightenment. The good news is that we have made progress. Women were liberated and slavery was abolished.

The idea that wisdom and virtue can cure tyranny predates the Enlightenment by over two thousand years. It was the solution proposed by the ancient Greeks, who give us the very language we will employ here, words such as *tyranny*, *sycophancy*, *democracy*, and *political philosophy*. The Greeks emphasized the need for virtue among the players in the political drama. Modern thinkers built upon this and emphasized the need for a rational system of government that prevents tyranny. Tragedy is avoided when leaders and citizens are virtuous, and when a stable constitutional system guarantees individual rights, divides power, and creates checks and balances.

We have known the cure for thousands of years. But the disease is genetic. Every generation or so, the conditions conspire to bring together an ugly cast of characters that includes a tyrant, his sycophants, and the moronic fools who cheer him on. Every so often a new plague breaks out. Albert Camus wrote, during the plague of Nazism, that the plague is never exterminated: it merely lies dormant, waiting for a lapse in attention.[6] That is why we must remain eternally vigilant in identifying and preventing the disease. Safeguards can be hard-wired into the system. But the tendency remains. Tyrannical people seek power. Sycophants suck up to them. The foolish masses cheer it on.

This is a political problem and also a spiritual one. Plato suggested that there is an analogy linking politics and psychology. Each of us can be tyrannical, inflated with ambition and pride. We can be sycophantic, sucking up to the powerful and ingratiating ourselves in cunning ways to those in power. And there are moments when we behave foolishly and embrace ignorance. There are tyrants in our families, sycophants in our places of work, and fools among our friends and relations.

The Trump years provide a potent example of this perennial problem. The cast is not new, even if the plot and setting are different. Today's drama involves fake news, political polarization, and a global pandemic. But the underlying story and its characters would have been familiar to Plato, Sophocles, Shakespeare, Jefferson, Madison, and Mary Wollstonecraft.

In this book I show how the tragic trio appears throughout the history of the Western tradition. A number of important authors have discussed the problem of tyranny. The unique contribution of the present volume is my account of the three characters who play a role in tyranny: the tyrant, the sycophant, and the foolish moron. This tragic trio is implicit in many discussions of tyranny. But no other account of tyranny that I know of highlights the fact that tyranny requires the company of fools and flatterers.

I consider two traditional remedies for this problem: a spiritual remedy and an institutional one. These remedies are well known. Again, my unique contribution is to understand these remedies in relation to the tyrannical trio. The spiritual or psychological cure is aimed at individual virtue and wisdom. Plato and the Greeks thought that education could create virtue and wisdom among the people. Enlightenment thinkers shared this belief in the power of education. The institutional solution is a system of checks and balances and a division of power. Aristotle pointed in this direction. But this remedy is really a modern invention, a product of the European Enlightenment's deep-seated concern to prevent tyranny. John Locke explained, "wherever law ends, tyranny begins."[7] James Madison believed that concentration of power was "the very definition of tyranny" (*Federalist* 47).[8] Democratic constitutions, human rights, the separation of powers, and the rule of law create structural impediments that limit the damage that can be done by tyrants, sycophants, and fools.

Neither of these solutions is perfect, and there is still work to be done. Recent history shows us this. We need to strengthen constitutional safeguards while carrying on the work of moral and civic education. My goal here is not to call for a return to Plato, Locke, or Madison. Rather, I turn to the past in order to imagine the way forward. It is important to criticize blind spots in the tradition and to consider non-canonical authors. Perennial wisdom must be developed in new and enlightening ways.

Authors like Wollstonecraft expose tyranny in gender and the family. She explained how tyranny breeds a slavish, stupid, and sycophantic social world. She helps us understand how tyranny infantilizes us. Patriarchal families teach women and children to be suck-ups and morons. Wollstonecraft's solution is to empower and educate women, as well as men. This inclusive vision is a crucial part of the solution. It was missing in Greek thought and in the thought of the American founders.

The Greeks permitted slavery, which is an obvious form of tyranny. So too did the American founders. This is why we cannot simply return to Plato or the Enlightenment. Rather, we should study this tradition and learn from its critics. Frederick Douglass is one of those critics. Douglass had a deep understanding of tyranny and sycophancy. He said, in the 1860s during the American Civil War, "The tyrant wants no law above his own will, no associates but men of his own stamp of baseness."[9] Tyranny breeds sycophancy because the tyrant will tolerate no one other than a suck-up who has debased himself. Douglass thought this helped to explain the corrupting nature of slavery, that peculiarly tyrannical institution. The tyrannical slave master's viciousness is facilitated by the yes-men and sycophants who benefit from the tyrant's rule.

And on the sidelines, cheering and jeering, is the foolish mob. Philosophers have long lamented the moronic masses and the conforming crowd. Ralph Waldo Emerson pinpointed the problem when he said, "Society wants to be amused."[10] This is the root of a culture of superficiality and celebrity. Emerson said the masses are "rude, lame, unmade, and pernicious in their demands and influence." We might say, as the existentialists do, that the "the crowd is untruth." The primary concern of the masses is emotion and entertainment—not truth, virtue, or wisdom. Hannah Arendt took this idea further in her critique of twentieth-century totalitarianism. She explained how propaganda functions in mob mentality and how "the mob always will shout for the strong man and great leader."[11] She reminds us that the mob is not shy about celebrating violence, crime, and evil.[12] One of Arendt's most disturbing observations is that the "dangerous fairy-tales" of racism and anti-Semitism are entertainments for bored people.[13]

The solution to these problems is an inclusive vision of enlightenment. The power to resist tyranny comes from educated and enlightened citizens. We also need institutional safeguards to prevent would-be tyrants from consolidating power. In both cases we need a vision and approach that includes those who were previously excluded from fully participating in social and political life.

I am a professor of philosophy and the humanities with a special interest in ethics and political philosophy. My studies remind me that nothing lasts forever and that virtue is rare. Athenian democracy was short lived. The Roman republic became a brutal empire. Socrates and Jesus were executed. The American founders owned slaves. And Germany, the home of Kant and Hegel, also adopted Hitler. History reminds us that tyrants rise, the powerful lack virtue, and the masses are often ignorant and indifferent. As a citizen of the United States, I have been fascinated and also terrified to watch tragedy come to life in recent years. As things unfolded, I have reflected on the history of the Western tradition, trying to glean some insight that can be applied to contemporary affairs. This book is an attempt to uncover perennial wisdom and push it forward. I remain hopeful that we can contain the worst disorders of the human soul.

The occasion for this book is the Trump era. I provide a number of examples of how this era brought tragedy to life. Luckily, Trump remained a would-be tyrant. The good news is that the American political system prevented full-fledged tyranny from taking root. There are sycophants and ignorant people among Trump's supporters. But there have always been such folks in all parties and at all times. Each of us contains the tragic trio. That is why each of us can benefit from virtue, wisdom, and enlightenment.

This book has three parts. In part I, I survey tyranny broadly. In chapter 1, I connect the Trump era to Plato. In chapter 2, I situate this problem in its largest context, viewing tyranny as a theological problem, arguing that the tyrant wants to be a god. Chapter 3 offers an overview of the tragic trio—and introduces a fourth character: the philosophical midwife who seeks to enlighten. Chapter 4 considers the question of how and whether we can use history as a guide in making recommendations for improving the world.

In part II, I examine each of our trio of characters in detail. Chapter 5 focuses in detail on tyranny and the vices of pride and ambition. Chapter 6 focuses specifically on the moronic masses and the dangers of stupidity. Chapter 7 discusses the problem of sycophancy in detail, including the problems of cunning and complicity.

The book concludes in part III, with two chapters offering remedies to our problem: a chapter about moral education and the citizen-philosopher (chapter 8) and a chapter about the wisdom of the constitutional system (chapter 9). A short summary of the argument is provided in chapter 10.

The book includes two appendixes. Appendix A analyzes Donald Trump's writings and speeches, in search of Trump's moral vocabulary. The results are disappointing. Appendix B provides a reference guide for readers, listing historical figures and events. You might want to consult that as you read.

This book need not be read in linear fashion. Each chapter is more or less self-sufficient. My hope is that when you are done reading, you will have a greater appreciation of the wisdom of the tradition, the danger of this tragic trio, and the possibility of making progress.

I

HISTORICAL, POLITICAL, AND THEOLOGICAL CONTEXTS

❶

FROM TRUMP TO
PLATO AND BACK AGAIN

Lack of wisdom is the worst plague.

—Sophocles, *Antigone* (1050)

Would-be tyrants are aided in their ambition to consolidate power by cunning sycophants and the foolish mob. Constitutional limitations and moral education can prevent the plague of tyranny from taking root. The case of Donald Trump teaches us this lesson. We also learn this from Plato and the Greeks. The Trump era sheds light on perennial issues. And ancient philosophy can help us make sense of current events.

TRUMP: 2021

Let's begin at the end of the Trump presidency, as a pandemic rages and the U.S. Capitol is under assault. The scene is one of American carnage; a broken nation has been left in disorder by a would-be tyrant who denies reality. A coterie of sycophants has brought the nation to this dark place by offering a raft of bogus arguments that flatter the president's ego, while the mob hoots and hollers, convinced by the president and his handlers that their man had won an election that he actually lost. Among the mob are those who believe the unbelievable QAnon conspiracy theories: that members of the opposing party worship Satan while practicing ritual pedophilia, and that the news media and the intelligentsia are enemies of the people colluding to destroy Trump, who is the savior of the nation.[1] These conspiracy theories are based upon a profound distrust of science that is manifest in the bizarre claim that governmental attempts to prevent the spread of COVID-19 were aimed at driving Trump from power. This conspiracy theory holds that scientists, the media, and the Democratic party used COVID-19 to destroy the economy, discredit the president, and change election rules in a way that allowed for purported cheating in the November 2020 election.[2]

On January 6, 2021, President Donald J. Trump gathered his supporters at a rally in front of the White House where he urged them to disrupt the U.S. Congress's procedural vote to confirm the results of the 2020 presidential election. With his urging, the masses marched down Pennsylvania Avenue and assaulted the Capitol. Protesters broke through police barricades, occupied congressional offices, and desecrated the halls of Congress. A protester was shot dead during the riot. She was a believer in the QAnon conspiracy theory, who once said that Trump was "one of God's greatest warriors."[3] Eventually the police restored order in the Capitol and Congress voted to affirm the result of the Electoral College, bringing the Trump era to an ignoble end.

Some called the events of January 6 a coup. Others called it an insurgency. This terminology is heavily politicized. Some Trump supporters even go so far as to maintain that the riot of January 6 was a "hoax," as one Michigan legislator did.[4] A poll taken in the spring of 2021 showed that one-fifth of Republicans believed that Antifa (a left-wing anti-Trump group) was to blame for the riot.[5] As we'll see throughout this book, polarization is a significant problem when it comes to accusations of tyranny, sycophancy, and stupidity. These terms are often used as rhetorical cudgels. Each side accuses the other, and the terms are divorced from reality. As we shall see, one obvious solution is to seek common ground in shared definitions and descriptions of tyranny.

As coups and insurgencies go, the January 6 event was minor and ineffective. The institutions of power in the United States proved to be fairly resistant to the mob. But despite the lameness of this insurgency, there is no doubt that the president of the United States incited his supporters to riot and urged them to assail the U.S. Capitol. And while

Trump's minions were marching and shouting in the streets, Trumpian sycophants in the halls of Congress were pushing Trump's false narrative about a stolen election. Among the sycophants who disgraced themselves during this sordid affair, none was more prominent than Rudy Giuliani, the former mayor of New York City. Prior to Trump's inflammatory address on January 6, Giuliani took the stage in front of the White House and bizarrely said, "Let's have trial by combat." The crowd cheered in response.[6]

The events of January 6 were not unprecedented, even though the riot in the Capitol took things to another level. Throughout the Trump years, we witnessed Trump play the part of a would-be tyrant. I say "would-be" because the constitutional system prevented him from consolidating power in a full-blown tyranny, as we'll see in more detail in later chapters. On the stage with Trump, we often saw sycophants like Giuliani urging him on and serving as a go-between linking Trump and the mob. But as I argue in this book, prior to Trump, Giuliani, and company, there has been a long line of predecessors. There have always been tyrants (would-be or otherwise), sycophants, and the moronic masses. This story has been replayed throughout history—from ancient Greece to the present. Before turning to the Greek precedent, let's pause for a moment to highlight two key points that we will return to throughout our discussion.

First, political tyranny is exorbitant, excessive, and extraordinary. The events of January 6 sought to disrupt the ordinary, rule-governed procedures of the American electoral system. Tyranny is a kind of rule breaking and norm busting. As Locke says, "Where law ends, tyranny begins." This makes it, by definition, criminal. But the tyrant believes his criminality is justified. The tyrant is not willing to be constrained by the rules because he believes himself to be exceptional. He thinks he is above the law and that he has the right to break the rules. The sycophant encourages him to believe that he is exceptional. And the adulation of the mob confirms him in this belief. The mob and the sycophant flatter the ego of the tyrant. At the same time, the tyrant flatters the ego of the mob. One of the strangest things said on January 6 was the president's message to his supporters as he half-heartedly disavowed the violence he had unleashed. "We love you," he said to the mob, "You're very special."[7] Not only does the tyrant believe he is exceptional, but he also convinces his supporters to believe the same thing about themselves.

This helps to explain the belief in conspiracy theories among the mob: they believe that they have special access to secret information.

Sometimes sycophants provide a political theory that justifies the tyrant's sense of his exceptionality. This could be based in a theory of sovereignty, such as Carl Schmitt's, that emphasizes the sovereign power to make and break the law.[8] But often this is just a marketing ploy intended to rationalize the tyrant's will-to-power. Indeed, the sycophant must be able to argue in multiple registers. When speaking to the legal authorities, the sycophant deploys legal and political arguments. But when inflaming the crowd (and soothing the ego of the tyrant), the sycophant must employ a different, more emotional language. Throughout all of this is the assumption that rules do not apply, laws should not constrain, and the tyrant and his friends have a right to make exceptions and commit crimes.

The second point to be emphasized here at the outset is that all of this is facilitated by emotional language that is often linked to violence. The tyrant's exceptionalism puts him at odds with the dispassionate rationality of the legal system. This leads to violence because there are no legal remedies for resolving disputes about the legal system itself. The sycophant likely understands this theoretically: he formulates arguments and rationalizations that seek to justify violence. But the tyrant grasps the power of violence directly in implicitly feeling the energy of the crowd and playing a game of incitement. Appeals to violence are ultimately emotional. The tyrant threatens and cajoles, berates and insults. The mob responds to these emotional appeals with roars and shouts and violent action.

We saw this unfold on January 6. Giuliani and another legal expert, John Eastman, provided some technical arguments that tried to lend credibility to their unfounded claims about a stolen election. But Giuliani's remark about trial by combat primed the emotions of the crowd. When Trump took the stage, he further enflamed the mob. Here is an excerpt from the end of his speech, which shows how Trump incited the crowd.

> We fight. We fight like Hell and if you don't fight like Hell, you're not going to have a country anymore. Our exciting adventures and boldest endeavors have not yet begun. . . . So we're going to walk down Pennsylvania Avenue, and we're going to the Capitol and we're going to try and give. . . . The Democrats are hopeless. They're never voting for anything, not

even one vote. But we're going to try and give our Republicans, the weak ones, because the strong ones don't need any of our help, we're going to try and give them the kind of pride and boldness that they need to take back our country. So let's walk down Pennsylvania Avenue.[9]

Admittedly, Trump never said, "Let's take up arms and invade the Capitol." There is some plausible deniability here. Later in the day, Trump called for peace and asked the rioters to go home. As I said and will argue throughout this book, Trump is only a would-be tyrant. But the recipe for violence is here. Giuliani gave some legitimacy to the claim that the election was stolen. And then Trump talked about pride, boldness, and the need to fight like hell. The masses responded to his message and took off down Pennsylvania Avenue. The insurgents burst into the Capitol. The violence that resulted was predictable.

Thankfully there are educated citizens and virtuous public servants in the United States, as well as a separation of powers and respect for the rule of law. The would-be tyrant was never able to become a full-fledged tyrant. And we are now able to learn some important moral and political lessons from the Trump era.

PLATO: 375 BCE

These lessons are not new. They are at least as old as Plato and Sophocles. The Greeks gave us the language I am employing here. Words such as *tyrant*, *sycophant*, and *moron* come to us from Plato and Sophocles. We also find a remedy for this problem in these ancient sources in the ideal of philosophy, virtue, wisdom, and the law.

In Plato's *Republic*, tyranny occurs when the masses submit to an unscrupulous demagogue who uses the mob to support his own criminality. Plato routinely condemns fools, idiots, and morons along with tyrants and sycophants. He has a number of unflattering names for the masses, calling them the "motley multitude," the "ignorant mob," and even the "great beast." Plato lambasts the sycophants and sophists who suck up to the tyrant and egg on the mob. Much of his work can be read as a critique of tyrants and of the tyrannical personality type. Plato had good reason to be critical of tyrants, sycophants, and morons. Plato was imprisoned by the tyrant king of Syracuse and sold into slavery. And

Plato's beloved teacher, Socrates, was linked to the tyrannical personality of Alcibiades, an Athenian golden boy who betrayed Athens during war. Socrates was eventually executed as a result of a trial in which the sycophants of Athens persuaded the moronic masses that Socrates was an enemy of the people.

Lest you take offense at the word *moron*, I use this as a technical term. The Greek term *moros* is often translated as "fool." A moron or fool lacks wisdom and virtue. The moron is ignorant—blind in a metaphorical sense—and often willfully so. In Sophocles's great tragedy, *Oedpius Tyrannos* (*Oedipus the Tyrant*), there is a heated discussion between the tyrant and the blind prophet Tiresias (lines 430 and following). Oedipus accuses the blind prophet of speaking *moronically* (often translated as "foolishly"). Tiresias responds by saying that even though he is blind, he sees better than the tyrannical king: it is the tyrant who is foolish and blind, and who is really the moron. A similar contrast between wisdom and foolishness is found in the Bible. In the book of Isaiah (chapter 23), the problems of the world are said to hinge upon the wickedness of scoundrels and the stupidity of fools. When Paul writes in 1 Corinthians that the foolishness of God is wiser than the wisdom of men, he uses the root word for *moron*. He suggests that moronic things are used by God to show the foolishness of human wisdom.

Moronic fools are tragic characters because they have the potential to overcome their stupidity. This is a common human flaw. Instead of seeking wisdom, we allow ourselves to become stupid and vicious. We foolishly close our eyes to things we should be able to see. In Sophocles's other great tragedy, *Antigone*, another tyrant, Creon, accuses Antigone of crime. Antigone responds (line 470) by saying that while Creon has accused her of being foolish, in reality he is the moron. In response, she says (in my own translation), "If I look like a moron to you, that's only because you are the real moron."

And thus we encounter the problem of polarization: each person accuses the other of being foolish or moronic. The same is true for the accusation of tyranny. Those in power are accused of being tyrannical. And those who want to grab power away from a tyrant are accused by the tyrant of behaving tyrannically.

In modern usage the word *tyrant* is a pejorative accusation. But this is a shift in meaning from the ancient origin of the term. At one point, the Greek word *tyrannos* simply meant *king*.[10] The Greek word *tyrannos* began its history as a name for any ruler.[11] Eventually it came to mean an evil, despotic ruler who seizes and maintains power by violence. In some cases, a tyrant simply slaughters his way into power. But outright violence and brutality are not effective without a more subtle form of political power. The masses need to be convinced that violence and brutality are somehow justified. And more importantly, the masses must be persuaded to put their own bodies on the line—to fight and die on behalf of the tyrant. It is the sycophants who help to accomplish this, as the go-between who translates the will of the tyrant into the movement of the crowd.

In contexts outside of the political arena, where tyranny is also a problem—in families, in civil society, or in business—outright violence is not the primary force. Rather, the subtle tyrant coerces and persuades by way of tricks and contrivances. The goal is not truth but power. Tyrants, sycophants, and morons are not restrained by consistency or by the facts of the world. This means that wild conspiracy theories will be entertained and a fantasy world will emerge in which values are upended and virtue is destroyed. Wrong becomes right. Falsehood masquerades as truth. And stupidity rules the day.

In the end, the masses *willingly* join in with the tyrant. The tyrant need never lift a fist or aim a weapon. It is the burgeoning and angry mob, inflamed by the tyrant, that is violent and dangerous. But the question to be considered here is how the mob is formed to begin with and how it becomes so angry. The answer has to do with foolish emotion. The morons are manipulated by the tyrant and often willingly allow themselves to be manipulated. The fools become the tyrant's compliant mob because they don't think things through, acting primarily on anger, fear—and even out of love of the tyrant. The mob is outraged or in love; but also often merely bored and looking for pleasure and excitement. As Plato suggested, it is licentiousness and appetite that lends itself to exploitation by the tyrant and his sycophants.

In the background are the sycophants, who shuttle between the moronic masses and the tyrannical autocrat. The sycophants connive and collude, whisper, cover up, and confuse. In Greek, the word *sycophant* has an etymology that links it to something obscene and degenerate.[12] A sycophant or *syko-phantes* is one who shows (*phanos*) a fig (*sykos*). Some authors claim that this has to do with revealing shameful things that ought not be revealed (e.g., genitalia). But "revealing a fig" may also have something to do with having access to secret information or with purported access to secrets, which fuel conspiracy theories. The sycophant uses rumor and innuendo to manipulate things.

The connection between sycophants and tyrants is made by Plato in *Republic* (line 575), where Plato points out that tyrants are served by henchmen and sycophants, who—unlike the tyrants they serve—commit "small evils." Plato explains that tyrants come to power in a variety of ways, and while some "steal, break into houses, cut purses, strip men of their garments, plunder temples, and kidnap," there are others who, "if they are fluent speakers they become sycophants and bear false witness and take bribes" (*Republic* 575b). The sycophant's crimes are subtle. Plato emphasizes that it is the sycophant's capacity for fluent speech that gives them their power. This is more dangerous than mere physical strength because it can manipulate the masses. Sycophants help the tyrant speak to the masses in the language that the masses long to hear. They also flatter the tyrant and refuse to question his power and authority. While some sycophants may later complain that they had no choice but to become bootlickers, the sycophant is not merely a victim of the power of the tyrant. The sycophant is a schemer. He inflames the tyrant's pride just as he fans the flames of emotion found in the mob. And although the sycophant may believe himself to be the most clever one in this wicked company, in the end the sycophant often bears the brunt of the blame. The tyrant may escape or retreat. And members of the mob can blend back into the background. But the sycophants are not powerful enough to escape and not small enough to fade away. In the end, it is often the sycophant who goes to prison or who is tarred and feathered. In a sense, the tyrant is purely a subject of id and libido; the same is true of the moronic masses. In a sense, each cannot help succumbing to their flaws. But with the sycophant, we say, "He ought to have known better."

Morons, sycophants, and tyrants are made for each other. They each lack certain virtues, including a sense of justice, courage, wisdom, and self-control. They are empowered when the political system lacks checks and balances and a separation of powers. Plato's solution was primarily focused on the first problem: the general lack of virtue and wisdom. He thought that political life would be made better when people were educated in morality. He also thought that since some were less able to be educated, there ought to be a hierarchical system in which philosopher-kings ruled over the compliant masses. This Platonic utopia is no longer worth considering. We know now that a stable constitutional system is useful for preventing tyranny. But even within this system, would-be tyrants will arise. And so we need to continue to be vigilant—both in protecting the constitutional system and in educating citizens and future leaders about the dangers of tyranny.

TRUMP: 2016

Now let's return to Trump and his rise to power in order to show how the warning signs of his potential for tyranny were present from the beginning. Many commentators warned of Trumpian tyranny, even before he was elected. Despite these warnings, Trump was elected. This election was facilitated by the sycophants of the Republican Party, who were threatened, cajoled, and berated until they fell in behind Trump—afraid, perhaps, of the power of what was called "Trump's base." This base was the mass of voters who truly loved Trump and cheered him on.

A number of examples could be employed to show that Trump's tyrannical streak was known from the beginning. Here is one. "I could stand in the middle of Fifth Avenue and shoot somebody, and I wouldn't lose any voters, OK," Trump said. "It's, like, incredible."[13] Trump said this at a Christian College in Iowa in January of 2016 on his way to the Iowa caucuses. This remark—and a variety of others about grabbing pussies, roughing up protesters, and so on—would seemingly disqualify Trump as a legitimate presidential contender in the twenty-first century. In 2016, Trump was already well known as a symbol of lust and greed. In *The Art of the Deal*, he bluntly said, "You can't be too greedy."[14] Perennial wisdom condemns the greedy soul as tyrannical. It would be difficult to imagine Thomas Jefferson or Abraham Lincoln giving voice to these kinds of statements. But Trump was elected to the same office held by Jefferson and Lincoln. Throughout his reign, he repeatedly offered outrageous remarks and verbal attacks. He bullied his opponents. He accused the press of being the enemy of the people. He hinted that the military, the police, and his own supporters should use extralegal violence. All of this indicates a soul pointed in the direction of tyranny.

After Trump gained power, a number of yes-men in the bureaucracy flocked to his cause, including those he had previously bullied. Senator Ted Cruz of Texas comes to mind as an example. Trump insulted him on the campaign trail, giving him the name "Lyin' Ted," accusing Cruz's father of being involved in the Kennedy assassination, and insulting Cruz's wife. Cruz called Trump a narcissist and a pathological liar. But Cruz needed Trump once Trump became president. So Cruz endorsed Trump and asked for Trump's support in Cruz's 2018 reelection bid.[15] And when Trump contested the election of 2020, Cruz was an ardent proponent of that cause—one of the few senators to register a formal objection to the election on the fateful day of January 6, 2021. A number of similar examples can be found among the Republicans who denounced Trump during his candidacy but who either failed to speak out against him or who actively supported him through the impeachment process that played out during 2019–2020. Senator Lindsey Graham once called Trump a "jackass" and voted for a third-party candidate rather than vote for Trump. Senator Graham said, during the 2016 election, "I have doubts about Mr. Trump. I don't think he's a Republican, I don't think he's a conservative, I think his campaign's built on xenophobia, race-baiting and religious bigotry. I think he'd be a disaster for our party."[16] But Senator Graham went on to become one of Trump's greatest champions.[17] Senator Susan Collins announced in 2016 that she would not vote for Trump because his "cruel comments" and "inability to admit error or apologize" make him "unworthy of being our president"; and even though some viewed her as a "swing vote" who might vote against the party line, Senator Collins voted with Trump most of the time, including during Trump's first, 2020, impeachment trial.[18] With a few notable exceptions, most of the "never Trump" Republican establishment bent themselves around Trump. There were some Republicans who resisted Trump. For example, Senator Jeff Flake, who spoke out against Trump, and Senator Mitt Romney, who voted against Trump in his 2020 impeachment trial and again in the second Trump impeachment trial in 2021. But mostly, the Republican Party coalesced around Trump despite the fact that Trump was registered as a Democrat from 2001–2009.[19]

Trump is an opportunist. His policies are reactionary and short sighted. Unlike traditional American conservatism, he was not a fan of American exceptionalism, free markets, or traditional religious values. Instead, Trump played around with porn stars, grabbed women's genitalia, undermined American international leadership, cozied up to Russia, and used tariffs to disrupt the global economy. Instead of using the power of the federal government to help during disasters such as hurricanes, COVID-19, and racial justice protests, he falsified hurricane maps, engaged in race baiting, and downplayed the pandemic to score political points. But the sycophants in the party were willing to overlook this. This is a crucial aspect of how sycophancy works: it is about power, connections, and partisan loyalty rather than about policy, ideology, or consistency. And while some Republicans have doubled down on Trump even after all of this, a number of Republicans have offered a damning postmortem of the Trump years. For example, Stuart Stevens, a conservative activist, wrote a book called *It Was All a Lie*, in which he lamented the fact that kooks, oddballs, weirdos, know-nothings, bigots, and fools had taken over the Republican Party.[20]

This brings us to the third character in this sordid drama: the moronic masses. The masses are not close enough to power to benefit from sucking up. They are simply along for the ride and enjoying the show. What is remarkable is that among the masses—among his so-called "base"—Trump remained popular, despite an administration that was plagued by scandals and controversies. In the summer of 2018, as outrageously embarrassing moments flowed from the White House, a Trump supporter in Cincinnati said the following: "I like Trump because he's hardcore. . . . He talks like I'm talking to you now. He's rough around the edges and that's what I am. I'm rough around the edges, and whatever comes to my mind, I just say whatever comes to my mind."[21] In December 2019, when impeachment hearings were unfolding, a young Trump supporter in Hershey, Pennsylvania, said, "I've always liked him. He just seemed like such a powerful person, all the way back to 'The Apprentice.' I think that's what we need."[22] These comments show that it was Trump's roughness and power that attracted his followers. Another typical claim among Trump supporters was that they like him because he is not a politician: they like his unfiltered and even obscene demeanor. When the world was talking about a video of Trump bragging about grabbing pussies, the actor Scott Baio went on Fox News to defend him, saying, "I like Trump because Trump is not a politician, he talks like a guy. And ladies out there, this is what guys talk about when you're not around. So if you're offended by it, grow up, ok?"[23] These comments indicate self-awareness. The people saying these things are not stupid or ignorant of the news or the political world. And yet these sorts of comments indicate a kind of moral blindness. This is moronic, in the technical sense of the term that I employ here. This is not unique to Trump voters. Rather, it is common to the masses in general. Most of us are morons, at least some of the time. We are more interested in style than substance. We enjoy emotional outbursts and the spectacle of power. We are not always interested in virtue or in the details of law and policy. In a sense, we simply want a politician or celebrity we can identify with and who will entertain us. And we appear to want a leader whom we can love and who tells us we are special and that he loves us in return.

CONCLUSION: TRAGIC LOVE AND THE PROBLEM OF POLARIZATION

It is the masses who suffer the most when the tyrant's circus comes to town. Tyrants and would-be tyrants leave victims in their wakes. In ancient Athens, Socrates was a victim. But so too was Meletus, one of the sophists who brought false charges against Socrates. According to legend, Meletus was eventually killed by the people of Athens, who regretted killing Socrates. The suffering of the mob became clear soon after January 6. In the aftermath of January 6, Trump disavowed the violence he had incited. This led some of his followers to feel that Trump betrayed them.[24] But some continued to believe in Trump, even tweaking the conspiracy in a way that falsely suggested that the violence in the Capitol on January 6 was not perpetrated by Trump followers at all, but by leftists who had infiltrated the mob. One Trump supporter put it this way:

> If it [the violence in the Capitol] did come from any conservatives, then I condemn it. There's no excuse for violence. It doesn't change my support for Trump. The people that love Trump, that's not going to change no matter if he gets a second term or not. It just means we're going to hold out for 2024 and hope either he runs again or his kids do.[25]

It is amazing that the tyrant (or would-be tyrant) inspires this kind of love—and that this love is transitive, translating also to love of the tyrant's family. As this Trump supporter suggests, love does not change, no matter what.

Some may suggest that this kind of ardor and passion is admirable. But Trump worship caused substantial damage. Those who believe that Trump is "one of God's greatest warriors," as the Trump supporter who was killed on January 6 had put it, suffered real-world consequences on his behalf: dying and going to prison. The worst damage that Donald Trump did during his regime was likely his mismanagement of the COVID-19 pandemic. Trump's hubris prevented him from admitting the seriousness of the pandemic. He blamed everyone else for his own failures of leadership including China, the news media, and state and local officials. As a result, by the time Trump's regime had ended, nearly four hundred thousand people had died. Many of those who died were Trump's supporters. While Trump, Giuliani, and others in Trump's inner circle came down with COVID, they had exceptional medical care and mostly recovered. The same was not true for those who live in poverty, lack medical insurance, and worked long hours in dangerous conditions. But even the pandemic did not diminish Trump's appeal. His supporters continued to love him, no matter what.

Some Trump supporters even appeared to believe that efforts to prevent disease—masking, shut-downs, and social distancing—were themselves a kind of tyranny. Senator Rand Paul quoted C. S. Lewis to make this point: "Of all tyrannies, a tyranny sincerely exercised for the good of its victims may be the most oppressive."[26] Senator Paul blamed state medical authorities for behaving tyrannically during the pandemic. Even more strange was the claim made by people like Trump's former National Security Advisor, Michael Flynn, that the COVID-19 pandemic was "fabricated" to gain control and undermine the November 3, 2020, election.[27] Here we reencounter the problem of polarization. Trump's critics blame Trump's tyrannical impulses (his lying and self-aggrandizement) for exacerbating the pandemic, while Trump supporters claim that the real harm of the pandemic was tyrannical overreach by state governments and medical authorities, which ended up harming Trump.

And so it goes. Trump cannot be entirely blamed for the deadly result of an infectious disease. But the link between tyranny and plagues has a deep history. This includes both the idea that tyrants are to blame for plagues and the awareness that polarization makes it difficult to sort out exactly who is to blame. Sophocles's play *Oedipus Tyrannos* is set in the midst of a plague. The plague is a curse from the gods, brought down upon Thebes as punishment for the crime of the tyrant's own incestuous, murderous, and tyrannical life. Oedipus seeks someone else to blame, unwilling to admit that he is the source of the pollution. He refuses to listen to Tiresias, who accuses him of being the cause of the plague. Oedipus goes so far as to suggest that Tiresias is working for Creon (who is at this point in the drama's timeline, merely a would-be tyrant) in an attempt to discredit Oedipus and stage a coup. The tyrant is blamed for the plague but he accuses his accusers of being tyranni-cal—and thereby makes matters worse.

The warning from Sophocles is clear. The deeper plague is lack of wisdom grounded in objective truth. Polarization is a significant part of the problem. The tyrant and his cronies are convinced (or convince themselves) that they are the good guys. The masses get pulled along and end up dying. Some of these characters may be downright cruel and evil. But tragedy is not melodrama. Tragic characters are more subtle than that—and therefore more insidious. The problem is that we are sick and believe ourselves to be well. We seek out an authority to save us. But he only makes things worse. The plot thickens, however, as truth is rejected as fake news and truth tellers are transformed into enemies of the people. This is not so much a problem of malice, cruelty, and deliberate evil as a problem of pride and ambition as well as ignorance and stupidity. The cure is obvious: wisdom, truth, and restraint under the law.

Of course, the stories told here are convenient myths. Real life and actual history are much more complicated. We no longer believe that the gods bring down plagues as punishment for a tyrant's ambition. But the moral of the story rings true. A leader's hubris can cause great harm. This harm includes the violence and disorder of the tyrant's regime as well as the polarization of truth that occurs when the tragic trio comes to power. The tyrant wants the world to conform to his own image. He denies reality and accuses those who speak the truth of being enemies of the people. The sycophants egg him on, flatter his ego, and reinforce the tyrant's fantasy. The masses are deceived and end up dying as a result.

2

TYRANNY AS A
THEOLOGICAL PROBLEM

God never made a tyrant, nor a slave.

—William Lloyd Garrison[1]

This is a book about tyrants, their sycophantic supporters, and the morons who get pulled along by them. The solution is wisdom, virtue, and a constitutional system set up to prevent tyranny. In this chapter, I look at tyranny from the broadest possible perspective as a theological problem. We saw this already above, when I quoted the words of a Trump follower who was killed in the assault on the Capitol on January 6; she said that Trump was "one of God's greatest warriors."[2] After considering this kind of thing in more detail here, I introduce some of the wisdom that offers a solution, including the wisdom of both ancient Greek thinkers and the American founding fathers. This wisdom is informed by theology. But it is also grounded in a modest humanism that rejects the idea that any human being should have God-like power.

MODEST HUMANISM

Let me begin by declaring that I don't think of any human being as a divinely appointed savior or holy warrior. As a humanist, I do not believe that any human being has divine insight or that the American founders (or any president or warrior) were saints or demi-gods, as some people do. Human beings muddle through and make mistakes. No one is perfectly good or perfectly wise. Nor do I believe that God has a special affinity for any nation. If there is a God, He is a cosmopolitan who likely views nationalism as idolatry. God is more likely more concerned with peace than with war, more focused on justice than power, and more concerned with the well-being of suffering individuals than the glory of any nation, prince, or president.

Political life can be understood as a game of human power. Tyranny is an attempt to win this worldly game and achieve the power and the glory of a god. It is about ambition, greatness, pride, and the unbridled desire for power and glory. The ancients understood this. Socrates described the ambition of Alcibiades as the desire to rule the world. He says that Alcibiades did not merely want to rule over Athens or over the Greeks but that he wanted the whole world to be filled with his "power and name" (*Alcibiades* 105). As Socrates explains, Alcibiades wanted to win the game of honor and glory: to prove to people that he was more worthy of honor "than any person who ever existed." The character flaw found in Alcibiades is ambition or "high-spiritedness." This is an inflated sense of one's own power, glory, and value. Thucydides describes Alcibiades in similar terms and explains that the people of Athens were afraid of his greatness and his ambition, which was why the people ultimately turned against him.[3] Alcibiades claimed, in his own defense—as explained in Thucydides's history—that he was worthy of ruling and had a right to rule. Alcibiades was from a rich family. He won more awards than anyone else in the Olympic games. And he had done great things for the city. He concluded that a great person should not have to lower himself and be equal to others who are less worthy of honor. After Alcibiades, Alexander the Great took up the task of ruling the world. Alexander turned out to be as much of a tyrant as Alcibiades. For example, Alexander adopted the mannerisms of the Persian emperors. He also killed those who refused to kowtow to him. Alexander even killed Callisthenes, a nephew of Aristotle's, for refusing to treat him like a god and grovel before him.

Machiavelli pointed out that tyranny is a pagan idea that is concerned with self-interest, material power, and secular glory. Machiavelli noted that the Christian religion values humility and contempt for worldly goods. Christianity, he says, "causes us to attach less value to the honors and possessions of this world."[4] Paganism, on the other hand, "deified only men who had achieved great glory, such as commanders of armies and chiefs of republics."[5] According to Machiavelli, in the pagan world, it was possible for people like Alcibiades and Alexander to become gods. The Roman Caesars were deified and worshipped in this way. Christianity could be understood in opposition to Roman political deification. Christians refused to worship Caesar. The Roman authorities killed them in response.

In this way, tyranny is a kind of blasphemy. This idea was made apparent in a sermon from 1750 by the American pastor Jonathan Mayhew, who said it was blasphemous to follow a tyrant. Mayhew had a profound impact on American founders, such as John Adams, who agreed with Mayhew's suggestion that there was a Christian duty to resist tyranny. Mayhew said:

> Tyranny brings ignorance and brutality along with it. It degrades men from their just rank into the class of brutes. It damps their spirits. It suppresses arts. It extinguishes every spark of noble ardor and generosity in the breasts of those who are enslaved by it. It makes naturally-strong and great minds, feeble and little; and triumphs over the ruins of virtue and humanity. This is true of tyranny in every shape. There can be nothing great and good where its influence reaches. For which reason it becomes every friend to truth and human kind, every lover of God and the Christian religion, to bear a part in opposing this hateful monster.[6]

The problem of tyranny is that the tyrant pursues his own glory without regard for morality, higher truth, or the common good. Mayhew and the American founders believed that they were justified in overthrowing tyranny. A less drastic solution was proposed by Socrates and Plato, who aimed to prevent tyranny by education focused on virtue, justice, and the common good. The plague of tyranny is avoided when the leaders, bureaucrats, and people themselves are honest, upright, and interested in justice. But since people often fall short of virtue, we also need a system of just laws. Of course, even laws can fail. For this reason, there is some wisdom in anarchism and the desire to find a separate peace that does not involve political power or coercive law.[7] But the anarchist dream remains merely that: an ideal of a world of virtuous people who rule themselves with dignity and responsibility. In the meantime—before we are able to rule ourselves with wisdom and justice—we need to keep working on the process of creating just laws and educating citizens and leaders alike. This work is up to us. It is not a matter of divine intervention. There are no saviors. We must save ourselves as best we can through vigilance, education, and strenuous labor.

I begin with this discussion of divine intervention in order to dismiss one of the strangest ideas of political philosophy, which is that somehow God gives a divine right to kings or that some party, person, or leader has divine sanction. This idea is foreign to modern liberal political philosophy. But it was also seen as a dangerous idea in the ancient world. Plato suggested that there is a close connection between a certain kind of theology and tyranny. In a dialogue with a young man named Theages, Socrates asked the youth what he wanted. Theages responded saying he would pray to become a tyrant, "if possible, over all men, and failing that, over as many as might be possible." He continued, "even more, I daresay, that I might become a god" (*Theages* 126a).[8]

Tyrants want god-like power: they want to rule the world. Those who aspire to tyranny also assume that this desire for divine power is what everyone else wants, projecting their lust for absolute power onto the world at large. The tyrant's dream of power extends to a misguided theological and psychological fantasy. The tyrant who wants to rule over everyone like a god, assumes that what makes God great is God's *power* and not His *goodness*. Socrates probes deeper, and Theages responds by saying that he does not want to "rule by violence," the way that actual tyrants do. Rather, he wants people to "voluntarily submit" to him. But the problem is that Theages wants people to love him and submit to him without understanding that people only love those who are noble, good, and virtuous. True leadership that creates "voluntary submission" comes from virtue—not from tyrannical power.

IS GOD A TYRANT?

This same idea is found in the theological problem about the relationship between God's omnipotence and his benevolence, which has been discussed in various ways by a wide range of thinkers in the Christian tradition. If there is a God, we should not obey Him merely because He is great and powerful. Rather, we should love Him because He is good and kind and just. In theological language we might say that it is not God's omnipotence we admire but his omnibenevolence. But let's be careful about saying "we" here—since there appear to be a lot of people who actually do admire omnipotence: people like Theages, who see the gods as tyrants and who aspire to be like them. As Charles Hartshorne once put it, asking ironically, "Tyrannical people may worship a tyrannical God but why should the rest of us do so?"[9]

And how do the sycophantic and moronic followers of a tyrannical God assume we should worship that divine tyrant? The answer is by offering fawning praise and obsequious flattery. The very idea of "worship" points toward the problem of the sycophant or suck-up. The word *worship* is related etymologically to the word *worthy*. To worship someone is to praise their worth. To worship is often also to suggest that the one who is giving praise is less worthy. This idea of elevating another above oneself is, however, unworthy of self-respecting human beings in relation to one another. No human being is worthy of being put up on a pedestal and worshipped as a God; and no human being ought to debase herself in this way by becoming a sycophant—even a sycophant to God. While some Christians emphasize humility and submission to God, a different enlightened theology holds that God ought not be worshipped in this obsequious fashion. It is the tyrannical idea of God that seems to suggest the need for sycophantic worship. This point was made by Immanuel Kant and others in the enlightenment tradition. In his lectures on ethics, Kant points out the dangers of zealotry and fanaticism. He says,

> Zealotry consists in endeavoring to revere God by using words and expressions that indicate submission and devotion in order to procure favor for oneself by such external tokens of respect and laudatory ejaculations. It is a hateful and repulsive thing to adopt this mode of honoring God, for in that case we think to win Him over without being moral, merely by flattery, and picture Him to ourselves as a mundane ruler whom we try to please by submissive acts of service, hymns of praise and sycophancy.[10]

Kant suggests that to praise God in this way as a sycophantic suck-up is to behave as if God is a tyrant who is susceptible to flattery and "laudatory ejaculations." This idea is, as Kant says, "hateful and repulsive" since it turns God into a vain tyrant, while debasing humanity.

It is worse still to praise a human being in this way, even though this is exactly what a tyrant desires: to be worshipped like a tyrannical god. In the modern liberal and humanistic tradition, the notions of omnipotence and worship have no place. Modern liberal, democratic political philosophy teaches that human beings are equal: no one of us is superior or worthy of worship. The modern tradition also calls for a separation of powers that is intended to prevent tyranny. In such a system, the notion that some individual or party has absolute power makes no sense.

John Adams, who was influenced as a youth by Jonathan Mayhew (quoted above), put a related point in theological language, saying this: "The fundamental article of my political creed is that despotism, or unlimited sovereignty, or absolute power is the same in a majority of a popular assembly, an aristocratical counsel, an oligarchical junto and a single emperor. Equally arbitrary cruel bloody and in every respect, diabolical."[11] Absolutism, despotism, and tyranny are viewed by Adams as the cruel work of the devil. This idea has deep roots in the modern tradition. John Locke said that slavery and war were the result or the desire for "absolute power" over another person.[12] Adams condemned absolute power as well. The Declaration of Independence condemned absolute despotism, while also proposing a remedy. The Declaration echoed Locke's words when it stated, "But when a long train of abuses and usurpations, pursuing invariably the same object evinces a design to reduce them under absolute despotism, it is their right, it is their duty, to throw off such government." One remedy to the problem of tyranny is thus revolution. Such a revolution has a theological underpinning: it is about asserting the God-granted worth of every human being over the tyrant's assault on human dignity.

Obviously Locke, Jefferson, and many of the others of that era did not take their own advice to its logical conclusion—since they supported the enslavement of African people and ignored the oppression of women. But eventually this light dawned. As mentioned in the preface, Frederick Douglass was among those who shed light upon the tyrannical darkness of slavery. In his widely quoted speech from 1852, "What to the Slave Is the Fourth of July?," Douglas linked slavery to a pernicious theology and a corrupt church, calling out the American clergy and theologians who supported slavery. He made the link to tyranny and a view of God as a tyrant very clear. He said that the American religion was "a religion for oppressors, tyrants, man-stealers, and thugs" that had converted "the very name of religion into an engine of tyranny."[13] Prior to Douglass, Mary Wollstonecraft pushed the critique of tyranny in the direction of a critique of tyranny in the family. When Wollstonecraft said, "Tyrants would have cause to tremble if reason were to become the rule of duty in any of the relations of life" (the quote with which we began this book), she was referring to tyranny in the family and the tendency of parents to tyrannize their children. Wollstonecraft suggests that good and kind parents do not need to act as tyrants toward their families, since reason and wisdom will serve to unite the family in obedience to morality. This idea had a theological implication that was made clear by William Godwin, Mary Wollstonecraft's husband. It was Godwin who most famously said, "God Himself has no right to be a tyrant."[14] If we insist on imagining God as a Father, He should not be imagined as a tyrannical father. Nor should God be seen as a slaveholding master.

The theology we find in Mayhew, Godwin, Wollstonecraft, and Douglass reflected the general critique of the tyrannical God that occurred throughout the Enlightenment period. We've already mentioned Kant in this regard. Let's cite one further source, the Baron d'Holbach, a central figure of the French Enlightenment. Holbach was an atheist who rubbed elbows with other important figures of the Enlightenment including Hume, Rousseau, and Benjamin Franklin. Holbach explained in 1761:

> If people imagine God as tyrannical, capricious or wicked, their religion will reek of slavery, inconsistency, and cruelty. But if they sincerely regard the divinity as an infinitely wise and good being, their religion will be reasonable and benevolent.[15]

In a work that he published anonymously for fear of persecution in 1772, Holbach suggested that the priests of Europe were behaving as sycophants, encouraging princes to be tyrannical, while keeping the people in slavery, which effectively made the masses into morons. He wrote:

> The idea of a terrible God, whom we paint to ourselves as a despot, must necessarily render his subjects wicked. Fear makes only slaves, and slaves

are cowardly, base, cruel, and think everything lawful, in order to gain the favour or escape the chastisements of the master whom they fear. Liberty of thinking alone can give men humanity and greatness of soul. The notion of a tyrant-god tends only to make them abject, morose, quarrelsome, intolerant slaves.[16]

This radical theology eventually made its way to the United States, although in less overtly atheistic fashion. Thomas Jefferson, for example, was influenced by Holbach's moral critique of Christianity, while, as mentioned above, John Adams was influenced by Mayhew.[17] In the theological imagination of the American Revolution, God was not a tyrant—even though the best theological impulses of the founders ran aground on the problem of slavery. Instead, the God of the revolution was a God who endowed persons with natural rights, including the right to liberty. As we've mentioned, this idea was limited in its application— and slavery and the oppression of women persisted. But eventually this kind of thinking was combined with the transcendentalist idealism of Emerson and the social and political movement for the abolition of slavery. Among the most prominent thinkers in this regard was William Lloyd Garrison, who said that "freedom is of God and slavery is of the devil."[18] Garrison was a hero for Frederick Douglass—Douglass quoted Garrison at the end of his famous Fourth of July oration. Garrison summed up the progressive theology of the American Revolution in his influential "Sonnet for Liberty": "God never made a tyrant, nor a slave."[19] Tyranny is ultimately rejected in the American political tradition and in the Enlightenment tradition of morality and theology— whether it is political tyranny, the tyranny of slavery, the tyranny of gender oppression, tyranny in the family, or the tyranny of God.

PAGANISM AND TRUMPISM

With this condemnation of despotism, tyranny, and absolutism in mind, let's turn to the contemporary world and consider President Trump's strange focus on worldly glory and his use of the language of absolutism. We will not focus here on Trump's unseemly relations with women. Nor will we focus on Trump's flirtation with racism. Those topics could form the basis for entire books.[20] These themes do offer a connection with ideas that connect to Wollstonecraft and Douglass. But here I focus on Trump's theology (to the extent that he has one) and the problem of Trump's ostentatious self-glorification. We see a pagan ideal in the gold and glitz of a billionaire who revels in his wealth and power, including the way that the Trump name is emblazoned on buildings and brands. Indeed, Trump's own theological commitment (to the extent that we can say he has any serious religious commitment) is derived from Norman Vincent Peale's gospel of self-help and worldly success.[21] Peale was Trump's spiritual advisor. He praised Trump for his success in real estate development. Peale was also a supporter and confidant of Richard Nixon. Peale's theology is focused on success in this world. His most famous book, *The Power of Positive Thinking*, begins by stating: "Believe in yourself. Have faith in your abilities."[22] While Peale tries to link this to Christian faith by channeling faith in self through faith in God, the idea of believing in yourself and having faith in yourself sounds quite a bit like paganism.

One poignant example of the strange religiosity of Donald Trump occurred in the summer of 2020 during social justice protests in response to the murder of George Floyd by police. Military force was used to clear protesters away from the White House. This allowed Trump, members of his administration, and some military advisors to walk to St. John's Episcopal Church, where the president posed in front of the church holding an unopened Bible. This symbolic action was widely condemned—because of both the military tactics used to clear Trump's path and Trump's use of the Bible as an idolatrous prop.[23] The image that the president sought to put forward was of his own religiosity connected to military power. He portrayed himself as a protector of the Christian faith, while ignoring the calls of Christians (including those who attend St. John's Episcopal Church) for social justice, nonviolence, and reconciliation.

Trump's "religiosity" is merely apparent—an image cultivated in order to consolidate political power. Related to this was the further problem of Trump's routine use of the language of absolutism. He declared that he had a variety of "absolute" rights: the absolute right to pardon himself, the absolute right to do what he wants with the Department of Justice, the absolute right to close the U.S.-Mexico border, and so on.[24]

Most notorious was Trump's claim in the speech in which he incited the riot of January 6. When President Trump repeated the false claim that Vice President Pence had the right to overturn the Electoral College result, he said, "He has the absolute right to do it."[25] Now the term *absolute* has become something of a linguistic tic in American English, with people often using the word *absolutely* as a kind of catchall word indicating affirmation and certainty. It might be that Trump's use of the word was merely this kind of affirmation—and certainly Trump uses the word a lot. But Trump really did seem to believe that his power was absolute—and some of his supporters seemed to believe it as well. During the COVID-19 pandemic, the president declared that his right to make policy decisions was total. At one press conference he said, "When somebody is the President of the United States, the authority is total and that's the way it's got to be."[26] Trump stated these sorts of things without any forethought and without indicating any deep understanding of the constitutional system. The idea of absolute power contained in these kinds of utterances is troubling.

The same is true of attempts to link religion and political power. In a secular system, a religious idea of political power makes little sense. Indeed, to bring religion into political life is to violate the basic idea that the state is a secular institution set up by human beings for our own benefit. Secular political systems provide an antidote to tyranny—as does the kind of education that Socrates provides, which teaches us not to want god-like power or to desire to be a tyrant.

One of the problems that I return to throughout this book is the way that a lack of education—about philosophy, theology, morality, and political thought—has led to current problems. President Trump and his supporters seem to misunderstand the wisdom of the Western philosophical and religious tradition. What is lacking is, in a word, enlightenment. The founding fathers of the United States were products of the Enlightenment, well educated in the wisdom of the Bible, the ancient philosophical tradition, and developments in modern (seventeenth- and eighteenth-century) philosophy and theology. This vision and comprehensive understanding of virtue, philosophy, religion, and political life was missing in Trump's worldview.

As an example, let's consider one of the most absurd ideas associated with the presidency of Donald Trump, which is that he is somehow ordained by God to lead the nation. It is undemocratic and untrue to believe, as Trump Cabinet member Rick Perry put it, that Trump's election was God's will.[27] Nor is it true, as former presidential candidate Michele Bachmann said, that Trump is a kind of savior of the Christian faith. Bachmann said of Trump, "He is highly biblical . . . we will in all likelihood never see a more godly, biblical president again in our lifetime."[28] This kind of thing has even influenced the president's view of himself. In 2019, he re-tweeted a comment about him that said he was "the King of Israel" and the "second coming of God."[29]

Did Trump really believe this nonsense? Who knows? But his sycophantic followers spread the idea. Christians like Bachmann may have been referring to Trump's appointment of conservative judges and other policies. But when they waxed biblical, they made use of a very flawed historical analogy. Some Christian Trumpians saw him as a figure similar to the Persian king Cyrus the Great.[30] According to some biblical interpretations, Cyrus was a great but imperfect man who was used by God for holy purposes. But this analogy appears to be a misunderstanding of both theology and the history of Cyrus the Great. For Christians to praise Cyrus is to focus too much on tyrannical power and not enough on virtue. Cyrus is an Old Testament figure who freed the captive Jews and sent them back to Jerusalem, viewed at the time as a messiah or "anointed king" (Isaiah 45). But Jesus points in a different direction, not to Jerusalem but to a kingdom that is not of this world (John 18:36): as Jesus says, the Kingdom of God is within (Luke 17:21). There is a debate within Christianity about the importance of worldly and political power, with a continuum that extends from the divine right of kings to Christian anarchism.[31] But let's leave theology aside and consider Cyrus himself. For the ancient Greek philosophers, Cyrus was an important symbol who provided a warning about the problem of tyranny. The Greeks saw Cyrus as a benevolent tyrant who brought liberty to the Persians, including freedom of religion. But Plato suggested, in his *Laws* (line 694ff.) that the seeds of disaster were found within Cyrus since even benevolent tyranny is unstable. After Cyrus's reign, Persia was taken over by evil tyrants—Cyrus's failed descendants—whose viciousness was understood in terms of Cyrus's failure to focus on moral education. Plato goes so far as to say that the problem of Cyrus is that Cyrus "the great" and his family and supporters were too focused on wealth and power and not focused enough on what makes for true "greatness." According to Plato, true greatness consists in virtue and not in political power, wealth, or physical strength. The story of Cyrus, for Plato, is connected to the way that political systems without a stable constitution, virtuous leaders, and a plan for moral education tend to degenerate.

A similar point was made by Xenophon, Plato's contemporary, who wrote an entire book, *The Education of Cyrus* (or *Cyropaedia*), about the problem of Cyrus. For Xenophon, the important point was that Cyrus needed to learn to be a benevolent ruler and not a tyrannical despot. Xenophon, like Plato, talks about the instability of governments and the way that democracies give way to oligarchies and monarchies—and how even despotisms fall apart. Xenophon explains that human beings tend to rebel against those who try to rule over them. In his story of the education of Cyrus, Xenophon has Cyrus's mother provide this warning: you must learn to be a king and not a tyrant.[32] This message had a profound influence on the founding fathers of the United States. Thomas Jefferson owned two copies of Xenophon's *Cyropaedia*, a book that was also read and discussed by John Adams, Benjamin Franklin, and others of that era. They understood the importance of virtue as well as the need for a stable system of laws to prevent the degeneration of political power toward absolutism, despotism, and tyranny. They understood that we do not need a new Cyrus. Rather than brandishing the Bible as a prop, the founding generation studied it and even criticized it.

INSPIRATIONAL MORAL LEADERS

The American presidency has included a number of wise and heroic individuals. None of these is a saint or an enlightened sage. No human being is perfect. Consider, for example, the problem of slavery—which is itself a form of despotism and tyranny. While the founders argued against the tyranny of England, they continued to tyrannize their own slaves. George Washington owned more than 300 slaves. Thomas Jefferson owned more than 600 human beings during the course of his life. And James Madison owned 100 slaves. Abraham Lincoln eventually freed the American slaves, but Lincoln did not believe in political equality between blacks and whites. Nonetheless, Washington, Jefferson,

Madison, and Lincoln set a high bar in terms of philosophical sophistication and political rhetoric. Despite the profound blind spot of race and slavery, they seemed to understand that political power ought to be restrained by morality and by wisdom. They were not philosopher-kings, in Plato's sense. Plato's vision of the philosopher-king is not useful in a democracy. But these wise presidents understood the dangers of unbridled political power, the need for a constitution to limit that power, and the related need for moral politicians and enlightened citizens.

Let's consider the importance of moral insight. This is one of the most important solutions for the tragedy of political life. Washington, Jefferson, and Lincoln were inspirational leaders because they were morally literate, despite the hypocrisy of slavery, racism, and sexism that was part of the inheritance of their time. They understood ethics and were able to connect moral insight to their governmental roles. Lack of moral literacy and ethical insight leads to the problem of tyranny and the rise of the tragic trio.

The tyrant's moral world is egoistic. He generally sees morality as something to be used to gain advantage. The sycophants are similarly self-serving. However, while the tyrant is basically a moral skeptic or nihilist, sycophants may actually think that by flattering the tyrant and playing to his vanity, they may be able to influence things in a moral direction. If the tyrant is a nihilist, then the sycophant is a realist and opportunist. The sycophant sucks up to power and thereby loses his integrity. The masses are fools and morons. The members of the foolish mob are not nihilists or realists since they do not really have a theory or set of commitments. They are simply not interested in morality. Instead, they want to be entertained, amused, and satisfied. Where the tyrant commands and the sycophants simper, the morons laugh, chant, cheer and rampage.

We will spend much of this book examining the flaws of those characters. But let's start with a more positive vision and set the stage by considering how thoughtful Washington, Jefferson, and Lincoln were about morality, power, and democracy. Washington said, "In politics, as in religion, my tenets are few and simple: the leading one of which and indeed that which embraces most others, is to be honest and just ourselves, and to exact it from others."[33] This commonsense moral insight provides a key to the solution to political tragedy: honesty, justice, and an all-around sense of responsibility are crucial. Washington understood that tyranny results from moral failure, when liberty runs rampant and becomes licentious. As he said, "Liberty, when it degenerates into licentiousness, begets confusion, and frequently ends in Tyranny or some woeful catastrophe."[34] This idea echoes Plato. Washington understood the ethical insights and political philosophy of the Western tradition.

Jefferson was even more of a philosophical spirit. He was inspired by John Locke, among others, whose thought inspired the Declaration of Independence and Jefferson's claim that all men are created equal and endowed by their Creator with inalienable rights. Jefferson explained his view of morality as one grounded in altruistic regard for the needs of others. Jefferson said in a letter from 1814, "Self-love is no part of morality. Indeed, it is exactly its counterpart." He continued, "Nature hath implanted in our breasts a love of others, a sense of duty to them, a moral instinct in short, which prompts us irresistibly to feel and to succor their distresses."[35] The moral instinct described here by Jefferson is a key to solving the problem of political tragedy. This moral sense or insight must be cultivated to cure tyranny, sycophancy, and foolishness. Jefferson's way of thinking about morality fits within the European tradition of Enlightenment thinkers and philosophers, including not only Locke but also Bishop Joseph Butler, Adam Smith, David Hume, and Immanuel Kant.

Lincoln was not as much of a scholar as Jefferson, although as a lawyer he understood the legal and constitutional system and the need for the rule of law. It was Lincoln who coined the phrase "the mobocratic spirit" to describe the danger of what happens when a mob takes the law into its own hands.[36] Like Jefferson, Lincoln also understood that a moral sense was needed as a guide and restraint on political power. He articulated this idea, for example, in his call for reconciliation in his second inaugural address, toward the end of the Civil War:

> With malice toward none, with charity for all, with firmness in the right as God gives us to see the right, let us strive on to finish the work we are in, to bind up the nation's wounds, to care for him who shall have borne the battle and for his widow and his orphan, to do all which may achieve and cherish a just and lasting peace among ourselves and with all nations.[37]

Lincoln calls us to charity to all, malice toward none in an ethical vision that is grounded in a clear vision of right and wrong, justice and injustice.

THE TRUMP DIFFERENCE

With these inspiring words providing a model, we can now consider how far we strayed under Donald Trump. Unlike his predecessors, President Trump is silent about morality, as I show in detail in appendix A. President Obama was fluent in the language of morality. So was President G. W. Bush. But Trump is different. One of Trump's greatest flaws is that he is morally illiterate and ethically inarticulate. Trump's silence about morality is different from the language of his predecessors.

As a point of comparison, consider John F. Kennedy's famous inaugural speech. Kennedy intoned, "My fellow Americans: ask not what your country can do for you—ask what you can do for your country. My fellow citizens of the world: ask not what America will do for you, but what together we can do for the freedom of man." President Trump's inaugural address articulated a completely different idea. Trump's movement is not based upon the idea of civic duty or social responsibility. He said, "At the center of this movement is a crucial conviction, that *a nation exists to serve its citizens*" (italics added for emphasis). This is the opposite of Kennedy's noble idea.

Unlike Kennedy, who asked citizens of the world to consider what we can do together for the freedom of man, Trump's America First rhetoric reversed course. Trump's inaugural speech concluded with a call to make America strong, wealthy, proud, safe, and great. But the desire for wealth and safety are not the same as the call of moral duty and the responsibility of civic virtue.

Perhaps all of this is not surprising, given that Trump's career and fame were built upon his image as a playboy, real estate salesman, and casino magnate. John Adams began his career as a schoolmaster and then a lawyer. Jefferson studied natural philosophy. Lincoln began his career as a lawyer. Washington was a general. Trump's pre-political career was as a television star and an impresario of unbridled capitalism. Trump's most widely read book, *The Art of the Deal*, was ghostwritten, which shows us a problem in terms of authenticity, honesty, and care for words and their meanings.[38] It is true that other presidents have speechwriters. Kennedy's Pulitzer Prize–winning book, *Profiles in Courage*, was mostly written by Ted Sorenson. The problem of authenticity is more difficult for modern presidents, who have public relations experts massaging their words. But there is no denying that Lincoln, Jefferson, Adams, and Washington were conscientious wordsmiths, who thought carefully about what they said.

In the era of Twitter and social media, things are quite different. We might explain the Trump difference by considering how Twitter functioned as a direct expression of Trump's unbridled self-expression. But Twitter alone is not to blame. During the course of his presidency, Trump was often careless in how he spoke in public settings, saying all kinds of absurd, false, and contemptuous things. At any rate, *The Art of the Deal* contains a recipe for unbridled capitalism and narcissistic self-promotion. The book stated: *"You can't be too greedy."*[39] It is impossible to imagine Washington, Jefferson, Lincoln, Adams, or Kennedy saying anything like this or signing their name to a ghostwritten book that affirmed such an idea.

Trump also explained that a key to the way he promotes things is to focus on "bravado." He said, "I play to people's fantasies. People may not always think big themselves, but they can still get very excited by those who do. That's why a little hyperbole never hurts. People want to believe something is the biggest and the greatest and the most spectacular. I call it truthful hyperbole. It's an innocent form of exaggeration—and a very effective form of promotion."[40] We have fallen so far: from Honest Abe Lincoln and the mythic image of George Washington and the cherry tree. Perhaps this works in sales and marketing. But in political leadership, it is dangerous and perverse. It is no surprise to learn that Trump regularly and repeatedly lied. By the end of his presidency, Trump had uttered more than thirty thousand falsehoods, including the repeated lie that he won the 2020 election.[41] Other contemporary politicians lie and exaggerate. Bill Clinton's affair with Monica Lewinsky comes to mind, as do the lies told by George W. Bush and his administration during the war on terrorism. But with Trump, we entered into a world of fake news and alternative facts, where hyperbole and lying became habitual, and truth itself became polarizing, as we'll discuss in the next chapter.

CONCLUSION: GOD IS NOT A TYRANT

Politicians all lie. Indeed, we all lie from time to time. The image of George Washington and the cherry tree is a myth. But an important difference for the problem of tyranny is the question of the justification of lying. Tyranny is encouraged when the tyrant believes that his lies are justified as part of his own exceptional power, glory, and wisdom. Plato encouraged the philosopher-king to tell noble lies that are used to manipulate people in his utopian society. This ideal of the philosopher-king can easily become an excuse for tyranny and violence (despite Plato's own hope that the philosopher-king was an antidote to tyranny). Machiavelli also flirted with lying and the other arts of tyranny. Despite his critical discussion of tyranny and paganism in his *Discourses*, Machiavelli is most famous (or notorious) for his book *The Prince*—where he encouraged the prince to be cunning as a fox and as violent as a lion. Machiavelli ultimately advised the prince to cultivate an *appearance* of virtue and Christian piety. Machiavelli suggested that the prince should conceal his lust for power and viciousness while cultivating an appearance of being "merciful, faithful, humane, upright, and religious."[42] There are hermeneutical difficulties in interpreting Machiavelli (and Plato)—for example, they may be offering their advice ironically.[43] But it is clear that tyrants themselves understand the importance of playing with appearances—of appearing powerful, of refusing to admit defeat, of doubling down on lies, of cultivating a sense of divinity and glory among their followers, and of using violence and the threat of violence as one of their tools. The sycophants help to cultivate the tyrant's appearance of power and glory. And the masses celebrate it, willingly playing along with falsehoods and appearances.

This returns us to the theological problem. Pagan religion is a religion of appearances and external power, including violence. The gods of the ancient world were engaged in battles with one another that involved deception, shifting alliances, and a play of appearances. Homer's *Iliad* and *Odyssey* provide obvious examples of the way that gods, demigods, heroes, and tyrants play a great game of strategy, glory, deception, and power.

A more developed theological idea teaches that God is not a tyrant, God is not a deceiver, God does not celebrate secular glory, God will not reward liars, glory seekers, and tyrants, and God condemns violence. Indeed, it was Norman Vincent Peale—Trump's spiritual advisor—who said, "Unless we are governed by God, we shall be ruled by tyrants."[44] Peale incorrectly attributed this inspiring phrase to William Penn, the founder of Pennsylvania. Whether Penn said it or not, Peale used the quote to support the idea that "you cannot make a slave of a man who

believes in the greatness of God."[45] Peale's self-help gospel was supposed to be limited by God. The idea is supposed to be that God will
help to support the cause of justice, liberty, and truth. We have seen
how Peale's self-help gospel can be warped when it is taken in a more
pagan sense that tries to enlist God in support of material glory and
greatness. One obvious antidote for tyranny is to understand the limits
of pagan glory.

These theological arguments are important. But they must be supple-
mented by secular arguments about the dangers of tyranny—especially
the danger of a tyranny that claims divine imprimatur. Secularism develops in a deliberate effort to limit the role of religion in political life.
A secular solution emphasizes the need for virtue and the limitation of
power, including restrictions on the way that religion can be employed
in political life. We need to promote and encourage education in wisdom, justice, courage, and self-control. We also need education about
tyranny, theology, and the modern democratic system and its struggle to
limit tyranny through a secular system of government.

The ultimate power to resist tyranny comes from the educated masses.
Tyrants prey upon morons. Their power increases as they manipulate
the masses. Sometimes this manipulation occurs by way of phony piety
and a masquerade of religiosity. One obvious solution is structural: we
need institutional safeguards against the tyrannical urges of would-be
despots, as well as ways to help prevent the masses from consolidating
into a mob. Such safeguards include a separation of powers, guarantees
of civil liberties, and the like. A central idea here is found in the First
Amendment to the U.S. Constitution, which establishes the separation
of church and state. But a less structural and more personal or ethical
solution is to empower the masses to resist the tyrants by transforming
would-be morons into enlightened, educated, and wise citizens. This
form of education should help to nip the tyrannical personality in the
bud. Would-be tyrants need to be educated so that they are less hubristic and less inclined to want to grab power. This education includes the
lessons of modern theology in which God is not a tyrant and God does
not glorify tyrants. The same lessons must be learned by the henchmen
and sycophants. In a democratic society, the political structure should
not reward sycophants. Sycophants should not create false idols and
exalt the tyrant. The heroes of democracy do not suck up to tyrants or
glorify their falsehoods.

3

THE TRAGIC TRIO AND THE
MIDWIFE WHO ENLIGHTENS

A Prince whose character is thus marked by every act which may
define a Tyrant, is unfit to be the ruler of a free people.

—The Declaration of Independence

A greedy bully grabs power. Bootlicking ass kissers swarm around him.
A mob of blind partisans allows itself to be seduced by his lies, propaganda, and virulent ideology.

This is a common tragedy. Tyrants rise to power. Sycophants suck
up. And the stupid masses cheer it on. We witnessed a version of this
tragedy during the Trump era. But this is an old story featuring a familiar trio: the tyrant, his sycophants, and the moronic mob. The hope is
that enlightened citizenship and a stable constitution can prevent the
tragedy of tyranny. For this to happen, we need moral gadflies to keep
us vigilant and philosophical midwives to open our eyes.

While the immediate impetus for the present account is the Trump
regime, Trump is only a symptom and an exemplar. Trump remained
only a would-be tyrant. The constitutional system provided a brake on
tyranny. Some suspect that Trump has a tyrannical personality.[1] But
personality alone is insufficient to produce full-blown tyranny. Tyranny
only takes root when there is a weak political structure, an extensive

class of compliant sycophants, and a substantial mob that supports the tyrant.

Tyranny has long been a subject of art, literature, religion, and philosophy. The Greek poets and philosophers named and condemned tyranny as the nadir of political development and the source of great tragedy. We have already mentioned Sophocles's tragedy *Oedipus Tyrannos* and Plato's worry that the ideal state would degenerate into the rule of the tyrant. Plato and Sophocles both understood that tyranny was a loaded and polarizing epithet. A millennium later, in the 1260s Thomas Aquinas said that tyranny is the worst form of government. Quoting the Proverbs of Solomon, Aquinas says, "Whence Solomon says (*Proverbs* 28:15) 'As a roaring lion and a hungry bear, so is a wicked prince over the poor people.' Therefore men hide from tyrants as from cruel beasts and it seems that to be subject to a tyrant is the same thing as to lie prostrate beneath a raging beast."[2] A few decades later, Dante put the tyrants in hell in his *Inferno*, where they were punished by being boiled in blood. In *Paradise Lost*, Milton sets up a contest between the power of God and the usurping aspirations of Satan, who waged "eternal war" against "the tyranny of heaven." These poets provide a working definition of tyranny. Dante said, in 1313, in his essay *On Monarchy*, that tyrants rule only for themselves and not in the interest of public welfare.[3] Milton explained in 1649, "A Tyrant . . . is he who regarding neither Law nor the common good, reigns only for himself and his faction."[4] Milton goes on to propose a revolutionary remedy for tyranny, saying that against this enemy of the people, the people may "lawfully" do whatever they may do "against a common pest, and destroyer of mankind." Lord Byron put it this way in *Childe Harold's Pilgrimage* where he asks, "Can tyrants but by tyrants conquered be"?

This is the stuff of war, revolution, sedition, and violence. My goal here is not to inflame but to understand. To do that we need a careful analysis of the tyrant and the characters who always accompany him: the sycophant and the moronic mob. Without sycophants and the mob, no tyrant can seize power. Understanding this tragic trio is the key to preventing tyranny and seeking the remedies provided by a stabilizing constitution and virtuous citizenship.

TYRANNY IS IN THE EYE OF THE BEHOLDER

These terms are complicated and politically charged. Tyranny is often in the eye of the beholder. Not everyone agrees that Trump is a would-be tyrant. While his detractors warn of full-blown tyranny, Trump's supporters see him as a hero who was elected to drain the swamp of a different cast of tyrannical characters and sycophantic insiders. Trump was impeached by Democrats who accused him of "abuse of power." Representative Adam Schiff said that to impeach Trump would be to stand up against "lawlessness and tyranny."[5] As might be expected, Trump's defenders accused Schiff and the House of Representatives of behaving tyrannically.[6] Before Trump, the charge of tyranny was leveled against Barack Obama. The accusation of tyranny is always politically contested.

The Declaration of Independence stated that King George III was a tyrant. But the authors of that document were not unanimous in this judgment. John Adams was reluctant to call George a tyrant: he thought that the accusation was too personal. Nonetheless, the Declaration unabashedly declared that George was a tyrant unfit to be the ruler of a free people. A revolution ensued. After it ended, both Thomas Jefferson and John Adams eventually met King George. Jefferson continued to view the king with disdain, while Adams thought him to be gracious.[7] As if to underscore the accusation of tyranny, George suffered from a kind of madness, the result most likely of an affliction known as porphyria. George's tyrannical madness was not only condemned by the American revolutionaries, it was also condemned by liberals in England, who despised him. The poet Shelley wrote a sonnet in 1819, which described England as being afflicted by "an old, mad, blind, despised, and dying King."[8] But not everyone agreed. For the celebration of George's fiftieth year as monarch in 1810, the Reverend Hollingsworth celebrated George for defending law and order against "the spirit of anarchy and rebellion" that had broken out across Europe.[9]

Abraham Lincoln was also accused of tyranny. Lincoln spoke of a nation conceived in liberty and dedicated to the proposition that all men are created equal. He actualized that ideal by eliminating the tyranny of slavery. In 1858 in a debate with Stephen Douglas, Lincoln suggested that slavery was a form of tyranny. There is a "tyrannical principle," he said, that underlies slavery. "No matter in what shape it comes, whether from the mouth of a king who seeks to bestride the people of his own nation and live by the fruit of their labor, or from one race of men as an apology for enslaving another race, it is the same tyrannical principle."[10] But Lincoln himself was accused of being a tyrant by the Southern states that felt they had a right to tyrannical rule over their slaves and thus seceded from the Union. John Wilkes Booth reportedly yelled *"sic semper tyrannis"* (thus always to tyrants) before shooting Lincoln. While most Americans view Booth as a sinister murderer, he was viewed as a hero across the American South. An editorial in the *Texas Republican* praised Booth, saying, "There is no reason to believe that Booth, in killing Lincoln, was actuated by malice or vulgar ambition. He slew him as a tyrant, and the enemy of his country. Therefore, we honor the deed."[11]

These examples of tyranny and accusations of tyranny—regarding slavery, Lincoln, and George III—remind us that accusations of tyranny are more complicated and politically loaded than we often admit. We live in the middle of history. Our capacities for judgment are finite and limited. But common themes, characters, and principles emerge.

The subject matter of tyranny has long been a focus of myth, tragic poetry, religious prophecy, and political philosophy. The tyrants of the historical imagination include a long list of characters whose names prompt fear and trembling: Oedipus, Herod, Tiberius, Nero, Caligula, Attila, as well as Hitler, Mussolini, Stalin, and Mao. This murderers' row shows us why Obama and Trump ought not be included among the tyrants. To suggest that Obama or Trump should be included among the tyrants of the ages underestimates the terrible misdeeds of the past, while overestimating the power of the modern American presidency. The good news is that our system of government works to prevent those in power from becoming full-blown tyrants. This system developed in response to the nearly universal condemnation of tyranny that we see in the Western philosophical tradition. The bad news is that we disagree about who is a tyrant. And thus, we are left with a tragic conflict.

OUR FUNDAMENTAL BROKENNESS

My goal in this book is twofold: to turn to the wisdom of the Western tradition in order to shed light on current affairs and to look at contemporary affairs in order to illuminate a prevailing theme in the tradition. We have already begun by turning to the sources mentioned above. The greatest thinkers and poets of the European tradition provide us with a substantial and perennial critique of tyranny. This reminds us that the threat of tyranny is always with us—a tragic possibility for human communities. The Trump era can be seen as playing out this tragedy again, although in subdued tones. Trump is far from a roaring lion or hungry bear, as the tyrant is depicted by Aquinas and Solomon. But the tragic narrative persists.

Indeed, political life is always tragic. I use the term *tragic* here in a technical philosophical sense. *Tragic* might mean sad or sorrowful—and even terrible and dreadful. But behind the dread and the terror is a fundamental human brokenness. Tragedy unfolds from fundamental conflicts among persons and values—and within the souls of human individuals. These conflicts are inevitable and unavoidable. We desire power. We are seduced by lies. We fail to think and to pursue virtue. The truth of tragedy is one that comes from Sophocles, who explains that human beings are strange, uncanny, and terrible; our foibles provoke terror and wonder (*Antigone* 322). The tradition holds out hope that in response to our brokenness, we may discover virtue and wisdom. But history never ends. Each generation must confront the fundamental conflicts of human nature.

Each generation lives through its own version of tragedy, as does each person. We are constitutionally conflicted. Each of us is, at times, a tyrant, a sycophant, and a moron. These are technical terms linked to specific moral failures. They have objective definitions and should be understood as describing archetypal human failings. The tyrant's ambition and selfish greed leads him toward a kind of moral nihilism. The sycophant's clever pursuit of self-interest makes him complicit in the tyrant's immorality. And the moron is a fool who cheerfully ignores morality so long as the tyrant entertains him.

We have the potential for each of these archetypes within us. We grab greedily after power. We suck up and play along. And we allow ourselves to be swept away by animal urges, emotional tides, and dumb ideas. We are finite and fallible. The same is true of societies. Nothing lasts forever. And nothing is perfect. Our world is fractured and fragmented. Things can seem to make sense—and go along well enough.

And then the unexpected happens: an earthquake, a storm, or an election. And what we take for granted is overturned.

These earthquakes are unpredictable moments of chaos. We cannot say exactly when such an earthquake will happen, even though we can predict that human history will continue to experience such earthquakes. The reason for this is that human freedom is a disruptive force. Our brokenness is connected to our liberty. Human beings are not content to take things as they come. We are not ants or bees who serve the hive without complaint. Instead, we reflect upon our condition and react to history—and to each other. In this process of reflection and reaction, liberty appears along with the possibility of disruption, revolution, and tragedy.

TYRANNY TRUMPS TRUTH

Consider as a primary example, the election of Donald Trump. The pundits predicted that Hillary Clinton would win the 2016 presidential election. Clinton appeared to be the obvious choice to succeed Barack Obama. She was riding a wave of historical change that brought new power to previously marginalized people and was expected to be the first female president. She was also part of a political dynasty, as the wife of former president Bill Clinton. On the Republican side, the pundits had predicted that some other more traditional candidate would rise to the top, perhaps Jeb Bush, another dynastic candidate. No one predicted that Donald Trump would make it through the Republican primary process or that he would defeat Hillary Clinton in the general election. But human beings are unpredictable, and liberty disrupts patterns. The pundits were surprised by how the people voted—a shock that was registered across the punditocracy as the election results came in.

People had seen enough of political dynasties, party machinery, and the political status quo. Yes, there were Russian trolls, the FBI investigation of Clinton, and a bunch of other shenanigans going on. The Democratic Party, for example, seemed to have rigged things against the insurgent primary challenge of Senator Bernie Sanders. But this is all part of the messy world of freedom. Human beings mix things up. We play games. We manipulate. We forge alliances. Some strive for power. Others poke holes in the powerful. Some get lucky and suck up to the eventual winner. Others hitch their wagons to losers. There are risks and gambles aplenty in human life. And most of the time, the masses have no idea about what is really going on. They (or we) jump on bandwagons. We are persuaded by lies and easily seduced by appealing images. That is the way that freedom works itself out in the messy world of democratic politics.

And in a world of freedom, people will disagree about everything. This disagreement is exemplified in the Trump era in the starkly partisan divide that displayed itself during the Trump years. The Democratic majority in the House of Representatives voted to impeach the president twice. The Republicans in the Senate voted to acquit him twice. There were few deviations from the party line on either side. This outcome was predictable. We know that the world is divided, siloed, and partitioned. Where one sees a tyrant, the other sees a hero. Where one sees a group of sycophants, the other will see a group of noble patriots. Where one sees a mob of deplorables, the other will see the embodiment of heartland virtue.

You would think that truth would provide a unifying force. But liberty allows truth to be politicized.[12] Different people describe themselves and the world in different ways. Some viewed Donald Trump as a con man and a scoundrel. Others saw him as a hero. Some viewed Hillary Clinton as a criminal who deserved to be locked up. Others saw her as one of the smartest and most qualified people ever to run for president. And Americans disagreed about the very world we lived in as Trump rose to power. Fans of President Obama believed that the world was rapidly progressing in a way that would produce international peace, racial harmony, and prosperity for all—and that Clinton would continue that trajectory. But Donald Trump said, as he launched his campaign, that all of that was false. He said, "Sadly, the American dream is dead. But if I get elected president I will bring it back bigger and better and stronger than ever before, and we will make America great again."[13] Trump described a world of "American carnage"—as he put it in his inauguration speech—that was at odds with what the Obama/Clinton voter saw. Each side in the ongoing debate about Trump seems to be living in a different world. Where one side sees an impeachable offense, the other sees a conspiracy theory and a witch hunt.

Indeed, under Trump, the phrase "alternative facts" came to be used to describe these divergent realities. Connected with this is the general politicization of truth in what some call a "post-truth" era. News reports that the president did not like were described as "fake news." The media was called "the enemy of the people." As president, Trump uttered a vast number of lies, including giving voice to outrageous conspiracy theories. By the end of his presidency, Trump had uttered more than thirty thousand false or misleading claims.[14] But this reportage, from the *Washington Post*, is viewed by Trump and his supporters as a hit job, more fake news from the "phony" media.

Trump was not the only president or politician to lie. Nor was he the only politician to attack the press. This is woven into the nature of democratic politics itself, which seems to require partisans to manipulate the opinion of the masses—often by sending out teams of sycophants who will "spin" things by touting their boss and denigrating the opposition. Truth is a problem in democracy. Plato noted this when he imagined democracy as a ship of fools who refuse to listen to the wisdom of the experts who actually understand important truths about life, virtue, and the world. As Sophia Rosenfeld explained in an analysis of truth in the Trump era, "Truth under the conditions of modern democracy has always been fragile."[15] Others have warned more strongly that the politicization of truth leaves us with the risk of tyranny and totalitarianism. Hannah Arendt, for example, said that totalitarianism does not depend only on the "convinced Nazi" (what we might call a fully committed sycophant); rather, she said that the real challenge is "people for whom the distinction between fact and fiction (i.e., the reality of experience) and the distinction between true and false (i.e., the standards of thought) no longer exist."[16]

It is easy to understand that substantial dangers flow from the denial of truth and a political (and personal) life built upon a worldview that does not properly distinguish between what is true and what is false. If the moronic masses are not concerned with truth, then they will throw their support behind whatever is pleasing or titillating. If the sycophant is not restrained by truth, then he will feel free to lie and exaggerate. And if the tyrant believes that truth is merely whatever the stronger party says it is, this will lead him to seek the power to determine what is true.

The antidote to this is a reasonable public sphere that allows for dialogue. In such a reasonable and civil dialogue, the truth would come out through a process of sifting and winnowing through which error is corrected and truth is sorted out. This dialogical process is supposed to work that way in science, for example, and in philosophy. Commonsense reasoning—in family life or in business—employs a process of dialogical reasoning. And a robust theory of democracy known as deliberative democracy emphasizes the importance of rationality in the public sphere. But political life may not be so rational, scientific, or even commonsensical. Plato saw this. And so do a growing number of contemporary political theorists. Achen and Bartels claim that folk wisdom about democracy as a process of enlightened decision making is a "fairy tale."[17] Empirical analysis shows that "most democratic citizens are uninterested in politics, poorly informed, and unwilling or unable to convey coherent policy preferences."[18] In other words, most voters are morons. We don't really know enough or care enough to vote rationally. Building a similar case, Jason Brennan concludes that democracy is a "dance of dunces."[19]

A significant problem for democracy is the fact that reason is not the only thing that matters: power is also on the table, and liberty allows unexpected things to happen. Bartels and Achen show that voting behavior is more about partisan affiliation and identity politics than about rational decision making. A rival theory of political reality—known as *agonistic theory*—reminds us that politics is about power. At its most primal root, agonistic politics is a game without rules, in which the goal is to outwit the system, to overpower your opponents, and to win. We are fortunate, however, not to live in such a completely agonistic state of nature. There are rules in our system, established by the Constitution and by norms of civility and decorum. But as we've seen in the Trump era, these rules can be bent and sometimes ignored by the would-be tyrant. And when this happens, the sycophants might jump on board the tyrant's ship, while the masses cheer him on. If the tyrant wants power and the sycophant goes along for the ride, the mob simply enjoys the show, using their liberty without much forethought. Political philosopher Robert Nozick showed how liberty disrupts patterns. Plato argued that liberty without reason and virtue is dangerous, unstable, and unpredictable. But a deeper problem is power without restraint. The Trump era shows us that power trumps truth. Trump lied and continues to lie. The fact that his most egregious lies were about democracy itself shows us the problem. In 2016, he lied about the popular vote count. In 2020, he lied about the election being stolen. He got away with these lies because he had the power to do so. Democracy was damaged as a result.

One of the primary mechanisms by which tyranny is enacted is through the manipulation of discourse, such that what passes for "truth" comes to be determined by the powerful. In such a situation, the game of truth and deliberation is changed. No longer are we interested in reasonable arguments aimed at disclosing truth. Rather, in such a situation, we are aimed at controlling the discourse and the flow of information. In such a situation, the most tyrannical character may be the most successful: he (or she) who is immune to the truth; he who is unashamed to lie; he who uses his opponent's commitment to the truth against him; and he who conceives of the game in agonistic terms instead of in terms of deliberative democracy. When truth gives way to power and impunity, we are on the way toward tyranny.

The antidote, of course, is to remain committed to truth—and to virtue and to the rules that limit power and establish an ethical code of civility and responsible citizenship. This is an old remedy for this ancient disease, known to us since the time of Socrates. The two mottoes from the Oracle at Delphi provide a useful guide: "know thyself" and "nothing in excess." The way to avoid tyranny trumping truth is to seek knowledge, including self-knowledge and to limit ourselves to a life of moderation and virtue.

TYRANNY OVER THE MIND

The problem of truth is a fundamental problem in a regime that guarantees liberty and allows for freedom of thought and speech. Democratic liberty allows people to believe and say whatever they want. In the United States, we have a free press, freedom of speech, and freedom of religion. This means that people can believe what they want and say what they will, short of inciting violence. Sources of news and information can report and publish what they choose (within very broad limits imposed by laws against libel and defamation). There is no requirement that what we say is true, that what we believe is reasonable, or that the language we use must be civil. Unbridled freedom creates a risk of degeneration.

The Enlightenment philosophers and statesmen who helped give form to modern democratic liberty believed that the cure for falsehood was more freedom. But liberty was supposed to be guided by norms of civility, rules of decorum, and the sincerity and good faith of human beings. The thinkers of the Enlightenment were worried about the tyrannical power of church and state. They wanted the tyrants to get out of the way and allow reason and liberty the space to achieve enlightenment. John Locke put it in a phrase that was also adopted by Thomas Jefferson: "The truth certainly would do well enough if she were once left to shift for herself."[20] But Locke assumed that those who were playing the game were guided by reason and the natural law. Jefferson reflected deeply upon Locke's ideas. In his "Notes on Religion" from 1776, Jefferson quoted Locke and explained that what Locke had in mind was that "truth is the proper and sufficient antagonist to error."[21] That same idea showed up in Jefferson's Statute for Religious Freedom for the state of Virginia. Jefferson linked this to a critique of a form of tyranny. Those who refuse to leave the truth alone are guilty of a tyranny of the mind. Jefferson explained this problem in a discussion of religious liberty that is inscribed under the dome of the Jefferson Memorial: "I have sworn upon the altar of god eternal hostility against every form of tyranny over the mind of man."[22]

Jefferson might have borrowed that phrase—"tyranny over the mind"—from Bishop Joseph Butler, who used it in a sermon from 1747. Butler advocated religious liberty—but within limits that were less liberal than Jefferson's ideal. Butler celebrated equality before the law and liberty as the genius of the British civil constitution. Unlike Jefferson, Butler defended the idea that there should be an established religion for a nation. Nonetheless, he thought that the religious and political authorities should allow toleration for dissenters. He explained, "A religious establishment without a toleration of such as think they cannot in conscience conform to it, is itself a general tyranny; because it claims absolute authority over conscience; and would soon beget particular kinds of tyranny of the worst sort, tyranny over the mind."[23] The issues arising here with regard to the separation of church and state are complicated. But the tradition that includes Locke, Butler, and Jefferson is generally interested not only in protecting against political tyranny but also in working to avoid a more general kind of tyranny that prevents free thought. This is what John Stuart Mill called the "tyranny of the majority" and also the "tyranny of prevailing opinion" in *On Liberty*. The solution, as Mill's title indicates, was liberty.

But liberty without restraint risks becoming yet another form of tyranny. Liberty trumps truth, especially when liberty is left without wisdom and virtue to guide it. Free people will say and believe anything so long as they only have what philosophers call "negative liberty" (i.e., freedom from external constraint). They will even contradict themselves, vote against their own self-interest, and turn a blind eye to the greater good. This is why freedom must be transformed into what we might call "moral autonomy." This is self-governance or self-control. It is not merely a negative form of liberty—although it depends in part upon freedom from external constrain. Rather, autonomy is the self-limitation of freedom out of respect for truth, respect for persons, and concern for the greater good. This is what the Enlightenment thinkers were aiming at, an idea that achieves its greatest expression in the work of Immanuel Kant, who understood autonomy as liberty that constrains itself out of respect for the moral law.

Autonomy requires cultivation. It results from moral education. If we lack moral autonomy in this sense, we remain broken. Liberty without limit produces political discord. It gives rise to tyranny or mob rule. In the life of an individual, unlimited liberty gives rise to internal conflicts that are not easily resolved or organized into a coherent pattern. When freedom is not cultivated, our passions push and pull us. We lack direction and a sense of justice. And we can be tempted to behave tyrannically, to suck up to those in power, and in some cases to simply give up and allow emotion to sweep us along.

To free ourselves of that kind of tyranny over the mind that Jefferson warned against, we need an enlightened sense of morality, psychology, and political reality. Ignorance, superstition, and moral indifference are connected to a lack of enlightenment. These failures are common. The work of autonomy and enlightenment is difficult. It is often easier to go with the flow and to give our freedom over to a dominant ideology or a tyrannical personality. The tyranny of the mind is cured by moral education that empowers us to be autonomous citizens.

TRUMP IS A SYMPTOM

There are many ways in which the world is tragic and in which things can be broken. In this book, I describe the unhandsome trio of tyrant, sycophant, and moron. I draw attention to this tragic triumvirate by focusing on current affairs. But this cast of characters is a mere example of a problem that extends beyond this moment and this configuration of personality, party, and political life. There are Democrats and Republicans with tyrannical aspirations, just as there are bootlickers and idiots in both the Republican and Democratic parties. The same was true in the Soviet Politburo, in Napoleon's Paris, and in Machiavelli's Florence. Trump is only an example or a symptom. We are fortunate that he remained a would-be tyrant who was constrained by enlightened citizens and a stable legal framework.

The tragic trio represents potentialities in each of us that are kept in check by virtue and by law. But no law or theory of virtue has absolute control. While we can construct political systems that prevent tyrants from seizing power, even the best system contains quirks and idiosyncrasies that allow rot to fester or to explode. To resist these tendencies, the human race needs justice, courage, and above all wisdom. The struggle to live well is both personal and political. There are tyrants, sycophants, and morons in our families, in our places of business, and in our churches and community groups. Plato directed our attention to an analogy between the city and the soul. This analogy links the external world to the internal. We learn bad habits by watching bad people. And political life reflects our own inner turmoil. In a democracy, people get the government they deserve—the government is the free creation of we, the people. The key to fixing our democracy must include dealing with the problems in our souls.

The path toward virtue requires education that produces wise citizens. This is an old path, clearly laid out by Socrates, who proposed moral education as the remedy for pride, stupidity, and complicity. But this old path must be revitalized with modern democratic values. Plato suggested that the solution to political tragedy was the philosopher-king. What we need today are enlightened democratic citizens and an inclusive public sphere.

If Trump is a symptom, the disease is a lack of virtue. The cure is a combination of structural/constitutional remedies that prevent would-be tyrants from seizing power and psychological/moral remedies that help us cultivate virtue. In the end we need both a strong separation of powers and a society of autonomous people whom we might call citizen-philosophers.

CONCLUSION: THE MIDWIFE WHO OPENS OUR EYES

Enlightenment implies waking up and opening one's eyes. But enlightenment is difficult, and some people prefer to remain asleep. The tragedy of tyranny develops out of a certain kind of moral blindness: the blindness of power. This is exacerbated by two other kinds of blindness: the blindness of willful ignorance and that of self-interested complicity. Deliberate blindness and foolish stupidity have always been problems—and are problems in all areas of life: in the church, in the family, in business, and so on. Thus, the problem of tyranny is not merely caused by moral failure in the heart of the tyrant or something unique about political power. Rather, tyranny is a social problem, facilitated by morons and sycophants. Without fools and suck-ups to support him, the tyrant cannot obtain power. Tyrannical power is not only the result of pride; it is also the result of complicity, compliance, idiocy, and incompetence.

Institutional safeguards can prevent tyrants from consolidating power. Tyranny becomes fascism and totalitarianism when the power structure permits it to happen (or is altered in a way that permits it). In a related fashion, democratic structures can empower demagogues when the masses are ignorant, foolish, and uneducated. The powerful few who run the bureaucracies and fill the political class become oligarchic cliques who serve their own interests when power is organized in such a way that it can be consolidated in the hands of sycophants. These institutional issues—and proposals for structural safeguards—are the focal point of most forms of political philosophy. We will discuss these structural safeguards in the final chapter.

But we are not only concerned with structural solutions to these problems. We must also focus on ethics and moral psychology. The ethical solution to the problem of tyranny is to cultivate wisdom and virtue—and to defend the objectivity of ethics and truth. Wisdom and virtue are assailed by the tyrant who is indifferent to truth and goodness, by the sycophant who deliberately abuses truth in order to flatter the tyrant, and by the morons who do not care or do not understand. Virtue, wisdom, and love of truth are needed at all levels of the political hierarchy: leaders, their supporters, and the masses of citizens all need education in wisdom and virtue. From a perspective that emphasizes moral education, the lessons to be learned here are not merely about political life; they also apply in other parts of human experience: in business life, friendship, and in the family. Fathers and bosses can be tyrannical. Some friendships and associations include much foolishness. And there are sycophants and suck-ups in every social group. The political iteration of this problem raises the stakes to the highest level. But the problem exists in all social relations.

One key to solving this problem is to learn to see it. The hoped-for resolution involves education and enlightenment. The solution is thus philosophical. We need to step outside of the struggles of political life and critically look at them. We need to raise our minds above the present moment. Only then can we diagnose the problem and imagine solutions. This is what Plato proposed in *Republic* in his myth of the cave: where the philosopher steps outside of the prison of daily life and sees the sun. Plato's ideal is a philosopher who returns from the vision of enlightenment, a benevolent sort-of tyrant, the so-called philosopher-king. Two millennia later, we know that this cannot be right, especially in light of the polarization we discussed above. The philosopher-king will also be, in a sense, in the eye of the beholder. Thus, rather than Platonic idealism, we need a more modest, Socratic kind of enlightenment. This idea can be found in another of Plato's dialogues—in the *Theatetus*—where Socrates explained that he had no wisdom to offer and that he was merely a midwife. The role of the philosophical midwife is to help people give birth to beauty, truth, and wisdom. Good seeds must be planted. They must be cultivated. And they must be delivered and nurtured. This is not the work of a tyrant, even a benevolent one; it is, rather, the work of the philosophical midwife.

In the modern era, the Socratic effort must be interpreted as a call for democratic education. The solution is for "we, the people" to be educated—about civic institutions and political philosophy. We don't need philosopher-kings; we need instead philosophical citizens, who give birth to wise and benevolent policies and who elect virtuous leaders.

Democratic peoples do not imagine a philosopher-king solving their problems. Rather, we believe that the educated masses have the capacity to choose well and wisely. But this only happens when the masses are properly educated—when they have been cultivated by the midwives of democratic virtue. In the ancient tragedies, the heroes were Antigone and Tiresias: blind prophets and dispossessed women. It is often the outsiders and strangers who enlighten us, playing the role of midwife to wisdom. That is why it is important to listen to critics, including especially the voices of those who are excluded, marginalized, and oppressed. Those ancient heroes failed to restrain the tyrant before it was too late. Truth tellers can suffer at the hands of sycophants, tyrants, and the angry mob. Socrates was accused by sycophants and executed by the Athenian democracy. Things seem better today. But the heroes of political life still are the truth tellers: teachers and educators, journalists, historians, and philosophers—those who open the eyes of the masses, inspire virtue, and cultivate wisdom. Ancient tragedy remains as a warning. There is no guarantee that people's eyes will be opened. The midwives and gadflies who enter the drama offering insight may end up in danger. Tyrants, sycophants, and fools often scapegoat those who shed light.

POLITICAL TRAGEDY
AND HISTORICAL WISDOM

Human-nature will not change. In any future great national trial,
compared with the men of this, we shall have as weak, and as strong;
as silly and as wise; as bad and good. Let us, therefore, study the
incidents of this, as philosophy to learn wisdom from.

—Abraham Lincoln, November 10, 1864[1]

The problem of tyranny, sycophancy, and moronic idiocy is an old one.
Understanding that this is an old problem puts things into perspective
and gives us some resources for responding to the problem. Some features of human nature remain constant, including lust for power and
lazy indifference. In the drama of political life, the details change but
the characters remain the same. We can make progress by cultivating
wisdom about human nature, derived from a careful examination of the
past and the present.

PHILOSOPHICAL HISTORY

We have already begun to trace this tragedy by looking at history and
literature. But philosophers do not merely repeat what the historians,

journalists, and poets tell us. Rather, we analyze general themes and propose solutions. This is a book of ethics and political philosophy. It has a normative task: it describes moral failure in order to consider solutions that can make things better.

Now, some scholars may not agree with this approach. Some may suppose that history should be merely descriptive. The same normative reluctance may be found in political science, sociology, and the like—even journalism, which purports to be the "history" or record of the present moment. The social scientist is reluctant to offer normative critique or prescriptions about what we ought to do. But philosophy includes normative analysis. Philosophical critique must be carefully grounded in facts and informed by history. But careful and self-conscious critique can and should offer suggestions for improving the world.

This approach has a noble lineage. Plato, Xenophon, and Aristotle derived their moral and political teachings from reflecting on history and the current affairs of their day. So too did Cicero, Seneca, and the Roman philosophers. Machiavelli offered an interpretation of politics with recommendations for the prince that was grounded in history. Montesquieu was a student of history whose writings resulted in normative ideas that had a deep impact on Madison and the other framers of the United States Constitution. And so on.

Philosophical critique is self-critical and modest in its prescriptions. It is more circumspect and less dogmatic than the ideological screeds of political partisans, the jeremiads of religious zealots, and the calls-to-arms of radical political actors. The philosophical approach looks for perennial themes in an effort to understand "human nature." I put this in scare quotes here because for philosophers, "human nature" remains a puzzle and a mystery. Although we can offer theories of human nature that appeal to universal features of our common humanity, we must acknowledge that humanity is complex and diverse. We are not all the same. And we are capable of change and improvement (as well as decline and failure). Despite this, philosophers attempt to derive larger conclusions, to see common themes, and to propose general solutions. Some critics may claim that philosophical normativity is problematic: that it is wrongheaded to offer a general diagnosis and a universal set of solutions. But we can diagnose and propose without being dogmatic and petulant.

Our analysis and critique must be modestly aware of the limitations of the subject matter. Historical examples represent concrete instances of universal problems. In each instance the details matter. In this regard it is important to reject facile historical analogies. Trumpism is not fascism. Trump is not Hitler. Nor is he George Washington or King George III, for that matter. It is also necessary to point out that Obama was not the anti-Christ; nor was Hillary Clinton. Political analysis occasionally falls into the fallacy of false analogizing. Outrageous analogies are provocative and fun. But it is easier to provoke than to think. One risk of the present account is that in employing a stereotypical cast of characters— the tyrant, his sycophants, and the foolish mob—we oversimplify. There is no perfect example of these characters in the real world. Thus, while I suggest that Trump is a would-be tyrant, this characterization can only be made in general and for the most part. Nonetheless, despite this substantial caveat, the characters discussed here do show up repeatedly in the history of political life.

The Western philosophical tradition has long been concerned with the problems identified here. Plato thought and wrote about tyrants, morons, and sycophants—as did Aristotle, Plutarch, and other ancient thinkers. Plato was imprisoned by the tyrant of Syracuse. He witnessed the trial of Socrates, where Socrates was accused of being a sycophant who sucked up to tyrants such as Alcibiades. After Plato, Aristotle is connected in the historical imagination with Alexander the Great, the conquering tyrant of Macedonia. And somewhere in the margin of this historical epoch is Diogenes the Cynic, who refused to kowtow to Alexander and the sycophants of Athens. Diogenes would likely include Plato and Aristotle among the sycophants, by the way, since they each flirted with a tyrant. And so it goes: philosophy has long been linked to the problem of tyranny.

Reflection on tyranny, foolishness, and sucking up is not confined to the Western world. My own expertise is ground in the Western European tradition. Perhaps someone more adequately versed in others of the world's traditions can add to my account—and decolonize my approach. I am sure there are lessons to be learned in a variety of traditions. Chuang-Tzu argued against sycophancy, flattery, and obsequiousness, as did Confucius. And so on. Tyrannical personalities, fools, and flatterers are also condemned in other traditions. Wisdom, virtue, education, and stabilizing political institutions are well-known as a common cure.

I limit myself here to the Western tradition. What I learn from this tradition is that wisdom, virtue, and the rule of law help to do the following:

1. to restrain the unruly impulses of tyrants;
2. to defuse the beguiling words of the sycophants; and
3. to cure the stupid ignorance of the moronic masses.

These are not neutral claims. They are grounded in a vision of human flourishing. Self-knowledge and self-restraint are keys to virtue, wisdom, and enlightenment. Education and law ought to help us develop knowledge and restraint. Not only does this help us overcome tyranny, sycophancy, and foolishness, but also, it helps us live well as human beings. Unlike historians, journalists, and tragedians who merely describe the problem and present it to us, philosophers propose the remedy, which ought to help us flourish.

ARISTOTLE, TRUMP, AND ALEXANDER THE GREAT

The Greeks struggled with issues that are similar to what we confront today. Aristotle, for example, spent much of Book V of his *Politics* examining the problem of tyranny.[2] He said that the tyrant loves vice and is a friend of the bad. The tyrant wants to surround himself with weak, bad, and stupid people. He finds good and wise people to be irritants because they do not support him in his viciousness. The tyrant also needs enemies and antagonists—those he rails against in order to rally his party and the party's base among the people. Aristotle explained: "The tyrant is a stirrer-up of war, with the deliberate purpose of keeping the people busy and also of making them constantly in need of a leader." Aristotle also understood that the tyrant needs his sycophants. He explained: "For tyrants enjoy being flattered, but nobody would ever flatter them if he possessed a free spirit." Aristotle continues to explain that a demagogue is what we call a tyrant in a democracy. The demagogue must, however, suck up to the people. He is, as Aristotle says, a "flatterer of the people" or as one translation puts it, "a sycophant of the commons."[3]

The tyrant wants power—as I pointed out above, he often wants god-like power. But according to Aristotle's analysis, one of the problems for the tyrant is that since he does not possess virtue, he lacks the kind of natural power that comes from virtue. Thus, the tyrant must cajole and flatter and manipulate things in order to get the power he desires. This leaves him resentful and jealous of those great-souled and virtuous people who possess moral authority and the power of the good. Thus Aristotle explains: "It is a mark of a tyrant to dislike anyone that is proud or free-spirited; for the tyrant claims for himself alone the right to bear that character, and the man who meets his pride with pride and shows a free spirit robs tyranny of its superiority and position of mastery; tyrants therefore hate the proud as undermining their authority."

These quotes could be applied quite easily to the tragedy of Donald Trump. He stirred up discontent (on Twitter, for example), while threatening war and violence, including a running list of those he viewed as enemies and traitors. He enjoyed flattery—especially from sycophants and media pundits who praised him. He rankled against those—like Senator John McCain, for example—who were proud and free and challenged his authority. His sycophants vied for the crumbs that fell from the tyrant's table, playing the game of power without possessing virtue. The "motley multitude"—as Plato put it—cheer and boo, enjoying the spectacle without really thinking about the ethical and political implications of what they are seeing.

The Trump regime did not invent the dysfunctional tragedy of political life. Nor is Trump the first would-be tyrant or vicious agent in American life. He was preceded—in recent memory—by Richard Nixon and Bill Clinton, who each defiled the Oval Office. The characters strutting on the stage today are familiar to us because they are us. The Trump regime is only the most recent example of a power-hungry would-be tyrant seizing power. Shakespeare saw this coming; so did Sophocles. There is dysfunction and family intrigue in the halls of power. A chorus of on-lookers encourages or criticizes. The party in power succumbs to the charismatic power of the tyrant—even those who once vowed "never Trump." Sycophants swarm to the powerful ruler, allowing corruption to grow and fester. The sycophant cleverly manipulates opinion, spreads rumors, creates alliances, and plays a game with the appearances of things. All of this is good fun for the moronic masses. Power and popularity titillate the mob, which sticks by a tyrant despite the lies, intrigue, and corruption. Of course, this is a bipartisan and common human problem. The opposition party hatches its own plans to take power, the mob swings to and fro, manipulated and deceived by propaganda, "fake news," and a system of justice that has devolved into a Machiavellian game. Each side (and there are often more than two sides) accuses the other of hubris, depravity, and stupidity.

As the drama proceeds, we hope that at some point a hero will arise who will set things right. This hero will point out that the emperor has no clothes. The hero will be an outsider to power: a blind prophet or a young woman or an old philosopher—a Tiresias, Antigone, or Socrates. This hero will defy the grandeur of power, speak the truth, burst the inflated ego of the tyrant, wake the sycophants up to their duty, and set things right. But of course this hero is also a myth. Tiresias and Antigone are *dramatis personae*. Socrates himself is a nebulous and vexing character. Plato created the Socrates of his dialogues as a mythic philosopher who would enlighten the world.[4] Plato also suggested that tyranny could be beneficial—so long as the tyrant was enlightened. But Plato showed us that the problem resides deep in human nature, since we are each tempted to be tyrant, sycophant, and moron. Thus, Plato's idea of a philosopher-tyrant, who would bring order to our ship of fools is a dream that rings hollow. The moral and political failure of humanity runs too deep for such a utopian solution.

In the modern world, we have given up on the dream of an enlightened philosopher-king. Instead, we have arrived at a more democratic solution—first suggested by Aristotle's discussion of "mixed government" and Plato's account of the flaws of each form of constitution. Monarchical rule is problematic because it puts power in the hands of one person who may be a vicious tyrant. Oligarchy empowers the few—who may in fact be partisan sycophants who are simply interested in feathering their own nests. And pure democracy empowers the moronic mob, which lacks the wisdom and self-control to govern things well. A mixed government imposes checks and balances. But beyond this structural solution, there remains a need for virtue, wisdom, and enlightenment. Each of us—whether ruler, bureaucrat, or individual voter—contributes to a better political world when we are enlightened and educated in a way that leads us to embrace justice, wisdom, courage, and virtue. Rather than a philosopher-king, what we need are philosophical citizens.

We also need the rule of law, as Aristotle emphasized. Aristotle witnessed the tyrannical turn of his pupil, Alexander the Great. On campaign in Persia, Alexander adopted the customs of the Persian emperors, forcing his subjects to grovel before him. Aristotle's nephew Callisthenes was a kind of philosopher-in-residence in Alexander's entourage. As a man of honor with a Greek education, Callisthenes refused to grovel and worship Alexander. In return, Alexander had the philosopher murdered. This episode may help to explain Aristotle's claim that it is best for the law to govern, rather than the will of the king. When the law governs, reason rules. But when the will of an individual governs, there is the risk of wild, beastly appetites gaining control. Aristotle warns that "passion warps the rule even of the best man" (*Politics* 1787a). He continues to explain that the law is "wisdom without desire." Tyrants like Alexander allow passion to rule. We have learned from history that one of the best ways to prevent tyrants and would-be tyrants from imposing their whims on people is to insist on the rule of law.

THE PROBLEM OF LIVING WITHIN HISTORY

Despite all of his talk about "greatness," Trump is no Alexander. Thankfully he remained only a would-be tyrant. Despite his tyrannical impulses, the checks and balances worked. One analysis claims Trump is an extraordinary person whose presidency was fairly ordinary.[5] His personality is unique among recent presidents; as is his approach to governing. And the system worked, more or less, to contain his mercurial and often vitriolic passions.[6] The good news is that a strong antidote for tyranny is a constitutional system that limits the power of any one individual.

Of course, we are in the middle of history today. Things may get worse. Historians will be sifting through the rubble of the present for decades. Reality is always more complicated than its initial interpretation. History offers insights that are not available to those who live through it. Subsequent historical narratives will give meaning and shape to the facts.

At some point, the present will work its way into legend and fable. Someone will write an opera or a stage play with Trump at its center. Perhaps this drama will echo themes and plots laid down by Sophocles or Shakespeare. Drama is central to the human experience. We love a good story. Dramatic re-creations are politically and psychologically beneficial. A drama can inspire action. Dramatic catharsis works to help us channel our emotions. This may purge us of negativity and leave us satisfied and complacent. But a dramatic retelling of things can also lead us to see why and how we must engage the political world. In the end, the observer must take action. Perhaps they choose to cheer on the tyrant. Or perhaps they follow along with Antigone, Tiresias, or Socrates—in acts of civil disobedience, by speaking truth to power, and trying to help give birth to wisdom.

For some revolutionaries, it may appear naïve to suggest that the remedy for social and political ills is dramatic reconstruction and ongoing moral education. It is true that institutional and structural remedies are also important. But beneath the structural changes is the ancient prescription of education. Any activism—including enacting constitutional remedies—depends upon the good will and wisdom of the human beings who take action. Moreover, the call for moral education comes from a hopeful analysis of human nature—one that believes that the remedy for tyranny can be found in the capacity of the human spirit to remain committed to truth, justice, and integrity. Revolutionary critics often worry that this is not true. They thus propose more radical and revolutionary remedies than moral education, civil disobedience, and democratic empowerment. But those radical remedies assume that the revolutionaries are somehow better than the rest of us at seeing the truth and knowing what virtue, wisdom, and justice require.

Our assessment of history is subject to dispute and polarization. Some view President Trump as a very substantial tyrannical threat to American democracy who misled the stupid masses and coerced and seduced the sycophants of the Republican Party into compliance. The staunchest critics of the president do not see Trump as a "would-be tyrant" but claim he was a full-fledged one. These critics long for a hero who will stand up to Trump and move the masses in a different direction.

Others see Trump as a hero whose pride and recklessness is a necessary feature of his heroic, world-historical mission. Some have even gone so far as to claim that Trump is doing the Lord's work. As we discussed at the outset of this book, some Christians appear to believe that Trump is, as Stephen Strang explains, "like the ancient Persian king Cyrus the Great, a pagan chosen by God for a purpose only he could accomplish."[7] Strang explains that several Christians told him that they had prophesied that Trump would win the election. And after the election, some Christians continue to believe that Trump was "chosen by God"—as Secretary of Energy Rick Perry put it—while also thinking that Trump's enemies are somehow in league with the devil.[8] Joseph Parker, a pastor and radio host who works with the American Family Association, said in December 2019, during the Trump impeachment trial, that this was "spiritual warfare" similar to what happened to Daniel in the Babylonian lion's den.[9] Earlier, in October 2019, Parker explained that President Trump was "very unpopular with the Devil and the kingdom of darkness."[10] On this version of things, Trump was standing up against the "deep state" and defying an ossified political establishment in order to make America great again (and perhaps to bring America back to God). In this version of the contemporary tragedy, the courageous loner shakes up a corrupt system with bold action. The moral courage of the rebel leads either to radical transformation or to a collapse into ruins. In this version of the tale, the sycophants who work for the status quo throw up obstacles along the way, impeding the hero's work. The faceless mandarins of the administrative state show up across the governmental and media establishment. Since the mob has been beguiled by the bureaucracy, the press, and the intelligentsia, the bold hero must fight for the soul of the nation against the many tentacles of a complacent establishment. That is one version of the story told by those who support Trump.

That is not, of course, the story I tell here. But let us note that when the history of our era is written, we will eventually tell some version of a familiar tale. Our interpretations of reality follow paths worn smooth by narrative forms, prefabricated concepts, and prior works of art and philosophy. If the Trump era looks like a Greek tragedy or Shakespearean drama or a biblical prophetic narrative, that's because history is replete with common character types and familiar plot lines. The most schematic formulation of these familiar characters reduces these to four: the tyrant, the sycophants, and the moronic masses, with a moral hero lingering somewhere in the wings. Reality may not exactly conform to this formula. But the formula helps us make sense of things by simplifying the chaos of history, transforming it into a narrative with dramatic form.

By analyzing these characters, we see how this set of *dramatis personae* creates a unique set of problems for political life. There are other ways to analyze political reality. One could offer a Marxist analysis that looks at class conflict and ideology. One could offer a feminist interpretation of political reality that exposes sexism and patriarchal power. Or one could look at political life from a Christian lens that sees an ongoing struggle between sin and salvation. And so on.

The interpretive framework explored in the present book focuses on the tragic trio and on the philosophical midwife who enlightens those who are engaged in the struggles of political life. Interpretive frameworks help us make sense of the world, even when they are conventional, "just so" stories. So we must admit that each situation is unique and there are blind spots. Despite this, common themes and story-lines can be observed.

THE COMMON STORY OF TOIL AND TROUBLE

When we see that this story is common, it means that the Trump era is not unique. Understanding this may help to defuse some of the angst that is afflicting the anti-Trump crowd. Some psychologists talked about "Trump Anxiety Disorder."[11] Trump and his supporters reject this as "Trump Derangement Syndrome"—an irrational negativity directed toward the president. When House Speaker Nancy Pelosi ripped up the president's speech after his 2020 State of the Union address, Trump accused her and the Democrats of suffering from Trump Derangement Syndrome: "That group is—you know, they say 'Trump Derangement Syndrome.' They've got it. They've got a bad case of it. You saw that. That was on display the other night when she ripped up the speech. That was terrible. It was a terrible—so disrespectful to our country."[12] But—and here is the problem—there is an open question of who is crazy and who is sane.

This question became even more acute after the 2020 election, when Trump and his minions were claiming that the election had been stolen. Most of the world accepted the reality of Joe Biden's win. But the

Trump faction lived in an alternate universe. The problem of falsehood and anxiety, derangement, and potential insanity is reminiscent of the dark and sinister world of tragedy. The drama of the 2020 election evokes and seems to echo images from *Antigone* or *Macbeth*. Reality itself seems torn and in dispute. There is always "toil and trouble," fires burning and cauldrons bubbling. "Fair is foul and foul is fair," as Macbeth's witches put it.

It might help to know that these kinds of questions—about truth and reality—and the turmoil of political life have always been with us. There were profound and fundamental disputes about Socrates, Jesus, and even the American revolutionaries. The followers of Socrates were viewed as strange and exotic. So too were the followers of Jesus. The American revolutionaries took a profound risk in rebelling against the world's dominant empire.

Knowing this does not make the turmoil go away. But it can help to defuse anxiety. There have always been tyrants, sycophants, and morons. There have always been plagues and pestilence. Our present troubles are not unique. And there have always been venal and vicious presidents. Before Trump arrived, Bill Clinton was committing adultery in the Oval Office and George W. Bush was looking for weapons of mass destruction in Iraq. The Bush debacle may be among the worst of recent history, since war broke out as the result of lies and incompetence. The Clinton family tragedy is however more significant for our present account because it is woven around that of Trump (in the struggle between Donald Trump and his nemesis, Hillary Clinton). The Clinton drama featured, in its first act, a charismatic man whose tyrannical sexual drive and tendency to lie and obfuscate resulted in his impeachment. In the second act, the president's faithful wife—a form of sycophant—remains loyal and seeks to redeem the family and herself by way of that loyalty. But in the third act, Hillary Clinton's own dreams of power are "Trumped" by the rival faction. And despite the dramatics, Bill and Hillary remain as popular among the party elite and the partisans of the Democratic Party as Trump does among "the base." The masses cheer and jeer from the sideline, saying either "Lock her up" or "I'm with her."

Before Clinton, there was Richard Nixon, whose character is often described in Shakespearean terms. Lyndon Johnson was crude and obnoxious. And John F. Kennedy had prodigious sexual appetites. Tyranny and tragedy have consistently haunted political life. In American history, presidents have lied. They have engaged in conquest. They have violated civil rights, set up concentration camps, and pushed the limits of power. The first president to be impeached was Andrew Johnson, who became president after the assassination of Abraham Lincoln. He behaved like an embattled tyrant, encountering resistance from the Congress and from General Ulysses S. Grant, who defied Johnson's orders.[13] But even Johnson had his sycophants and moronic partisan loyalists—which helps explain why, like Clinton and Trump, he was not removed from office despite his impeachment. As we discussed above, a heroic figure like Abraham Lincoln was accused of being a tyrant for suspending the right of habeas corpus and declaring martial law. John Wilkes Booth made that accusation against Lincoln, shouting "sic semper tyrannis" as he assassinated Lincoln. This Latin phrase means "thus always to tyrants." It is what Brutus is supposed to have said when he killed Julius Caesar. While this does not make Booth's murderous assault on the president defensible, it shows that the accusation of tyranny recurs throughout our history and follows familiar patterns.

Thus, there has always been tragedy, tyranny, and the temptations of power. Our political situation is not new. Our situation has many historical precedents. Plato described the ethical and philosophical problem of tyrants, sycophants, and the moronic masses a very long time ago in his book *The Republic*. So too did Aristotle in Book V of *Politics*. Sophocles and Euripides—the great tragic poets of ancient Greece—showed us this problem in dramatic form. Since then, Machiavelli, Shakespeare, and a variety of others have considered the nature of power, politics, and populism. Trump is a new entry into the historical record, to be made sense of with reference to the tradition of political philosophy, political art, and political science.[14]

We might like to think, however, that there is something unprecedented about the way that political power is obtained, manipulated, and distributed in the contemporary age. It is true that in the era of secularization, globalization, and modernization, there are new challenges and technologies. Communication is much faster today. Systems of artificial intelligence and virtual reality have created new problems. The entire world is caught up in a common network of economic, cultural, and political life. And our challenges—from nuclear weapons to climate change—pose existential risks. But some features of human nature and political power remain constant. The problems created by new communications technologies and other evolving tools and techniques are not unprecedented. Before Twitter and Russian trolls, there was yellow journalism and political pamphleteering. And before that, the masses were riled up by sophists and demagogues speaking in the forum or agora.

Each generation must learn that power, pride, ambition, ignorance, and corruption often walk hand in hand. We are shocked when we discover this. But what helps the shock to wear off is a glance at history. These problems are not new. And there are solutions and models from the past that can help us work through them. New technologies do transform these problems. Fake news, media silos, Facebook, and Twitter allow direct communication between the tyrant and the masses. And constitutional structures channel sycophantic urges in ways that are convoluted and often hidden. But the human psyche and its social relations remain familiar. Despite all that is new in the past centuries and decades, it remains perennially true that those who seek power are easily seduced by its temptations. It also remains true that the masses allow themselves to be manipulated by those who are willing to lie to them and use their ignorance against them. And in every epoch, there have been yes-men and suck-ups who facilitate the interaction between tyrants and their moronic followers. The Trump era has opened our eyes anew to a set of human problems that are universal and as old as human culture and civilization. It also reminds us of the perennial solution, which is wisdom, virtue, and enlightenment. A sense of history and a glance at human nature can give us a bit of hope that we, too, will survive the present crisis.

TYRANTS EVERYWHERE

Tyrants and morons have always been with us. They have always been identified as human failures. And we each contain a bit of the fool and the bully. All human beings can behave autocratically. Infants can behave like tiny tyrants. Adults can manipulate one another in an effort to gain power and satisfy their urges and ambitions. When tyrants encounter one another, there is a struggle for power. But the tyrant's preferred prey is the moron, the blind and stupid fool who is easily manipulated. The combination of stupidity and power is deadly and dangerous. And let's admit that stupidity is a common human failing. Human beings—each of us—behave foolish and stupidly from time to time. We, the gullible fools, are easily manipulated by unscrupulous rogues who prey upon our foolishness. But we morons do not know any better and so we willingly submit to—and even encourage—the bully.

Along with tyrants and fools, there are also sycophants. This is often overlooked, perhaps because the tyrants and the fools form a two-sided coin that is easier to conceive. The world would be easier to comprehend if there were only morons and tyrants. Sycophants form a third element. The sycophant is not as narcissistic and overtly brutal as the tyrant, even though the sycophant is motivated by the desire for power. And the sycophant is not as stupid as the fool, even though he cultivates a sort of deliberate blindness and dumbness—strategically keeping his mouth and his eyes shut. The sycophant knows the dangers of power and stupidity—and plays along anyway. Unlike the tyrant, who is a bullheaded bully, the sycophant is clever. He plays with words. He adjusts his behavior to the social situation. We might hold the sycophant responsible in a way that we do not with the tyrant or the fool.

It is easy enough to locate these three character types in the contemporary world. Donald Trump is easily understood as a would-be tyrant. His most zealous supporters among the masses are fools and morons. And the staff members of his political machine are the sycophants of this era.

Consider, for example, how Trump ranted and raged on Twitter. His rants reflected unbridled and uncensored outbursts of id. And from time to time in public speeches, Trump lets us know that "political correctness" is a mask that hides the tyrannical impulse. He said that he could speak like a regular politician—and then he would stiffen his spine, arch his eyebrows, and mock the polite language of the masked politician. Trump told us that politics was a game and show. He implied that it was not a moral endeavor based in principles, ideas, and morality.

Trump's sycophants supported the show. When the mask of political correctness falls too far off, his staff readjusts it or tries to explain away the tyrannical outburst. Trump's clique was careful not to offend him, since he rewarded loyalty and turned quickly against those who betrayed him. And while Trump was mostly a toothless tiger, the lesson of Alexander's murder of Callisthenes lurks in the background. Those who are close to a tyrant can end up dead if they don't kowtow and grovel.

But we risk oversimplifying. People in power supported Trump for a variety of reasons. Some were sycophants and would-be sycophants who benefited (or hoped to benefit) in some way from Trump's power—knowing full well what they are doing. Others "held their noses" (as media reports often put it) and went along. They knew that Trump was flawed but supported him for their own reasons. Thus, evangelical Christians, who should have been appalled at his marital infidelities, misogyny, and crudeness, held their noses and went along in order to get social conservatives appointed to positions of power including the Supreme Court. Thus, businesspeople who recognized serious flaws in Trump's policies—say, his trade wars and tariffs or his antagonism toward European and North American trading partners—went along because of tax cuts or other self-interested economic reasons. These people are like the sycophants of the inner circle. They wanted something from Trump. They understood his flaws. But they played along out of self-interest.

Finally, let's consider the outright fools and morons. They didn't merely hold their noses and go along. They didn't seem to know that there was something here that smelled rotten. Or they didn't bother to find out. Instead, they cheered on the tyrant because it was fun and it felt good. They didn't really care about the policy implications. They were not really strategizing their own self-interest. They were merely along for the ride, pulled by the emotions of the moment. They didn't bother to think carefully or inform themselves about the details. Instead, they joined in cheers and jeers—from "Lock her up!" (referring to Hillary Clinton) to "Send her back!" (referring to Rep. Ilhan Omar). The cheering and jeering masses often do not even know the details of the case. They are simply swept along with the tide of emotion. At its most extreme, this moronic behavior devolves into conspiracy theories such as QAnon's, which are so outrageous that they beggar belief.

All of this came to a head on January 6, 2021, when Trump insurrectionists marched on the Capitol, motivated by outrageous falsehoods.

Some thought Biden and Pelosi were communists. Others thought COVID-19 was a sinister plot. Some believed pedophiles, Satanists, and lizard people had infiltrated the government. While those lies appear to be so bizarre that no serious person could believe them, there were other more plausible and insidious lies. There was the lie that the election had been stolen. There was the false belief that the Congress and vice president could overturn the Electoral College. Most important was the false belief that violence would work. And as this broth of bullshit boiled over, the world was appalled and surprised. But we should not have been that surprised. Human beings have believed—and died and killed in the name of—all kinds of bizarre bullshit.

One typical analysis of the "Trump voter" focused on the sense of grievance felt by white males, whose status has been challenged by globalization, immigration, and so on. But this assumes that those white males are bothering to think carefully about status, identity, and economic policy. There may be some Trump voters who carefully weigh out the pros and cons. But most of the people at a political rally are not thinking. They are emoting and reacting. Consider, for another example, the taunting of journalists that occurred at Trump rallies and the cries of "fake news." If pressed to explain what this means, there is no depth of understanding of the issue—especially since the news reports about fake news are themselves often fake, coming from the wingnut fringe of conspiracy theories and from trolls who sow distrust for a living. These rallying cries do not reflect careful study. They are just plain fun. They are taunts, slogans, and chants. There is no thinking behind these outbursts. This is foolish and moronic: the unthinking grunts of the crowd.

I repeat that although the Trump era is the occasion for this book, this book is not a single-minded attack on Trump and his people. These same *dramatis personae* are found in other times and in other places: the details change but the masks and roles remain the same. This is a problem for all of us—of whatever party and whatever stage of history. A simple way of putting this is that it is always the age of Trump. Tyrants, sycophants, and morons have always been with us.

We mentioned the era of Bill Clinton above, as well as a variety of others in the American tradition. Nixon had his sycophants; and many morons were ignorant of what was going on in his White House. Hitler was surrounded by yes-men, and the "good Germans" were swept along by fascism. Most of Alexander's entourage gave in to his desire for worship and groveling. And so on. Tyrants, sycophants, and morons fill the stage of political life. Sometimes what we watch is more comedy than tragedy: a stage filled with porn stars and reality-show caricatures. But at other times, the farce becomes atrocity when the will of the tyrant becomes genocidal, when the sycophants are racists and anti-Semites, and when the moronic masses provide material and political support for murder.

CONCLUSION: WISDOM, VIRTUE, AND DEMOCRATIC EDUCATION

The structural cure for all of this is separation of powers and the rule of law. But behind that is the need for virtue at all three levels—at the level of the ruler, the bureaucracy, and the people themselves. The theory of virtue is complex—and there is a rich and extensive literature in "virtue ethics" that is presumed here. We can simplify this by focusing on the four virtues identified by the ancient Greeks as cardinal or primary virtues: wisdom, courage, justice, and moderation. These four virtues are mutually supporting. Of the four, wisdom is the broadest and most important. Wisdom is an obvious remedy for foolishness. That wisdom is the cure for tyranny may not be as obvious. Wisdom must be accompanied by virtues such as moderation and a sense of justice, which prevent people from becoming tyrants. But it is wisdom that keeps the would-be tyrant's eyes open to his own selfish impulses and the fatal flaw of hubris. And wisdom clues the would-be tyrant in to the sweet and beguiling words of the sycophants. Sycophants, of course, need to be wise enough to know how to manipulate and cajole. But in addition to lacking the courage to "speak truth to power" (as the contemporary saying goes), they also lack the wisdom to see that in supporting the tyrant at the expense of the masses, they are sowing the seeds of their own future demise. The sycophant is in a precarious position. The tyrant can turn against him at any moment. And the foolish masses will not understand the machinations and calculations that motivated the sycophant. When the tides of history change, the masses will also turn against the sycophant.

In conclusion, let's return to Aristotle and the importance of the rule of law. Tyrannical power cannot be consolidated in a democracy when the masses are wise—awake and aware—and when the law prevents it. The temptations of sycophancy are weakened when potential sycophants realize that the short-term rewards of sucking up are often outweighed by the long-term risk of linking their lives and careers to a tyrant in a system that prosecutes law breakers and accomplices.

The prescriptive thesis of this book is grounded in a broad defense of democracy and moral education. We prevent tyranny by cultivating wisdom—and other virtues. We cultivate wisdom and virtue by way of education. In order to be effective, education must be broadly democratic, inclusive, and empowering. For democracy to work, there must also be legal structures in place that prevent a would-be tyrant from consolidating power.

In this broken and tragic world, there are no panaceas. There is no guarantee that democratic education and wisdom will permanently fix things. It is difficult to find virtuous friends and wise teachers. History shows that things fall apart. With each new generation, the task of education and self-knowledge reemerges. And so, while we ought to remain hopeful, we must also acknowledge the sense of tragedy. We should work to cultivate wisdom and support democratic education; we should seek out virtuous friends and wise teachers. But we must also reconcile ourselves to the fact that tyrants, morons, and sycophants will always be with us.

II

THE TRAGIC TRIO

5

THE TYRANT'S PRIDE

On Ambition, Power, and Greatness

Hubris gives birth to tyranny.

—Sophocles, *Oedipus Tyrannos* (873)

A number of people have called Donald Trump a tyrant.[1] The same charge has been leveled against Barack Obama and a number of other contemporary leaders.[2] In April 2021, a congresswoman called Joe Biden a tyrant for calling for gun control.[3] And so it goes. On one very simple and subjective definition, tyrants are those we hate. One of the goals of the present chapter is to separate *ad hominem* hyperbole from the reality of tyranny. Unbridled ambition may indicate a tyrannical personality. But a tyrannical personality does not become a full-blown tyrant unless the legal system permits him to consolidate power. Luckily, the American legal system has so far prevented real tyranny from taking hold.

FASHIONABLE TYRANNY

When Trump was impeached the first time, Democrats accused him of behaving tyrannically. The impeachment charges against Trump included "abuse of power." Democrat Adam Schiff, who led the House's impeachment inquiry, accused Trump of behaving lawlessly and tyrannically. Schiff's Democratic colleague Jerry Nadler said Trump was a "dictator."[4] Trump's defenders, as might be predicted, accused his accusers of behaving tyrannically. Representative Mark Green said that Nancy Pelosi, the House leader, was "tyrannical" and "out of control."[5] While these accusations hung in the air in 2019, they were even more urgent in the aftermath of the 2020 election and the debacle of January 6. In Trump's second impeachment in the House of Representatives, the word *tyranny* was flung again in the direction of the White House. Representative Ilhan Omar said, "For years we have been asked to turn a blind eye to the criminality, corruption and blatant disregard for the rule of law from this tyrant in the White House."[6] Representative Rashida Tlaib said, "Donald Trump is a tyrant that has continued to endanger and bring harm upon the people in the United States."[7]

Tyranny—or more specifically accusations of tyranny—has become fashionable today. But the accusation of tyranny has always, in a sense, been fashionable. This point was also made twenty-five hundred years ago in a comedy by Aristophanes—*The Wasps*—where a character says that these days every other word is "tyranny" and "conspiracy." He had never heard the word *tyranny* for fifty years, he said, but now it is as common as sardines. Aristophanes is onto something: the more you are primed to see tyranny, the more likely you are to see it. But some of this becomes absurd. To say that Trump, Obama, Biden, or Pelosi are tyrants seems to diminish the power of the epithet. I do not want to downplay the damage wrought by Trump. Nor do I deny that Trump has a personality that appears to be tyrannical. But I reiterate that Trump remained a would-be tyrant—thanks in part to the pushback from the House of Representatives. If Trump and Obama are tyrants, they are pale versions in comparison with Alexander, Nero, and other famous tyrants. The reason for this is that the American system does not permit tyrants to consolidate power. The United States is set up with constitutional checks and balances. We understand the importance of rule of law. And although slavery was a uniquely American form of tyranny, it was abolished by Abraham Lincoln—who was himself accused of being a tyrant by Southern slavers.

Tyranny is not only fashionable. It also seems to be in the eye of the beholder. Thomas Hobbes made this point in the seventeenth century in his *Leviathan*. He suggested that a tyrant is simply a ruler we do not like. He says, "The name of Tyranny, signifies nothing more, nor less, than the name of Sovereignty, be it in one, or many men, saving that they that use the former word, *are understood to be angry with them* they call Tyrants" (emphasis added).[8] Hobbes's point is crucial for situating the difficulty of the present chapter—and book. When we describe someone as a tyrant, is this merely an expression of disapproval based in emotion: Is a tyrant merely a ruler we don't like or are angry with? Hobbes points toward an emotivist account of the ordinary usage of the term *tyrant*: the accusation of tyranny is understood as merely a kind of emotional outburst. As Shakespeare might suggest, the tyrant is he whose name blisters our tongue.[9] But is this merely a matter of our own taste, or is there something objectively poisonous about certain rulers? A subjectively oriented account of tyranny would say that when we dislike a ruler's policies or ambition, we describe him as a tyrant. As a subjective pejorative, the word is intended to discredit the so-called tyrant by linking him with treachery, deceit, and murder of the cruelest despots of history. But if we remain at the level of subjectivity, we are left with the problem that one person's tyrant is another person's heroic leader. A central question must be whether there is an objectively valid definition of tyranny, which can be used to evaluate the leader and decide whether the person we accuse of tyranny is in fact a tyrant.

History shows us that the word *tyrant* is politically loaded. At one point in England under Henry VIII, for example, it was illegal to use *tyrant* (along with other terms such as heretic, schismatic, infidel, or usurper) to describe the king. The punishment for calling the king a tyrant was death.[10] Henry VIII was, of course, a tyrant. The fact that he executed those who called him a tyrant seems to make this point clear: a tyrant is a ruler who murders his enemies (and his wives!). The politicization of the term does not mean that there is no objectively valid definition of tyranny. We must understand that objective definition first. And then we can attempt to apply it in an impartial way to particular cases. As I show here, such an objective approach shows that none of our modern American presidents is actually a tyrant—whether Nixon, Obama, Clinton, or Trump. Some of these individuals may have tyrannical urges—or a tyrannical soul, perhaps. But they are not tyrants. The reason for this is that the political structure prevents tyranny from forming. This is, however, a contingent point. That tyranny is prevented depends upon the vicissitudes of political life, including the role played by bureaucratic sycophants and the moronic masses. A tyrant cannot fulfill his tyrannical wishes without the support of sycophants and morons and a compliant political structure.

DEFINING TYRANNY

There is a long tradition of thinking about tyranny and a long history of the term, which can be traced back to the Greeks. We will turn to the Greeks in a moment. But since we mentioned Henry VIII above, we might begin with Thomas More, who was executed for treason by Henry VIII in 1535. More is famous for his book *Utopia*, which explores an ideal political society. The other side of this ideal is More's study of the tradition of thinking about tyranny that can be traced back to Aristotle and the Greeks. He explained that a true king "respects the law" and thus differs from "a cruel tyrant" as follows: "A tyrant rules his subjects as slaves, a king thinks of his subjects as his own children."[11] The good king is a benevolent father, while the tyrant is predatory and exploitative. More puts this metaphorically by saying that a good king is a watchdog who guards his flock from the wolves, but a tyrant is the wolf. This was also what Plato suggested when he explained that a tyrant was transformed from a man into a wolf (*Republic* 566a).

Shakespeare picked up this metaphor. He has Brutus explain that Caesar became a wolf who learned to prey upon the Roman sheep. The theme of tyranny is found throughout Shakespeare's work. He pins the blame on ambition. Shakespeare's Brutus says that Julius Caesar's ambition ran wild. And through cruelty and callousness, ambition turned into tyranny. After Brutus stabs Caesar, he says, "Ambition's debt is paid." Brutus offers us a poetic definition of the tyrant's abuse of power; he says, "Th'abuse of greatness is when it disjoins remorse from power."[12] Remorselessness is the result of ambition and pride run amok. The tyrannical soul is so sure of itself that it cuts off compassion and fails to restrain itself under the moral law. One remedy for tyranny is tyrannicide, which is the subject of *Julius Caesar*, *Macbeth*, and others of Shakespeare's works. After Caesar is killed, Cinna exclaims, "Liberty! Freedom! Tyranny is

Dead!" But the audience knows that this is only a temporary respite from a perennial problem. As Shakespeare implies in *Henry VIII*, the mighty eventually all fall down: "How soon this mightiness meets misery." And while it might give us hope to know that every tyrant eventually dies, it is also a source of the tragic sense of life, since history shows us that new tyrants continue to rise and take the place of those who fall.

A more permanent and proactive cure for tyranny must involve structural changes that prevent would-be tyrants from assuming absolute power, as well as moral education that puts pride in its place. Constitutional remedies are not the purview of a poet. But the poet can show us the spiritual problem. What is needed—and what the poet provides—is an understanding of human nature, which shows that the sort of unbridled power the tyrant seeks is the shadow of a shadow. This does not mean that there is no such thing as a benevolent usage of power or that justice (or tyranny) is in the eye of the beholder. Shakespeare does flirt with this idea. However, the lesson we take is that beyond these mere opinions, there is some larger reality in which justice and moderation rule. When Hamlet discusses the prison of Denmark under his tyrant uncle, Rosencrantz and Guildenstern provide us with the thought that ambition (and power and justice as well) is but a shadow's shadow.[13] This may seem like a kind of nihilism. But it echoes the idea that we find in Plato's *Republic*, where the goods of the cave (power, glory, etc.) are seen as mere reflections of a reflection of genuine good. In Shakespeare, as in Plato and More, the desire for a utopia in which there is an unambiguous concordance of liberty, justice, and virtue remains merely a hope. That hope must be guided by an ideal of good government that also tells us why tyranny is unjustified and immoral power.

Philosophers have offered objective definitions that make this clear. Locke said, "Tyranny is the exercise of power to which nobody can have a right."[14] A tyrant exercises power in a way that goes beyond what is right or lawful. Locke explains, "Wherever law ends, tyranny begins."[15] He also says: "That is what happens when someone employs the power he has in his hands, not for the good of those who are under it but for his own private individual advantage."[16] Locke also introduces the word *despot* into our discussion. Both *despot* and *tyrant* have Greek etymologies; and both are connected to the idea of a person with unlimited power.[17]

For the most part, *despot* and *tyrant* can be used synonymously and in connection with other terms such as *autocrat* and *dictator*. *Autocrat* is a Greek term that reflects the idea of a singular source of power or ruler who embodies the state in himself. *Dictator* is a Latin term that has come to mean a central source of power, typically united in the person of the dictator. But a dictatorship can also be united in a party as in Karl Marx's idea of the "dictatorship of the proletariat." We might also note that the term *tyrant* can be extended in such a way that it can apply to a party, as in John Stuart Mill's discussion of the "tyranny of the majority." At any rate, *tyrant* seems more decisively pejorative than *despot* (it is possible to say that there is a "benevolent despot" in English while the idea of a "benevolent tyrant" seems oxymoronic).

Locke explains that despotic power is absolute and arbitrary—and in violation of the natural law: "Despotical power is an absolute, arbitrary power one man has over another, to take away his life whenever he pleases; and this is a power which neither Nature gives, for it has made no such distinction between one man and another, nor compact can convey."[18] The example of despotic power that Locke provides is of captives taken in war, who are subject to the will of their captors without recourse to some prior agreement or social "compact." In the background of Locke's discussion of tyranny is this account of despotism. Tyranny takes despotic power to its nadir: it is absolute and arbitrary power that is exercised selfishly and solely for the benefit of the tyrant. This leads directly to Locke's discussion of revolution. If the tyrant exercises power unjustly and despotically, then the people have the right to rise up and depose the tyrant. It is important to note that one could desire exorbitant power without actually having that power: one could want such power but be foiled by circumstance. When there is a system of checks and balances and the rule of law, which limits power, a would-be tyrant may be limited.

Thus, we ought to properly say that a tyrant is a person who combines an ambitious and prideful soul that wants absolute and arbitrary power with the real capacity to exercise power in unbridled ways. There are three components of tyranny then. A tyrant is a person:

1. who *desires absolute power* in exorbitant ways that are not constrained by moral or legal limits;

2. who *actually does use power* in that way; and
3. whose *interest in power is based upon ambition, pride, and self-interest*, without regard for justice, benevolence, or other moral concerns.

This threefold rubric helps rule out people who are forced to use power exorbitantly or immorally (because they are coerced, for example) or who accidentally (or unintentionally) violate moral/legal limits. It also rules out would-be tyrants who want to use power in extra-legal ways but who are not able to (because they are not able to grab power or get elected—or are prevented by the separation of powers). Finally, this definition rules out someone who uses power in exorbitant ways but who believes that this usage is justifiable in moral terms (say, in the case of someone who breaks a rule for what they earnestly believe is the greater good—Lincoln comes to mind, as an example here of a president whose extra-constitutional actions were undertaken for benevolent purposes). Applying this definition will depend upon a number of factors including both external deeds, public discourses of justification, the legal system, and the putative tyrant's intentions and state of mind. Despite these difficulties, it is possible to apply the term *tyrant* in an objective sense.

One crucial factor here has to do with motivation and intention. Locke says that the tyrant is concerned with self-interest and his own personal advantage. But if we push deeper, we might say that for the tyrant, moral justification is irrelevant—or the vocabulary of morality is meaningless. At any rate, the tyrant is simply not concerned with moral and legal limitations. He sees these as merely conventional restraints that either lack objective reality or that do not apply to the sort of exemplary and exceptional individual he takes himself to be. In the first case, the tyrant is a moral relativist or nihilist of sorts. He views the social compact and the moral law as something that lacks substance and that can be abrogated by his own willful ambition. In the second case, the tyrant's relativism is linked to his own narcissism, his inflated sense of importance, his own self-glorification, and his desire to be God (as discussed in chapter 1).

The Western tradition links tyranny to pride—or better to *hubris*, which is a negative kind of pride. Each of our tragic characters has flaws that can be stated in simple general terms: the tyrant is afflicted by pride, the sycophant by cunning, and the moronic masses by stupidity. But pride only gets a would-be tyrant so far. Tyranny is in fact the conjunction of pride and power. The tyrant wants power for the sake of pride, which helps explain the tyrant's understanding of power as an outgrowth of personality. The tyrant may pridefully think that he himself is the source of law, for example, or that his very existence is the sun around which political life ought properly to orbit. This is what we might see in Louis XIV's motto *"L'État, c'est moi."* But a different kind of pride places the tyrant, in his own estimation, somehow above the law. This is the conclusion that a tyrant might draw if he thinks that the law is merely conventional and is only obeyed out of self-interest. Rousseau explains this in drawing a subtle distinction between a tyrant and a despot. He says, "The tyrant is he who thrusts himself in contrary to the laws to govern in accordance with the laws; the despot is he who sets himself above the laws themselves."[19] We could nitpick the difference between Locke and Rousseau on their technical usage of terms like *tyrant* and *despot*. But whatever we choose to call it, the problem of exorbitant power is the essential issue. A would-be tyrant wants power; his pride, ambition, and greed lead him on. A system of checks and balances can prevent the tyrant from gaining the power he wants. But when the tyrant gains power, his pride is reinforced. It comes to seem to him that he is in fact the exceptional one to whom conventional morality does not apply or the one who deserves to exist in the liminal space beyond the law.

A TYRANNICAL SOUL DOES NOT A TYRANT MAKE

Let's return to the question of whether this definition and analysis can be applied objectively. It is difficult to establish an objective evaluation of political life from within political life. Our evaluations are easily biased by our point of view, our limited access to information, and our orientation to action.[20] While this chapter attempts to consider tyranny from an objective point of view, the examples we examine—especially when they come from the contemporary world—always risk bias. Nonetheless, it is helpful to consider real-world examples, since those examples can inform our judgments and normative concepts through a process of reflective equilibrium.

So let's apply this standard to Donald Trump. Trump has been described as an egoist and narcissist. He is easily angered. He appears to be obsessed with popularity and loyalty. He lies and exaggerates. He is promiscuous, relentless, and inflammatory. His personality seems quite similar to what the Greeks warned about with regard to tyranny. Furthermore, like Thrasymachus in Plato's *Republic*, he seems to view morality and the law as a matter of power and self-interest rather than a question of justice or goodness (see appendix A). We see this in Trump's motto "Make America great again." What matters for Trump is greatness—not goodness. Unlike goodness, which is correlated with virtue and morality, greatness is correlated only with power and popularity. This is what matters for the tyrant who schemes to obtain power—often by flattering the masses.

But was Trump really a tyrant? The answer is no. He may have wanted exorbitant power and he may be narcissistic. The sycophants in Trump's party tried to help him keep power, and Trump's "base" supported those efforts. But the constitutional system prevented Trump from establishing a full-fledged tyranny. This shows us why we need strong constitutional limitations on power. A would-be tyrant such as Trump shows us the risks and dangers of full-fledged tyranny.

Trump is not the only contemporary politician who has been accused of being a tyrant. Before Trump, President Obama was accused of tyranny. Senator Ted Cruz accused Obama of consolidating power in a way that appeared to be tyrannical: "What the Obama administration is doing to harm the American economy is the sort of power grab that our founders would have recognized as tyranny."[21] One focal point of this complaint was Obama's effort to create health care reform through the Affordable Care Act—which critics call "Obamacare." In the foreword to a book titled *Lawless: The Obama Administration's Unprecedented Assault on the Constitution and the Rule of Law*, Senator Cruz explained that Obamacare was an example of the way that Obama went around Congress and put "ideology above fidelity to the law."[22] He cited other examples of Obama's "usurpation" of power such as the DREAM Act—and he generally describes "Progressives"—beginning with Woodrow Wilson—as engaged in a long struggle against the limits of the Constitution. Cruz quotes James Madison (*Federalist* 47), who said that "the concentration of executive, legislative, and judicial power in the same hands is the very definition of tyranny." He continues: "President Obama's actions suggest that he does not believe (or just does not care) in the truth Madison described."[23] The charges against Obama are further explained by the author of the book, David Bernstein. Bernstein explains that by appealing to an "end-justifies the means" kind of reasoning Obama employs "exactly the rhetoric and reasoning used to justify tyranny around the world."[24]

One of the questions at issue here is our conception of the American presidency. The American system has gradually evolved in the direction of what Arthur Schlessinger called, during the Nixon era, "the Imperial presidency." There is an open question about whether the contemporary American system makes it possible for the president to act tyrannically. There has been a tendency of presidents to avoid congressional oversight, for example, by using executive orders, signing statements, making recess appointments, and so on. In this regard, the accumulation of power in the presidency is a bipartisan problem. For example, with regard to executive orders, recent presidents have all widely used them.[25] To cite a very important example, presidents send troops to fight without formal declarations of war from Congress, which are required by the Constitution (article 1, sec. 8, clause 11). An important question is how the other two branches of government (and the states) can and should respond to the accretion of power in the hands of the president. Political scientists can help us answer that question. Here we are focused on philosophy, ethics, and moral psychology. This leads us to consider the character (or soul) of the person who is president—his virtues, his wisdom, and his understanding of power.

In this moral sense, I suggest that there is something unique about Trump. Trump seems to exemplify the kind of greed, ambition, and egoistic pride that is typical of the tyrant. He appears to have a tyrannical soul. While Senator Cruz claims Obama behaved tyrannically, the personalities of Trump and Obama are different. It is difficult, of course, to peer inside the soul of another person. But Trump's words and deeds seem to indicate the character flaws we have been describing. As I show in appendix A, Trump appears to be morally inarticulate. Trump touts his accomplishments and celebrates his "greatness." He brags of his intelligence and skill. He is acutely aware of those who attack and insult him—and he returns the favor, constantly vying for power and vaunting his success.

It is thus not surprising that a number of prominent thinkers have accused Donald Trump of being a tyrant or even a fascist. For example, in 2018, Jeffrey Sachs, a professor at Columbia University, published an opinion piece titled "Trump Is Taking US down the Path to Tyranny."[26] In the summer of 2019, Jason Stanley, a philosopher at Yale University warned of "fascism" appearing at a Trump rally at which Trump's followers chanted "Send her back!" when Representative Ilhan Omar was mentioned.[27] In popular usage, fascism, tyranny, and totalitarianism are often synonymous. But the difference between fascism and tyranny has to do with the role of the party and nationalism. In general, a tyrant seeks self-aggrandizement, while a fascist party seeks national unity and strength. At any rate, tyranny is often linked to a disorder of the soul. Consider Angel Jaramillo Torres and Marc Benjamin Sable, the editors of a work of political philosophy titled *Trump and Political Philosophy: Leadership, Statesmanship, and Tyranny*. Torres and Sable conclude:

> Classical political thought, with its emphasis on virtue, typically presented tyranny as a function of the tyrant's base character. By contrast, modern and postmodern interpretations tend to emphasize the tyrant's willful imposition of political goals contrary to the common good. We believe that Trump has a tyrannical soul, in both senses, and that he vacillates between knave and factionist.[28]

This claim about Trump's tyrannical soul is worth considering. I reiterate that it is very difficult to psychoanalyze someone at a distance. Nonetheless, we do see a kind of tyrannical pride and ambition in Trump's behavior and rhetoric.

Ambition and pride are not merely problems for politicians. This is a broadly human problem. We can all be tempted by power and seduced by pride. Fathers can be proud and tyrannical; the same is true for ambitious CEOs and priests. Hubris can afflict each of us. Hubris as a vice that is uniquely antidemocratic, cruel, and vicious. Hubris is contrasted with justifiable pride. Arrogance, narcissism, and aggressive self-assertion come from a mis-estimation of one's value and worth. In its more pernicious form, this is linked to a kind of relativism and nihilism that are antithetical to the rule of law and moral restraint. Tyrannical pride focuses on greatness without concern for goodness. The solution is found in the virtue tradition, which teaches that the source of authentic pride is goodness, not greatness.

EXORBITANT POWER

A tyrant is one who wants power that is exorbitant and whose actual power allows him to behave in excessive ways. Exorbitant power is outside of the normal course of things. The word *exorbitant* literally means to be outside of the orbit: to be outside of the ruts and channels in which life ordinarily proceeds. As Leo Strauss put it, echoing the passage from Locke we quoted above, tyranny is "essentially rule without laws."[29] This is what makes tyranny violent, unruly, capricious, uncanny, and strange. In a sense, tyranny is like a stroke of lightning or an outburst of freedom. It arises from some mysterious externality and arrives in the world as an alien force. A somewhat benevolent face may be put upon the tyrant if we see him as striving to establish a new norm. Something like this can be found in Nietzsche's thinking about "the Overman" (*Übermensch*), who creates a new order of things based on his will-to-power. The tyrant is not interested in morality or justice (or even in the fascist ideal of "the nation" or "the party"). Rather, the tyrant wants to aggrandize himself and rebuild the world in his own image. And when the prideful soul of a person inflamed with tyrannical desire finds himself with power, there will be a tendency to set aside morality, truth, and the rule of law—those constraints that prevent the tyrant from fulfilling his wish to establish new norms, to be the source of truth and the foundation of law.

When stated this broadly, it is easy to see that the tyrant has a God complex: he wants to be the savior, the creator, and the source of things. Or rather, he has such a deep and prideful belief in himself and his own powers that he comes to think that he is actually a god, a superman, or a messiah. In the summer of 2019, this sort of language did in fact show up in the Trump tragedy. At one point President Trump suggested that Jews who vote for Democrats are either ignorant or disloyal. The president then re-tweeted a comment attributed to Wayne Allyn Root that said Jews in Israel love him like he was "the King of Israel" and the "second coming of God."[30] Now Trump likely does not believe that he is the Messiah (of course, how would we know . . .?). But the fact that he would re-tweet such a blasphemous claim shows the problem. This problem extends to Wayne Allyn Root and other Trump supporters who say these sorts of things. The sycophants around Trump exaggerate his virtues in ways that would seem to be sacrilegious.

This begins to sound extreme. But the Western tradition has tended to view pride as a sin because it does in fact tend toward sacrilege. When Thomas Aquinas addressed the question of whether pride was a sin, he made the connection with God explicit.[31] God's power and goodness are justifiably a source of God's pride—and of human pride, insofar as we are created in the image of God. Good pride glorifies God (and thus also is humble), while sinful pride glorifies the self and seeks to put oneself into the place of God. As Aquinas says, following Jerome, sinful pride resists God. But humble pride (if such a thing is not an oxymoron) is self-esteem that nonetheless submits to God, the moral law, and so on.

Like a god, the tyrant operates in a realm that is beyond the law and that rejects the moral and cultural norms of ordinary life. In Plato's *Republic*, the character Thrasymachus describes tyranny as the excessive power of consummate injustice. The tyrant is the one who does exactly what he wants, who demands that others do what he wants, and who is able and willing to make his enemies miserable. Thrasymachus explains: "This is tyranny, which both by stealth and by force takes away what belongs to others, both sacred and profane, both private and public, not little by little but at one swoop" (*Republic* 344). The tyrant takes power and lords it over all things, inserting himself like a new god. We saw at the outset that one of Plato's other characters, Theages, thought that tyrannical power would be godlike. We saw that in another dialogue, Plato suggested that Alcibiades wanted to rule the whole world. What Thrasymachus adds to this discussion is the idea that the tyrant's godlike power gives him the power to establish a new moral norm. As Thrasymachus suggests, the tyrant establishes an idea of a "justice" based upon what he says. The key to this is strength and power. The tyrant wants power because it is power that allows him to establish a new law created in his own image. Thus the idea of tyranny points us toward the foundation of the legal and moral universe. In the passage quoted above, Thrasymachus hints at the religious implications of tyranny. And indeed, according to the Liddell Scott Greek lexicon, the Greek term *tyrannos* is associated with the gods.[32] The gods are the original tyrants. They rule the universe. Their power is exorbitant—outside of the orbit of moral life. They establish norms, laws, customs, and the good itself.

The gods are more than human. With their excessive power, they appear as tyrants. We might also say that animals are tyrants. They do

what they want, existing in a world of power and interest that is not ame-
nable to moral education. Thus, when Aristotle suggests that gods and
animals are not political, since they do not live in cities or think about
justice, there is an indirect suggestion that gods and animals are tyrannical. When humans behave tyrannically, we either revert to the level of
the beasts or we attempt to transcend humanity and become like gods.

There is a connection between tyranny and sovereignty.[33] This connection is political, religious, and psychological. Sovereignty becomes
tyranny when it appears to declare a kind of power that is exceptional or
exorbitant. In the Christian tradition, it is God that is the sovereign of
the universe. This sovereign power allows God to establish and enforce
the moral law. Ideally there is supposed to be a necessary connection
between God's power and His goodness. God's omnipotence (his glory,
power, or greatness) is connected to his omnibenevolence (his perfect
goodness). But not everyone agrees. In Milton's *Paradise Lost*, Satan
complains that God is a tyrant whose "Sole reigning holds the Tyranny
of Heav'n" (Book 1, line 124). On this cynical view (it is the view of Satan
after all . . .), God's power is primary and not limited by God's goodness.
Leaving this critique aside, we should note that there is supposed to be
an analogy between religious sovereignty and political sovereignty.[34] In
the political realm, as understood in the natural law tradition, legitimate
sovereignty is supposed to be based on the connection between power
and morality. Tyranny occurs when there is a disconnect between greatness (power) and goodness (morality).

REVOLUTIONS AND TRANSITIONS

When Thomas Jefferson and the American revolutionaries declared
their independence from England, they invoked the natural law tradition and declared that the king had become despotic and tyrannical. The
Declaration states: "The history of the present King of Great Britain is
a history of repeated injuries and usurpations, all having in direct object
the establishment of an absolute Tyranny over these States." It continues: "A Prince, whose character is thus marked by every act which may
define a Tyrant, is unfit to be the ruler of a free people." The revolutionaries drew their inspiration from Locke. They believed that the king

of England was behaving tyrannically and justified their revolution as a legitimate response to tyranny. This shows us the importance of this conversation: the stakes are quite high. But it also throws us back to the Hobbesian worry that tyranny is in the eye of the beholder. Some of the colonial loyalists did not believe that King George was a tyrant. Others may have been sycophantically engaged with the British power structure. And the masses on both sides likely struggled to make sense of the whole thing.

When a new sovereign is declared, there will be deep questions and divided opinion. This is obviously true in the case of revolutions. But it is also the case in democratic transitions. When your candidate wins, you celebrate. When your candidate loses, you grouse about how the other side grabbed power. You may even complain, as Donald Trump has, about election fraud, which is ultimately a complaint about the legitimacy of the transition of power in a democracy.

Discussion of the question of sovereignty, revolution, and democratic transitions leaves us with questions about the source or foundation of the law and the consent of the governed. In the Christian political tradition, the sovereign was a person who existed outside of the law as the source and administrator of law. But in the social contract tradition, the notion of sovereignty shifts toward claims about constitutions, majoritarian political structures, and legal/moral principles that are either independent of the law (as in natural rights) or are the result of some original agreement. In liberal-democratic theory, questions still exist about the status of the executive power. Non-tyrannical power is limited and functional. In modern political life, ordinary power is determined by roles and functions within the constitutional system. Tyrannical power aims beyond the law and its functionally limited power to a kind of exceptional power that rests with the person and not with the role. This relates to the issue of sovereignty beyond the law, as formulated by Carl Schmitt, who said, "Sovereign is he who decides on the exception."[35] The sovereign's power is in a sense outside of the constitutional system since—on Schmitt's view—the sovereign would be entitled or empowered to make exceptions to the law (supposedly on Schmitt's view in defense of the legal system itself). In Schmitt's analysis, this happens in times of crisis or emergency. Furthermore, the exceptional act or decision is in the most profound sense a genuine decision: it is not guided by law or norm; it is based on the will of the sovereign. However, when the will of the sovereign is the sole power, tyranny arrives. We might hope that the sovereign exception is benevolent. But exceptional power can encourage the sovereign to think that it is *he himself who is exceptional*.

The questions raised by Schmitt, Thrasymachus, and Strauss have come to the fore in the Trump era. We have been forced to consider whether the president can be indicted for possible illegal behavior that included threats to the electoral system and thus to democracy itself. The question of whether a sitting president can be indicted is about the nature of sovereign power. A practical question exists: Can the president properly execute his duties while under investigation; and for the good of the functioning of the government, is investigation or indictment practically useful? But the deeper question is about the status of the law itself. Is the person who is the president subject to the law, while serving as president? Can he pardon himself—as Trump suggested he might?

These questions point us toward the depths of political philosophy and questions about the status and source of the law. Now let's turn to the psychological question, following up on a point made above with reference to Schmitt. Schmitt suggests that true sovereignty is a power of decision: the sovereign is he who decides to administer the law and who decides when to suspend the law in time of crisis or emergency. The issue of decision connects us with the idea of autonomy and the sovereignty of the individual. Human persons are autonomous insofar as they have the capacity to decide; and this decision power extends up to the point of the autonomous person giving themselves the norms that he or she will abide by. The word *auto-nomy* can be translated literally as self-rule or giving oneself norms (*nomos* is a word for law or norm). Now, in the Western moral tradition, especially in the tradition associated with Immanuel Kant, autonomy is supposed to be subject to the moral law. We are autonomous, on Kant's account, when we give ourselves a rule that conforms with the moral law. Moral decisions are thus not capricious, willful, egoistical, self-interested, or anarchic; rather, moral decisions are autonomous even though, when making a moral decision, we voluntarily subject ourselves to the moral law.

Thus, we can say that tyranny occurs when autonomy becomes capricious, arbitrary, and anarchic. A tyrannical person refuses to submit to the moral law. Instead, he substitutes self-will for law. His choices are capricious: they lack order, coherence, and continuity. Returning to Thrasymachus's account of the tyrant, we might say that tyrannical persons are only interested in a version of "morality" that is entirely self-oriented. They declare their will as law. They want what they want and declare it to be good. They thus also refuse to accept the moral law as legitimate. Like Satan in Milton's account, they wage war against morality and the sovereignty of the moral law. The tyrant is narcissistic and egomaniacal. He or she is indifferent to the moral claims made by others. He is indifferent to demands for consistency and truth. He pursues his own selfish desires. And here is the important point: the tyrant lacks guilt or remorse. He understands what the legal and moral systems demand. But he views those norms as restraints that are not legitimate or justified. Ordinary non-tyrants who break the law and feel guilty accept that there is value in the norms they violate. But the tyrant does not accept the normative structure as definitive and so feels no guilt. He may practically work within that structure. But fundamentally, he rejects the structure as having any legitimacy: the moral and legal structure is powerful but it is not legitimate. This is why the tyrannical personality can be understood as either an animal or a god. Animals can be brought to heel and taught to conform to the expectations of their trainers without any kind of autonomous consent. The tyrant can also respond to threats and rewards, working within the system of norms—but without accepting those norms as definitive or, as in the case of the animal, without understanding those norms. The tyrant sees himself as a god who is better than the law, whose greatness gives him the power to break the law, and whose sense of self gives him the right to establish a new law. The tyrant may negotiate and cajole—and play within the norms of the established structure—as a matter of expedience. But ultimately, he asserts his own will; and when the chance comes for him to grab power and establish a new set of norms, he will take it.

HUBRIS

The chorus in *Oedipus the Tyrant* declares that hubris gives birth to tyranny (*hubris phuteuei tyrannon*—line 873). Some scholars suggest that this phrase can also be translated in a reverse sense to mean that tyranny begets hubris. In other words, it is power that leads to excessive pride, and it is pride that leads us to grasp power. An English translation from 1887 uses the word *insolence* to translate *hubris*. "Insolence breeds the tyrant. Insolence, once vainly stuffed with wealth that is not proper or good for it, when it has scaled the topmost ramparts, is hurled to a dire doom."[36] Whether we translate hubris as insolence, arrogance, or pride, the image here is a useful one: of a person who is overstuffed (*hyper-pimplem*) and who climbs high above the earth—and is then hurled back to earth. When we turn the verse around so that it says "tyranny begets hubris," we can see the problem: power leads us to become over-stuffed. Power creates arrogant pride; and it is pride that leads people to pursue power. The would-be tyrant wants power. He believes that he deserves power. He is sure that he is superior to those he will rule. At the same time, the powerful are convinced that since they are powerful, they must somehow deserve their power. A self-catalyzing cycle occurs. Those with inflated self-assurance seek power; when they obtain power, they feel justified in their self-assurance; and so on.

The Western tradition teaches that hubris, ambition, and vainglory cause crime and lead to ruin. In Shakespeare's *Macbeth* we hear about, "vaulting ambition" that overleaps itself. The Bible's book of Proverbs explains (16:18) that pride goeth before the fall. The King James version puts it less succinctly: "Pride goeth before destruction, and an haughty spirit before a fall." The Greek word *hubris* shows up in the Greek translation from the Hebrew along with the term *kakophrosyne*, which means bad judgment or folly. In the Latin Bible, the term *hubris* is translated as *superbia*, which means conceit, pride, or haughtiness. The word *haughty* (in its connection with *superbia*) provides another clue: it is related to the word *height* (or in French *haut*). Hubris is a vice of the heights. We might call it a "superiority complex." It occurs when one places oneself above others—when one vaults above them, as Macbeth might say. The idea that hubris comes before the fall thus contains the idea of falling from a height.

While the term *hubris* is translated as *pride*, pride is not always a vice. Indeed, there are times when lack of pride is a vice—as the case of a so-called inferiority complex. Justifiable pride occurs as a reflec-tion of worth. When someone wins a race, they should be proud. When someone discovers something, they should be proud. When someone has lived a good life, they should be proud. But proper pride involves appropriate self-estimation or self-esteem: it involves a truthful understanding of where you stand, what you've achieved, and how high you have climbed (and *deserve* to have risen). Proper self-esteem is related to Aristotle's consideration of the virtues connected to honor. The virtue of proper pride, magnanimity or *megalopsychia* ("greatness of soul") is opposed to false humility and immodest vanity (*Nicomachean Ethics*, 1123b). It is also immune to flattery and sycophancy—since the praise of those who are not virtuous is meaningless to those who know themselves to be good and who have a proper understanding of where they stand. Goodness and virtue are needed for proper self-esteem. False humility and low self-esteem fail to take credit for goodness. But hubris and vanity want credit when in reality the person is not worthy. It is good to consider yourself good when you are in fact good. It is hubris to think you are superior when you are not.

If we dig a bit deeper, we come to the related concepts of self-esteem and self-respect. Self-esteem can be distinguished from self-respect.[37] Self-esteem results from judging yourself to be good. Self-respect results from considering yourself as an autonomous moral agent worthy of basic moral respect. In a sense, all human beings deserve self-respect; but not everyone is worthy of esteem. It would be odd, for example, for criminals to have high self-esteem (although they sometimes do because of excessive pride or hubris!). A criminal should have low self-esteem, even though he should recognize his worth as a human being and respect himself enough to see that he deserves to be punished. Importantly, as we learn from Kant, all human beings are worthy of respect, since we all have the capacity to be autonomous.

This discussion of a criminal's excessive self-estimation helps explain how hubris is connected to crime and to tyranny. The problem for a criminal with high self-esteem and for the tyrant is that they misestimate their own value. They do not admit their moral failures. Instead, they somehow think that they deserve what they take. This belief in their superiority is mistaken. But hubris is a kind of delusion. It confuses greatness for goodness. It also fails to properly understand the idea of dignity and respect. The tyrant believes that only he is worthy of respect. Thus, he disrespects others, insulting and abusing them. He has no moral regard for other people. He may "esteem" them, in the sense that he values their support—as he values the sycophants and morons who support him. But this sense of esteem is strictly instrumental. For the tyrant, other people are tools to be used. A truly tyrannical soul has an inflated sense of self-esteem that puts his dignity and worth on a higher level than that of other human beings.

Hubris is sometimes translated as "overweening pride"—where *overweening* means presumptuous, overconfident, or conceited. The word *ween* that forms the basis of "overweening" comes from a Germanic root; it is related to the German word *Wahn* or *Wahnsinnig*, which means insane, delusional, frenzied, or demented. Hubris can thus be defined as the delusional belief that one is worthy of power, that one is fundamentally superior to others. This is insane and delusional because it flies in the face of the fact that "all men are mortal" and that no one of us is a god.

Hubris is also linked to violence, cruelty, and tyrannical behavior. The standard Greek dictionary definition of hubris explains that hubris is "wanton violence, arising from the pride of strength or from passion."[38] Further entries connect it to outrageous and cruel behavior, including rape and acts that injure others. A recent article by Mark Button emphasizes that hubris contains violence and cruelty. Button explains:

> Hubris entails the assertion of superiority through the exuberant, unabashed, and contemptuous violation of another person's equal moral standing, often through violence (such as rape, or torture) or other forms of ill-treatment designed to denigrate or diminish others. Hubris is marked by a settled disposition to reduce, shame, or humiliate others as a means of asserting, consolidating, or relishing in one's own relative preeminence.[39]

Button's discussion shows us that hubris is an essentially anti-democratic vice. It is disrespectful of others, causing the tyrant to treat others as less than fully equal. The tryant is focused on power without goodness. He wants praise and accolades as external confirmations of his power. The sycophants give him this, as do the moronic masses. But the hubristic individual fails to understand that flattery from sycophants and morons is worthless. He also fails to understand the source of justifiable pride is virtue, justice, and the good—and not external accolades.

GREATNESS IS NOT GOODNESS

Now let's apply what we've learned here to Trump. We can see the problem of hubris, I suggest, in Trump's slogan, "Make America Great Again." The MAGA slogan is not "make America good again." Instead it is about greatness. Note the echo here of the Greek word "mega" (great) in the MAGA slogan. Trump's vocabulary includes a lot of synonyms for greatness: tremendous, terrific, huge, and so on. These are terms of quantity, not quality. They are about glory, power, and superiority. Now, it might be the case that Trump and his sloganeers simply assume that America is good and they want to return this good nation to its former greatness. But the focus on greatness is a typical trope of Trumpism. And it shows us the moral problem that is connected to tyranny and hubris. Greatness is external and pagan (as discussed in chapter 2). It is connected to the kind of power that made Alexander the Great so great (in Greek he is *Megas Alexandros*). Greatness is a matter of power and not a matter of ethics. It is measured in external terms. Goodness is internal. It is about moral principles and virtues rather than political power. Goodness is about respect, dignity, and moral worth—not about power or glory.

A variety of Trumpian issues can be explained by employing this schematic distinction between an external/quantifiable focus and an internal/qualitative focus. We might begin with Trump's use of language. He repeatedly talks about the size of things and other evaluative measures that are quantifiable. He is focused on wealth, IQ, height, and beauty. He looks at the outside of people. He is obsessed with crowd size, television ratings, Twitter followers, stock market valuations, and lists of accomplishments including, especially, wealth. This leads to hyperbole and outright lying. When Trump was a real estate developer, he inflated his own wealth and employed a variety of public relations techniques to create the sense that he was incredibly wealthy. This helped him establish his credibility and allowed him to expand his business. Lying and exaggeration are essential techniques for those who are focused on externalities and so-called greatness. Trump explained this clearly in his business manifesto, *The Art of the Deal*. He wrote in a passage that I quoted at length above, about bravado and "truthful hyperbole" as a form of self-promotion (58). Trump admits that bravado, bluster, and hyperbole are an essential part of his self-promoting strategy. Trump also explains why sycophants and morons fall for all of this. He says people want to get excited by big and great and spectacular things. They (we?) enjoy the fantasy of power, glory, and greatness.

Trump offers here an account of our moronic tendency to be beguiled by fantasy and power. We enjoy power vicariously through the greatness of the celebrity we identify with. We focus on the most superficial or external measures of greatness because these are obvious and spectacular. Notice that none of this has anything to do with reality or with virtue. Trump does not sell goodness; he sells greatness.

A further issue flows from this, which has to do with the unsatisfactory nature of quantitative measures. When greatness is the focus, there is no end to the pursuit of quantity. This explains why Trump would say, as he does in *The Art of the Deal*, "You can't be too greedy."[40] Greed, envy, jealousy, and hubris are all connected to the seemingly endless pursuit of external greatness. Greatness is comparative. If someone else has something that is bigger than mine, I have to enlarge what I've got. If someone else has a bigger pile of money, I need to get more. If someone else has a more beautiful wife or a faster jet or larger crowds at their rallies, I lose and they win. This explains Trump's interest in sports, for example—including his tendency to cheat. Rick Reilly explains in his book about Trump that Trump's father insisted that he be a "winner" and that the cutthroat viciousness in pursuit of winning leads Trump to lie, exaggerate, and cheat. Not only does Trump cheat at golf, but he also exaggerates his wealth. Reilly also explains that Trump even lies about the number of floors that exist in buildings he owns. Trump World Tower has only fifty-eight stories; but Trump and the Trump organization claim that it has sixty-eight.[41] Reilly also points out that Trump exaggerates his own height. Reilly claims that Trump is about 6'1". But Trump—and his doctor—claims that he is 6'3".[42] This is a minor point, but it is related to the focus on quantitative measures of greatness. In order to feel great, the tyrannical personality exaggerates everything, including facts about himself, that are easily verified. And when called out for these lies and exaggerations, the tyrant doubles down and accuses those who challenge him of vicious behavior. For the greedy person focused on externalities, it simply does not matter whether it is true that you are actually richer or taller than someone else. Rather, what matters is that other people think you are richer and taller and treat you accordingly.

This is why sycophantic flattery works on the tyrant. The tyrant wants his greatness confirmed. He needs his flatterers and the morons who cheer him on. The external confirmation of his greatness provides a sense of value and worth. But since these external and quantitative measures are fleeting and ephemeral, the tyrant always feels he is on the edge of losing power. He must continually ask for flattery to confirm that he is great. There is obvious instability in this. The truth eventually comes out, and the naked emperor is eventually exposed in his absurd façade. Consider, for example, all of the trouble that has arisen from the question of Trump's tax returns. It is not clear why Trump conceals his tax information. Some suspect that ties to Russian mobsters will be found in them. But the likely story is that Trump is not as rich as he pretends to be. This is not to say that Trump is not incredibly wealthy. He likely has a net worth of several billion dollars. But he has claimed that he is worth ten billion or more. If it turned out that he had much less than that amount, it would undermine the essence of his claim to be extraordinary and great. The mystery about his own wealth actually fits well with the idea of "truthful hyperbole" that he advocates: the fantasy of wealth is enough. If real numbers came to light, the fantasy would collapse. Furthermore, the tyrannical personality knows that eventually there will be someone who is taller, younger, or wealthier. The tyrant senses this and constantly lashes out against those who might challenge his greatness. The morons, of course, find this to be quite fun and amusing. And the sycophants struggle to figure out which bandwagon to jump on.

CONCLUSION: THE GOODNESS OF GOODNESS

In this chapter we have considered some of the problems of tyranny and the tyrannical personality. We've looked at Trump as an example and shown how the idea of tyranny and a tyrannical personality help explain some of what we witnessed during the Trump era. Trump remained a would-be tyrant. He may have a tyrannical soul. But constitutional structure limited the impact of his worst impulses.

There is a kind of instability woven into hubris and the focus on external measures of greatness. The solution is obvious: to focus on the internal/qualitative goodness of truth and virtue. Those who tell the truth do not need to worry about being exposed. Virtuous people live good lives that have a modest dignity that is worthy of respect. They have nothing to hide and no need to exaggerate or cover up. They do not need to worry about gossip and rumor. Indeed, if there is gossip and rumor of wrongdoing, the virtuous person opens himself up to scrutiny. This means that the virtuous person has already subjected himself to self-scrutiny. The remedy for each of our three problem types (the tyrant, the sycophant, and the moron) is self-examination. Through self-examination, we discover that external measures of greatness are irrelevant. Hubris is cured by self-conscious awareness of our own faults and failures. We come to understand through this process that the flattery of sycophants and the cheers of the morons are worthless.

The point is this: if the tyrant is not really worthy of praise (because he lacks goodness), then the praise of the sycophants and morons is abjectly pathetic. As Hegel pointed out in his master-slave dialectic, there is a structural problem in relationships that are not based on real recognition and respect for moral worth. We want to be recognized by other human beings who acknowledge us as having dignity, value, and worth. But in pursuit of recognition, we can end up forcing others to conform to our own will. When those others submit to us and offer us recognition, we end up in a position of mastery over them, and they become inferior and slavish. This is a terrible problem for the slave who is forced to submit. But it creates a structural problem for the master. The master wants to be recognized as having dignity and worth by full-fledged human beings who are worthy of giving praise and recognition. But the praise and recognition the master gets from the slave is deficient since it comes from those who have submitted to his will and who are no longer free persons of dignity and worth. Social theorists have examined and applied the master-slave dialectic in many ways. We might offer a more colloquial explanation here in conclusion. What the tyrant would discover if he took the time to examine himself is that the external confirmation of his "greatness" is a pale reflection of moral worth. Either the morons and sycophants are so stupid that they don't know that he is not worthy of praise or they are so selfish that they suck up and cheer anyway, hoping to gain something in return. In either case, the accolades and flattery prove to be a further sign of the dysfunctional tragedy that unfolds around the tyrant. The solution, of course, is for the naked emperor to open his eyes and look in the mirror. The solution to tyranny is self-knowledge and enlightenment.

6

THE FOOL'S STUPIDITY

On Willful and Vicious Ignorance

Nothing in the world is more dangerous than sincere ignorance and conscientious stupidity.

—Martin Luther King Jr.[1]

We foolish morons lack the desire to be wise. We want to be entertained and amused. We do not lack intelligence. We drive cars and pay our bills. But we acquiesce to our foolishness and succumb to stupidity. When we behave moronically, we do not care about truth as much as we care about laughter, excitement, rage, and violence. I say "we foolish morons" here because everyone can be a fool or a moron at times. We get drunk and say dumb things. We get carried away by the crowd. We let anger, gluttony, and lust get the better of us. Sometimes we give in to anger, hatred, and violence, which is the most moronic and dangerous thing of all.

By saying that we give in to violence and allow ourselves to be stupid, I am asserting that we do, after all, have a choice in the matter. When I speak of fools and morons and their stupidity, I am not talking about an organic brain deficiency. Rather, this is the sincere ignorance and conscientious stupidity that Martin Luther King Jr. referred to in relation to racism. Some racists have brain deficiencies. Others have been taught racist lies by a racist society. For a few such racists, we might say, as King does echoing Jesus, "Forgive them, for they know not what they do." But most racists are not like this: they knowingly choose to embrace stupid ideas. The same is true of most of the morons of political life. We can say of them that they ought to know better. Whether we choose to forgive those who chose ignorance and stupidity is a deeper question than we can consider here.

Perhaps a loving Christian might extend forgiveness this far. But King also makes another point. We must never tire, he says, "of reminding men that they have a moral responsibility to be intelligent."[2] King suggests that this is a Christian duty. But the same point holds in secular philosophy. Plato told us that the great evil of ignorance is that the ignorant are satisfied with themselves: foolish morons do not desire to be wise and do not value things they lack (*Symposium* 204a). We ought to become wise. We ought not succumb to our moronic urges. And we ought to enlighten others. This is the gist of that motto of the Enlightenment that Kant borrowed from the Roman poet Horace: "Dare to be wise" (*sapere aude*). Kant encourages us to grow up, become autonomous, and enlighten ourselves. We are reasonable beings. But we lack courage and resolution. Sometimes we are afraid of knowledge. But often we merely enjoy our stupidity. And so we embrace our own foolishness and choose to enjoy violence, fun, and pleasure. When we do that, we are morons, more interested in amusement than in wisdom.

VIOLENCE IS FUN

To make this point concrete, consider a Donald Trump rally in Lowell, Massachusetts, in January 2016. Protesters in the crowd disrupted the rally. There was yelling and shouting. Trump urged the removal of the protesters. The crowd began shouting "USA." Trump said, "Isn't this more fun than a regular boring rally?" If you view the video, it is clear that this was a lot of fun for the audience: people smile and cheer as this transpires. Now, as I've been arguing, Trump is only a would-be tyrant. The January 2016 mob was not as frantic and violent as a lynch mob. Nor was the 2016 mob as violent as the mob of January 2021. But throughout his campaign, there was a kind of menace that seemed to appear, along with Trump subtly encouraging violence—toward protesters, toward the media, and so on. Luckily, most people resisted the temptation to engage in outright violence. The notorious "Unite the Right" rally in Charlottesville, Virginia, in August 2017 brought out white supremacist symbols and a threat of violence that ended up with a counter-protester being killed. This was a prelude for the attack on the U.S. Capitol on January 6, 2021. And while the January 6 insurrection was terrifying, there was also a kind of gleeful joy seen in photos and videos from the scene. The mob was inflamed. They exerted themselves violently. As it unfolded, members of the violent mob appeared to be enjoying themselves.

One rioter who was interviewed in the immediate aftermath of January 6 said, "It was really fun." That rioter was filmed wearing a Trump cape on the floor of the Senate. He was later arrested and charged with violent entry, disorderly conduct, and obstruction.[3] Another rioter who was later arrested and charged with assaulting a federal officer as well as obstruction of Congress explained his participation in the events of January 6 to an undercover FBI official as follows: "It was fucking fun."[4]

The rioters of January 6 are not the only people who describe participating in violence as fun. One eyewitness reporter described the anti-Semitic violence of *Kristallnacht* (November 1938) as an "orgy of destruction." The reporter continued: "I saw fashionably dressed women clapping their hands and screaming with glee, while respectable middle-class mothers held up their babies to see the 'fun.'"[5] This is not merely a phenomenon of right-wing extremism. The Long Beach, California, band Sublime commemorated the Rodney King riots of 1992 with the song "April 29, 1992," which celebrates the fun of anarchy and looting with a chorus of "Let it burn." Conservative critics have said that participants in urban riots such as erupted in 2020 after the murder of George Floyd are "rioting for fun and profit."[6] And it was Hunter S. Thompson who pointed out that riots often erupt after sporting events, whether the home team wins or loses. And why does that happen? Thompson explains, "Riots are fun."[7] Quentin Tarantino, the Hollywood director, put it simply: "Violence is fun, man."[8]

Violence is obviously related to tyranny. Real tyrants engage in brutal violence: executing their enemies and controlling the masses with purges, pogroms, and holocausts. This is horrifying and wrong. But we misunderstand violence if we view it only through the lens of power, terror, and moral outrage. Violence is also amusing, fun, and entertaining. Violence is, of course, also stupid and irrational.[9] Violence makes no arguments. It does not do its work on ideas or appeal to logic. Rather, it dwells in immediacy. It manipulates bodies with brute force. The better angels of our nature teach us that violence is inferior and subhuman. But at times we give in to the brutish stupidity of violence. And we enjoy it. This is why violence is closely linked with sex, as Freud and others have pointed out. There are a variety of ways we could explain the pleasure of violence: in terms of power, innate aggression, or learned behavior. But there is no doubt that human beings experience a kind of joy in destroying things and watching them burn. Tyrants know how to manipulate and channel this kind of thing. And the moronic mob is glad to participate. This is not only because the mob is duped by the tyrant (although this happens). Nor is this because the mob is cajoled or threatened into becoming violent (although this happens too). Rather, the most important point to notice is that the mob joyfully joins the violence.

The Greeks understood this. Violence is an important theme in Greek tragedy and philosophy. Homer's *Iliad* is a poem about rage and violence. Achilles goes on a rampage of destruction. We should rightly condemn this excessive violence. But Homer is giving voice to an essential feature of human nature, which is that violence can become an excessive celebration. A similar point is made by Euripides in *The Bacchae*, which links violence with madness, drunkenness, and stupidity. The victim of this tragedy is Pentheus, who is described as a mad and wretched fool. The wise prophet Tiresias tries to warn Pentheus about the violent power of the god Dionysus. But Pentheus rebels, saying that he does not want this foolishness to rub off on him (343–44). The word for foolishness here is the Greek word *moros*. Tiresias responds with an ominous warning, fools speak foolishly, which could be translated as "morons say moronic things" (369). This passage echoes what we discussed earlier in relation to Sophocles's *Antigone*, where the same problem appears: the foolish or moronic person does not listen to reason and, indeed, accuses the wise person of being a fool. In both cases, violence follows. In Euripides's play, this violence is of utmost brutality: animals and human beings are slaughtered and torn apart. In his madness and stupidity,

Pentheus participates in the violence and is himself torn apart by it. His own mother participates in his dismemberment, marching madly with Pentheus's head on a stake. When she finally comes to her senses and realizes what she has done, she laments her madness and folly. What is fascinating is that before the tragic awareness dawns, there is a kind of joyful glee in all of the violence. This is similar to drunkenness and demonic possession (after all, we are talking about Dionysus here). The implication is that stupidity and foolishness, like drunkenness and madness, are closely related to violence.

And of course, the audience enjoys the show. While we might blame the foolish morons who actively participate in violence, there is another level of analysis worth considering. The fun of violence can be transformed into art and show. The spectators cheer it on in the name of amusement and fun. This point was made by Diogenes the Cynic, who called the Dionysian festivals of ancient Athens "a spectacle for morons."[10] Diogenes used the word *moros* here in a phrase that has also been translated as "peep-show for fools." Perhaps we could call this "moronic amusement." Moronic amusement includes much of popular culture, pornography, gossip, and so on. Violence and sex and rude and raunchy behavior are entertaining. Quentin Tarantino is a master of this. But before Tarantino, there was the cornball violence of professional wrestling, kung fu movies, and spaghetti westerns. Prior to that—and much more serious—were the spectacular festivals of violence associated with lynchings, public executions, and the like. This is what one author has called, following Nietzsche and Foucault, a "carnival of atrocity."[11]

Unlike a lynch mob, where the audience is witnessing tyrannical cruelty unleashed upon the living flesh of a real person, the audience for a play by Euripides or a film by Tarantino knows that this is art and amusement. We put aside moral judgment and enjoy the show. But this tendency is also linked to the problem of violence in the real world and the moronic urge to be entertained. There is a kind of voluntary suspension of moral judgment that happens when the moronic urge comes forward. There are some evil and deranged people in the world. But the violent mob is made up of ordinary people, having a good time participating in violence. They should know better. But when formed into a mob, the moronic element takes over. And so otherwise normal, smart, and decent people end up cheering on violence and madness.

When we let our guard down, we become morons—more interested in amusement than anything else. Political ideas can inspire violence.

Some of the tyrant's supporters are evil and cruel. Trump was no doubt supported by racists, anti-Semites, and misogynists. But those who believed that the 2020 election was stolen were not merely evil and cruel. To focus on evil transforms this tragedy into a simple melodrama. The problem of tragedy is that seemingly decent people end up doing indecent things. The reason this happens is not because of a malicious soul but, rather, because of a failure of wisdom and virtue.

That is why we must recognize that the actions of a mob are not wise or enlightened or logical or reasonable. The mob is not making arguments or espousing a dogma. Rather, the mob is a movement of bodies, more like a mosh pit than a debate. The ideas that give movement to the mob are less important than the action and emotion. That's why fake news and untruth can wreak havoc. Truth is not a concern for the mob as much as movement, action, adrenaline, and amusement. The mob may chant slogans, but it is not the content of the slogan that matters as much as the energy and emotion of the chanting.

Enlightenment, virtue, and wisdom are difficult and frustrating. It is more fun to be a fool. This unhandsome tendency is a common human failing, which puts us at risk of falling prey to tyranny. There is an erotic element to this—a strange attraction and desire that leads the moron to fall into the tyrant's clutches. Plato recognized the erotic element in tyranny, connecting it to a warped and misplaced love. The tyrant loves only himself, of course. He claims to love the mob. But what he loves about the mob is the fact that the mob loves him. And thus what is exceedingly strange about all of this is the fact that the moronic masses do not seem to care about the tyrant's indifference. It is not that the mob is so stupid that they cannot see that the tyrant is using and exploiting them. Rather, the mob willfully ignores what is plain to see. The moron does not care about the tyrant's lies and deceitful love. What the moron wants is some excitement and fun. The lies and deceit are part of it. Tyrannical love makes life interesting for the moronic mob. That is why the process of enlightenment must involve education about love, as much as it requires critical thinking about truth.

WHO ARE YOU CALLING A MORON?

The word *moron* is contentious, divisive, and dangerous. If you want to provoke a fight, call someone a moron. The word may appear to be an epithet without any objective content. To put this simply, we might say that stupidity is in the eye of the beholder. Like the accusation of tyranny, the accusation of idiocy and foolishness can be used to express a subjective and emotional evaluation not grounded in objective reality. Words like *moron*, *imbecile*, and *dummy* are used as insults. These kinds of words do not usually express a serious evaluation of a person's intelligence. Rather, they are disparagements that express contempt and hate.

Consider, for example, Donald Trump's use of the word *dummy*. In an interview in June 2019, President Trump said, "Joe Biden is a dummy."[12] While Trump disparaged candidate Biden as "Sleepy Joe" and suggested that he was suffering from senility, none of this was based in an objective evaluation of Biden's cognitive faculties. This was typical Trumpian bombast, sarcasm, and invective. The word *dummy* is commonly employed by Trump. His Twitter archive indicates that he called a number of people dummies: Bill Maher, Jon Stewart, Rosie O'Donnell, Russell Brand, Bill Kristol, Beto O'Rourke, Brian Williams, Juan Williams, John Bolton, and the unnamed mayor of Portland.[13] The word *moron* was also frequently employed by President Trump. A search of the Trump Twitter archive returns thirty-seven tweets in which Trump tweeted (or re-tweeted) *moron*. The most recent one occurred on January 22, 2020, when Trump re-tweeted an insult directed at Congresswoman Alexandria Ocasio-Cortez that read, "AOC is such an embarrassing, barely literate moron."[14] The ad hominem attacks flow in both directions. Senate minority leader Chuck Schumer called President Trump a "moron" while blaming Trump for the coronavirus pandemic in the fall of 2020.[15] Former Republican speaker of the house John Boehner blamed the rise of extremism in the GOP on an influx of morons. He said, that in 2010, as the Tea Party rose to power in Republican circles, "you could be a total moron and get elected just by having an R next to your name."[16] Most famously, President Trump's former secretary of state Rex Tillerson reportedly called Trump a "moron" in July of 2017 (some reports say that Tillerson called him a "f***ing moron").[17] Trump eventually retaliated in a tweet (December 7, 2018) where he said, "Rex Tillerson, didn't have the mental capacity needed. He was dumb as a rock and I couldn't get rid of him fast enough. He was lazy as hell."[18] Trump clearly does not reserve his invective for members of the other party. In 2021, he called Mitch McConnell "a dumb son of a bi∗∗∗."[19]

Polarization appears here even within the Republican Party. You are either with Trump or against him. The larger problem of polarization depends upon what you take to count as wisdom or stupidity and who you are referring to as "the people" or "the mob." Conservatives view liberals as stupid, and vice versa. Hillary Clinton once said that half of Trump's supporters could be put into a "basket of deplorables" because of ideas that she said are "racist, sexist, homophobic, xenophobic and Islamophobic."[20] But Trump routinely accused liberals of being stupid. As Newt Gingrich explained, Trump is anti-left, anti–political correctness, pro-American, and anti-stupid. Gingrich explains that the bureaucrats think that they are smarter than the average person and that Trump uses this strategically: "One of his favorite tactics is to accuse the ruling class of stupidity."[21] Trump's accusations against Democrats involve a visceral and insulting vocabulary. The Trumpians use words like "lib-tard" to describe their opponents. This word is intended to be offensive, as a combination of "liberal" and the schoolyard slur "retard."

This kind of tit-for-tat ad hominem poses a difficulty here. The term *moron* can be an offensive slur. I do not use it here in the long-discredited way that it was employed in the twentieth century, as a way of categorizing and disparaging people with mental disabilities. *Moron* was in fact only introduced into the English language in the early part of the twentieth century in an attempt to categorize undesirable mental defects.[22] The term was associated with related terms: *idiot* and *imbecile* in a schematic system with *idiot* as the most "feeble-minded," *imbecile* as the next level of development, and *moron* defined as "those whose mental development is above that of an imbecile, but does not exceed that of a normal child of about twelve years."[23] This schema was employed in eugenic policies in the United States that were connected to ethnic prejudice, racial stereotypes, and moral judgment—as well as to pseudo-scientific evaluations of intelligence.[24]

Obviously, we must be careful with the word *moron*. Furthermore, what appears to be moronic to me may look like inspiration to you; what

I view as genius, you may see as foolish and idiotic. The most famous example of this is found in the New Testament when Paul says (1 Corinthians) that the wisdom of the world is foolish, while the foolishness of God is wise. The Greek word Paul uses in a number of places in 1 Corinthians is *moros*—the same word used by Plato and Sophocles in this regard. Paul is saying that those who go with God will appear foolish to nonbelievers. And he says that those who reject Christ will turn out to be the real fools. A literal translation of these passages reads: "The wisdom of this world is moronic" (1 Corinthians 3:19); and "Let wise men become morons" (1 Corinthians 3:18).[25]

Accusations of foolishness, idiocy, and stupidity are found throughout the Western tradition. Before Paul, the 14th Psalm stated, "The fool says in his heart that there is no God."[26] Hobbes played off of this and said that the fool says in his heart that there is "no such thing as justice."[27] Dramatists and poets have played with the difference between foolishness and wisdom—as for example in the role played by fools and jesters (in Shakespeare and opera, for example) and in the person of the blind prophet (especially in Sophocles). Some radical critics, such as Nietzsche, have accused the whole tradition of being stupid and idiotic. Nietzsche said of Christianity that "it takes the side of everything idiotic, it utters a curse upon intellect."[28] I mentioned this problem of perspective and conflicting points of view already with reference to Sophocles's *Antigone*, where we see an exchange of accusations of stupidity and of tyranny. Antigone says (at 470) that while Creon has accused her of being foolish, in reality he is the moron. She says (my translation), "If I look like a moron to you, that's only because you are the real moron."

This polarization creates a significant problem leading to profound conflicts of religion and political life. We disagree about what counts as wisdom and enlightenment. We also disagree about who is the real moron. With this worry in mind, however, we will probe deeper. The problem of the tragic trio is not simply a matter of conflicting perspectives and points of view. The tyrant (or would-be tyrant) aspires to have exorbitant, absolute, or godlike power. And the morons who support the tyrant really are blind, ignorant, and stupid. While the morons may claim that they are actually smart and enlightened, in reality they are not.

The key to sorting this out is an objective standard of justice, wisdom, and virtue—and a regime of responsibility that relies upon this objective standard. The solution for the problem of tyranny, sycophancy, and idiocy is philosophical enlightenment as well as a rational constitution and shared standards of moral accountability. Those solutions are not merely a matter of perspective. Relativism and perspectivalism lead nowhere. The philosophical tradition assumes that there is some truth to the matter of justice, that absolute power is unjust, and that moronic people really are blind and ignorant. This assumption of objectivity is manifest in the person of Tiresias, the blind wise man of the Sophoclean dramas; it is also found in a more complicated sense in the objective commentary of the chorus. We see the assumption of objectivity in Plato and Aristotle (and in the character of Socrates). We also see it in the assumptions of the Enlightenment, which focuses on the objectivity of truth. The moral and political ideals of Enlightenment philosophy depend upon the idea that there are human rights, that governments are instituted to protect those rights, that wisdom and virtue are objective, and that we are responsible for our own misdeeds and stupidity.

INFANTILIZATION AND ACCOUNTABILITY

Critics of the Enlightenment and of the Greek philosophical tradition have called some of this into question by noting that this long tradition allowed for slavery and the oppression of women. This was connected to the problem of infantilization and authoritarianism directed toward those who were excluded from the political community. Women and slaves were treated as children, idiots, and morons by the tyrants who ruled over them. As Jean Bethke Elshtain has influentially argued, Greek philosophers such as Plato and Aristotle reflected the Greek notion that "the private person or *idiot* was a being of lower purpose, goodness, rationality, and worth than the *polites* or public citizen."[29] Among the class of the *idiotes* were women, slaves, and children. Aristotle held that women and slaves were inferior and that they ought to be governed or ruled by those who are superior. One of the distinguishing features in Aristotle's account is the supposed lack of reason (*logos*) in slaves and women (*Politics* 1254b).

It is not only the lack of reason that is at issue here. A further problem is a general lack of accountability granted to morons and idiots. In the Greek world, private persons (the *idiotes*) were those who were *not* held to public account. Women and slaves were excluded from serving in the assembly and thus from taking part in the political process. As a result, they were not subject to public justice and accountability. This two-tiered system continued for thousands of years in the West, up until a hundred years or so ago, when slavery was abolished and women were granted the right to vote, serve on juries, own property, and so on.

The treatment of women and slaves was indeed a form of tyranny. Furthermore, the tyrant himself enjoys a privileged lack of accountability in this system.[30] The domineering husband and the cruel slave master got away with cruelty and violence because they ruled with impunity over those who had been reduced to the status of being "idiots" (private things not granted the full rights of real persons). For long centuries, there was no legal recourse for abused wives and slaves. The impunity of the domestic tyrant was envied by those who desired political tyranny. As we saw, the tyrant dreams of being a god. This dream includes the kind of impunity provided by he who rules over idiots. This dream of impunity is brought into being by those foolish morons who willingly give themselves over into the tyrant's embrace. What the Greek tradition worried about was the fact that morons choose ignorance over wisdom and vice over virtue, and willingly vote the tyrant into power. Using the language developed here, the result is that the morons reduce themselves to idiocy, infantilizing themselves in deference to the tyrant.

Arguments in favor of the liberation of women and slaves maintained that it was not true that women and slaves were really moronic and idiotic—it was the system of tyranny that caused ignorance, servility, and infantilization. This argument presumes objectivity: both that slaves and women are not objectively inferior and that it is the system that causes infantilization. Today we no longer believe that women lack reason or that a race of inferior human beings deserves to be enslaved. We aim for an inclusive public sphere that is aided by public education for all and a democratic system that allows for all adults to vote and participate in the electoral process. We also understand how infantilization works.

But the problem of accountability persists, in a different sense that is endemic to democracy. The problem is that morons are allowed to vote, without any system for holding them accountable when they support sycophants and tyrants. Plato and Aristotle understood that this was a problem. Each warned that democracy was rule by the moronic mob. Plato and Aristotle feared that the morons would support a tyrant, who would take advantage of them. In *Republic*, Plato describes the rise of the tyrant as involving the participation of sycophants and fools. He says that the tyrant will gather a group of thieves and sycophants and other vicious types around him. But this alone is not enough for him to seize power. The tyrant needs his gang of supporters to also have the support of the "foolish masses" (*Republic* 575c). The term Plato uses here is *anoia*, which means lacking in reason. Plato connects this term in other places (*Republic* 382c) to madness (the Greek term is *mania*). For Plato the problem is that mad, foolish, morons throw their support to the tyrant and succumb to the lies and flattery of the sycophants who make up the tyrant's clique. Plato preferred aristocracy, which he understood as rule by wise and virtuous people. We know today that aristocracy also has its flaws. Our system is democratic and inclusive. But what do we do when morons vote for tyrants?

The solution ought to be education that prevents infantilization while encouraging autonomy and accountability. We do not want voters to be moronic. But a tragic flaw is woven into democracy: fools are free to participate without much accountability at all. This is a problem of the ballot box as well as the jury box. In a culture that lacks intelligence and accountability the idea of a "jury of one's peers" is another iteration of Plato's worry about the democratic ship of fools. We might think that systematic solutions could prevent the fools from wreaking havoc—such as requiring education or testing for literacy at the polls or in jury selection. But attempts to limit participation or make voters and jurors more accountable can be discriminatory and undemocratic. To set up a literacy test or a civics test to screen out voters or jurors would reiterate the problem of exclusion and infantilization we have discussed here.

Plato brought this problem home in his *Apology of Socrates*. Socrates stated in his defense speech that he avoided public service and led a private life, which can be literally translated in the way I am emphasizing here as the life of an idiot (in Greek, an *idiotes*). Socrates understood that his commitment to reason and virtue would get him into trouble in the public sphere. His attempt to remain aloof was unsuccessful. He was put on trial, found guilty, and executed by the moronic mob of Athens. In his final speech to the assembly, Socrates suggested that the mob would be held to account by history and the gods. Of course, this admonishment did not prevent his death. The conclusion is a tragic one. Democracies that include fools can do terrible things; but democracies that exclude people from voting or serving on juries can also be terrible.

DEFINING FOOLISHNESS

As stated already, terms such as *moron* and *fool* are not meant to mock or denigrate those who have serious cognitive deficiencies. Our focus is deficiency understood as a lack of virtue and wisdom. This is a normative term, grounded in an account of human flourishing. We live better when we are enlightened. We live better when we resist foolishness and dare to be wise. Unlike those with organic cognitive deficiencies, a moron, in my sense, has the processing power to become wise—but fails to do so. To be a moron is to be ignorant or blind in a *moral* and *intellectual* way. In this sense, a moron is a person who is able to be wise but who fails to do so. Foolish morons have the potential to overcome their stupidity and blindness. But they allow themselves to be infantilized. That is why they can be subjected to moral critique.

There is a large and growing literature on cognitive issues and their connection with political life and moral judgment.[31] We know quite a bit about cognitive failures such as perceptual blindness or inattentional blindness. This can be linked to related issues such as unconscious bias, partisan bias, confirmation bias, the persistence of early belief, and other problems of judgment. While there is a growing body of literature focusing on these cognitive failures, these are very old problems. Plato understood the problem as did Francis Bacon. Bacon described the problem of confirmation bias in his *Novum Organum*, where he explained, "The human understanding when it has once adopted an opinion draws all things else to support and agree with it."[32] Bacon explained that this tendency to believe helped explain the persistence of "superstitions" including belief in astrology, dreams, omens, divine judgments, and so on. He even recognized that this same failure afflicts science and philosophy: "The first conclusion colours and brings into conformity with itself all that come after, though far sounder and better."

Given all of these problems, there may be no real way to achieve enlightened rationality. One significant problem is that we shape our intentions and values in response to emotional responses and other unconscious processes. Jonathan Haidt argues that the emotional dog wags the rational (and moral) tail. He has applied this emotivist and intuitionist theory to political judgment. He suggests that political partisanship is addictive: the mind gets addicted to the feel-good experience of making partisan judgments. Haidt says that "rationalism" is a delusion. For example, Haidt explains that individual reasoners are extremely limited in their capacities: "each individual reasoner is really good at one thing: finding evidence to support the position he or she already holds, usually for intuitive reasons. We should not expect individuals to produce good, open-minded, truth-seeking reasoning, particularly when self-interest or reputational concerns are in play."[33] This problem afflicts all of us. Even those of us who think we are wise, enlightened, and rational can at times be moronic.

This diagnosis only makes sense if we assume that something other than stupidity might be possible. If we are all morons, and there is no hope of being more rational, then we might just give up with a shrug on the project of moral education and the goal of making political progress. A kind of nihilism can creep in with this diagnosis, which can make things worse morally and politically. The moron diagnosis can become a self-fulfilling prophecy. If we are not able to make rational and enlightened decisions, then we might as well just go with the flow, give vent to our emotions, and give up on the need to cultivate character, civility, and wisdom. The philosophical tradition has, since Socrates, resisted this kind of nihilism. Socrates thought that there was value in self-examination—so too did Plato, Aristotle, and the rest. The value of this process is that it can cure us of our stupidity. There is no perfect solution or panacea. But understanding our tendency to be moronic is surely part of the cure. If we know that we tend to be biased, we can take better care to avoid bias—and work to become more reasonable.

With this in mind, it is now possible to formulate a definition of the moron. As with our definition of the tyrant, there are three components. A foolish moron is a person:

1. who *does not reason in a way that is impartial, accurate, and objective*;

2. who is *able to think and reason in a reasonable* way; but
3. who *does not desire to reason* in that way.

The first condition directs our attention to the actual reasoning processes of a moron. A moron is biased, partial, subjective, emotional, as well as ignorant, irrational, and uninformed. We could pile on synonyms for stupidity and ignorance here. But the point is that a moron makes bad judgments. This does not mean that a moron always holds false beliefs. But the truth or falsity of a belief is not a focal point of a moronic judgment. Sometimes a stupid person accidentally gets things right. The problem of moronic judgments is that they are made for bad reasons—they are not impartial, objective, wise, studied, or based in reality. Again, we could pile on adjectives here for what ought to happen when beliefs and judgments are rational, objective, impartial, and true. The point is that the moron will mostly not get things right—and will be subject to manipulative powers that appeal to subjectivity, emotion, and so on.

The second condition rules out those who really are cognitively deficient in an organic or physiological sense. Those with severe cognitive impairment or dysfunction are simply not able to reason well. In this case, we ought not blame them for their inability to judge well. This condition may also rule out those who are unable to reason well due to circumstances that prevent them from doing so—such as a poor education, lack of information, or political manipulation. Haidt suggests that our cognitive apparatus makes it so that no one is able to think and reason in a way that is as impartial and objective as we might hope. Other critics of this idea may suggest that there are deep and pervasive social and political circumstances—such as oppression and ideology—that prevent proper reasoning. There are important issues to be considered in both cases—with regard to our brains and with regard to social and political circumstances. But the second condition in my definition stakes a normative claim: we ought to be able to work our way beyond ideology and to improve our cognitive capacity. This "ought" should be interpreted weakly. Those who lack education should strive to educate themselves. Social circumstances can leave people with severe cognitive disadvantages. But unless we believe that we can rise to some degree above our cognitive limitations, we will remain stuck with a kind of nihilism.

This leads us to the third condition, which is linked to the normative claim. Those who desire to overcome their own ignorance and bias are to be applauded and encouraged. But some people lack that desire (or their desire for wisdom is so weak as to be inefficacious). This brings us to the heart of the judgment. Morons lack the intellectual virtues associated with education. They are intellectually lazy. They lack curiosity. They are closed minded. And so on. They may falsely believe that they are unable to overcome their own stupidity—and so affirm their stupidity in a moronic effort at self-congratulation. Or they may be so comfortable in their ignorance and selfishly sure of themselves that they have no interest in critical thinking. Again, there may be organic and social or political circumstances that need to be accounted for. But the big problem of the moron is that he chooses to be dumb and is resistant to new ideas, education, and improvement.

This is a problem for democratic politics. John Locke—to cite an important historical example—spent significant time considering the problem of what he called "lunatics and idiots." It is likely that Locke meant those with organic brain damage or other physiological maladies, as we currently understand them. Locke's discussion must be taken with a historical grain of salt—since we have made substantial progress in thinking about cognitive diversity and various forms of cognitive dysfunction.[34] Locke's discussion of idiocy and lunacy is linked to his political philosophy. According to Locke, idiots (and lunatics) are like children insofar as children are subject to the ruling authority of their parents: "Lunatics and idiots are never set free from the government of their parents."[35] But this is a rare and sad case. Normal children grow up. They develop the capacity for reason, learn about morality and the natural law, and are eventually capable of self-government. The problem for democracy is those who refuse to grow up, who embrace infantilization, and who fail to actualize their potential for wisdom, autonomy, and virtue.

People with organic cognitive deficiency should be kept under the "tuition and government of others," as Locke puts it. But beyond that small subset of people, everyone else should be "set free" (again using Locke's language) to participate in democratic government as set up under the social contract. We might note that Kant also discusses what he calls "mental derangement" as something that requires confinement to a madhouse. Kant provides a detailed description of various kinds of deficiency that reflects some of the callousness of the Enlightenment. He considers "idiocy" to be "complete mental deficiency," saying: "it cannot be called sickness of soul; rather it is absence of soul."[36] Kant points out that mere fools do not belong in a madhouse because the madhouse is a place to confine those who must be "kept orderly through someone else's reason."[37] Stupid people—according to both Kant and Locke—can rule themselves enough to live freely. But one wonders, should those stupid buffoons be allowed to vote and participate in self-government? On Locke's view, the requirement for such participation is maturity of reason, which Kant further explains as rational autonomy. For both thinkers, the key is to be able to know and understand the moral law, the law of nature, and the nature of freedom.

The liberal-democratic tradition assumes that most human beings can become free and self-governing, that is, that we are not doomed to be morons who lack reason and virtue. Kant, Locke, and others in this tradition limited the scope of humanity in ways that we can no longer accept. They did not think that women and non-White persons were able to achieve the level of maturity necessary for self-rule and democratic participation. We have made considerable progress in the past few hundred years. But this progress hinges upon the belief that human beings in all of our fascinating diversity are capable of wisdom, virtue, and autonomy. Liberal-democratic citizenship depends upon the belief that we can overcome partiality, bias, and unreason. It rests upon a democratic faith in human nature that assumes that we are capable of enlightenment and that we ought to desire to be enlightened.

IGNORANCE AND THE BIG LIE

To say that we are morons is to admit that we often fail to be self-aware critical thinkers. A moron is not simply stupid or dumb. The problem is not a literal inability to think. Rather, morons fail to employ their critical faculties in a variety of ways. They are ignorant, illiterate, and innumerate. There are other ways we could describe what is lacking in moronic thinking, but these will suffice.

Let's begin with ignorance. Someone who is ignorant is not simply unable to think. Rather, their thinking is limited. Sometimes this limitation is self-imposed because the moron is not willing to question or challenge deeply held beliefs. This kind of willful ignorance explains a variety of other ills. Racists who cling to stereotypes despite counter-evidence are willfully ignorant. Superstitious people who refuse to consider critical objections to their superstitions are willfully ignorant. And political partisans who stick by a party, a candidate, or a national identity despite evidence of corruption and evil are willfully ignorant. Willful ignorance of this sort is typical of the sycophant: the sycophant ought to know better, but he deliberately chooses to affirm lies for partisan purposes.

A related but less severe problem is what we might call "uncultivated ignorance." Unlike willful ignorance, uncultivated ignorance is not a deliberate choice. Rather, this is the ignorance of those who lack education, those who have not been exposed to certain critical ideas. We could imagine, for example, a young person who has grown up in a racist society. This person thinks, for example, that Whites are superior to Blacks. But he has never met a Black person. Nor has this person ever really encountered a book or an educator who challenges his racism. A similar scenario could be imagined with regard to sexism, religious belief, political ideology, and so on. The uncultivated ignoramus has not encountered any ideas or experiences that challenge his ignorance. In a sense, we cannot blame the uncultivated ignoramus for his lack of education. But if, upon discovering new evidence and ideas that challenge his beliefs, the uncultivated ignoramus chooses to deny or discredit what he has discovered, the uncultivated ignoramus becomes willfully ignorant. With the uncultivated ignoramus, a reasonable response might be compassion combined with an effort to correct his ignorance. But even though we can understand the psychological and social mechanics of someone who remains in denial in the face of counter-evidence, willful ignorance is not excusable. With regard to the willfully ignorant, we can say that they *should have* known better or that they *ought* to reject their prior ignorance. Human beings ought to grow up, seek wisdom, and question their own beliefs.

A typology emerges, then, based upon the difference between willful ignorance and uncultivated ignorance. The moronic mob is mostly made up of uneducated ignoramuses, while the class of sycophants consists of the willfully ignorant. There will be overlap among these categories depending upon the degree of ignorance, the depth of one's corruption, and the seriousness of one's belief in lies, falsehoods, and nonsense. But in both cases, the problem is distance from the truth and a malfunction of virtues such as honesty, sincerity, and integrity. We might add that the tyrant can also be located in this typology as a person for whom truth is simply irrelevant. The tyrant maintains that what matters is his own power and personality. He appears to believe either that truth does not exist or that truth is simply whatever he says it is.

This brings us to the problem of what pundits and scholars have called "the big lie." This idea has been traced back to Hitler's *Mein Kampf*, where he explains the power that enormous and impudent lies have over the masses.[38] The masses fail to imagine that lies of such magnitude are actually lies. In Hitler's words, they fall prey to big lies because of "the primitive simplicity of their minds." The Nazi propaganda machine used this notion to its advantage, propagating anti-Semitic lies as a way of gaining power. When a lie is boldly stated by those in power, the masses shrug and say, "well, maybe. . . ." This does not mean that they believe every part of the lie. Rather, enormous lies leave a residue, as Hitler explained: they stick in the minds of the ignorant masses. This causes doubt and distrust, on the one hand, while also leading the masses to fall back upon faith. The strange and seemingly paradoxical outcome of the big lie is that when the masses are encouraged to disbelieve the evidence of their senses and the testimony of "the experts," they throw up their hands and simply choose to believe whatever myth is convenient. The shrug of "well, maybe . . ." opens the door to conspiracy theories and cults of personality. It creates a moronic situation in which truth and enlightenment are set aside in favor of what is titillating, fun, violent, and self-affirming.

Contemporary marketing and advertising are different from Nazi propaganda, even though there are similarities. The strategy of the big lie appears to morph and adapt to new circumstances. Trump's critics maintained that his complaint about the 2020 election being stolen is a "big lie": a strategic effort to disseminate falsehood and to undermine the masses' faith in democracy. But this became more convoluted as Trump himself appropriated the language of the big lie for his own purposes. In May 2021, Trump proclaimed, "The Fraudulent Presidential Election of 2020 will be, from this day forth, known as THE BIG LIE!"[39] Representative Liz Cheney, a leading Republican, reportedly responded, "The 2020 presidential election was not stolen. Anyone who claims it was is spreading THE BIG LIE, turning their back on the rule of law, and poisoning our democratic system."[40] It is reassuring to see a Republican stand up to Trump, even though Cheney was ousted from her leadership role. But this kind of exchange remains damaging to democracy, since the ignorant masses will be left confused and not knowing who to believe. When that happens, tyrants and would-be tyrants can take advantage. Doubt and distrust can lead the ignorant masses to simply "go with their guts" and choose to believe whatever they want.

Let's move on to talk about illiteracy. One may simply be illiterate—actually unable to read. The illiterate are in a similar situation as the uncultivated ignoramuses: they lack access to information. But the concept of illiteracy has been applied in a variety of contexts that extends it metaphorically. When we say that someone is illiterate about science or religion, we mean that they have not read about science or religion. It is not that these illiterates are unable to read. Rather, they choose not to read about certain topics. Or more generally, they have not been educated about these topics. As in the case of ignorance, one might be a victim of circumstances here. Some people lack access to education about science or religion. Thus, they are not fully to blame for their illiteracy. But others refuse to read, when the content challenges deeply held beliefs. Thus, we might distinguish between those who are involuntarily illiterate and those who are deliberately illiterate.

A related concern is that there are some who are able to read and who do read but who are unable to properly interpret and understand what they are reading. In this category, we might place those who have been miseducated. Their teachers have not helped them develop hermeneutical skill. Their reading has been kept narrowly focused. And they have not been forced to deal with the challenge that occurs when conflicting texts require careful interpretation. In this category of morons, we might find those who have been educated in narrow traditions that provide a skewed interpretation of American history. We should also mention here those who suffer from civic illiteracy: those who do not understand the Constitution, the electoral process, and so on.

Finally, let's consider the problem of innumeracy. Innumeracy is a lack of mathematical ability and understanding. Innumerate people are not good at understanding very large or very small numbers. They are not good at understanding percentages and ratios. They don't understand statistical reasoning. They succumb to logical fallacies. And so on. This can be the result of bad education. But a different type of innumeracy is deliberately cultivated for partisan purposes.

In connection with the big lie, a kind of innumeracy is at work. One of the moronic claims made about the 2020 election had to do with changing vote tallies in the days after the election. Some people, including Trump himself, claimed that this indicated election fraud. But even prior to the election, experts predicted a "blue shift" as votes were tallied.[41] Early vote tallies tended to point in Trump's direction, while later vote counts tended toward Biden. This blue shift (also called a "red mirage") was predictable, based upon the demographic trends of mail-in ballots. Democrats are more likely to vote by mail than Republicans; and it takes longer to tally mail-in votes. This kind of thing led Trump to claim that the election was stolen in states such as Pennsylvania—and many continue to believe him. In order to defuse this moronic conspiracy, we need better understanding of how votes are tallied and how demographic data can explain discrepancies.

We could go further into a discussion of all kinds of fallacious reasoning. Let's conclude this section by noting that the remedy is better education about civics, mathematics, and virtue. But it is not enough to merely provide information and education. What is also needed is a change of attitude such that information and education are taken to heart, and citizens will seek to be better informed, more literate, more logical, and more critically aware.

CONCLUSION: FOOLS WANT TO BELIEVE FAKE NEWS

As we conclude this chapter, let's admit that in some cases it is very difficult to sort out the truth. Scientific information is not easily understood. And as I've argued here, people are lazy. We are often more interested in a titillating piece of false information than in a complex explanation of what is really going on. This is why people fall for magicians, psychics, and con artists. Charlatans understand our foolishness and use it to take advantage. This helps explain why fake news works and why it is such a problem.

"Fake news" is yet another term that can be used as a subjective and polarizing epithet. President Trump would often call stories that he did not like or that portrayed him unfavorably "fake news." But just because someone—even the president—says a story is fake, does not mean it is fake. Sometimes, President Trump appeared to use "fake news" as a synonym for "false." But there is a difference between false stories and fake news. Fake news is primarily something that looks like a news story but isn't. For example, there are links on webpages that look like news stories but are really advertisements. This shows up in print media also, with text that appears to be news but is really an advertisement. State propaganda can also function in this way. Notice, by the way, that a "fake news" story (understood as an advertisement) could in fact be true. The fakeness of the story is not necessarily in its content but in the fact that it appears to be a real piece of journalism. This distinction implies that genuine journalism is something other than advertising. Journalists are professionals who have standards of proof and who adhere to a basic code of journalistic ethics. One important principle for journalists is that they are not supposed to write stories that involve conflicts of interest: journalism is not advertising, nor is it supposed to be overtly partisan. Journalists are supposed to be oriented toward the truth—and when they make a mistake, they are supposed to admit it and correct it.

Tyrants and the sycophants who support them understand that ordinary people are easily confused by the kinds of subtle points made here about advertising, propaganda, journalism, and truth. The tyrant and his sycophants know that we morons are interested in amusement. We often click on links in order to be entertained, not informed. In the old days, we would glance at the tabloids in the checkout line at the grocery store or in the newsstand at the train station. These days, social media and its algorithms bring the titillation of fake news straight to our smart phones. In some cases, outrageous lies gain traction through repetition and the echo chamber of social media. This helps explain the QAnon conspiracies. It also helps explain why Trump lied and continued to lie even when he was caught in a lie. Trump lacked shame with regard to untruth. And he discovered that many of his followers did not seem to care about truth at all. One study showed that even when Trump's lies were exposed, his partisan supporters did not waver in their support of him.[42] The point here is that truth was less important than loyalty—and

I would add amusement and fun. Trump explained his idea of "truthful hyperbole" in *The Art of the Deal* in relation to telling people what they want to believe, which is, as Trump notes, a very effective form of marketing and promotion.[43]

Trump most likely does not know that his idea has roots that can be traced all the way back to Aristotle and to Julius Caesar. Aristotle noted that rhetorical persuasion is not simply a matter of logic. It also involves ethos and pathos: emotional connections, trust, identification, lifestyle, social connection, and psychological disposition. We want to believe those we trust, who share our values, and with whom we identify. We'll stick with them, even if we know they are lying. We'll treat their "fake news" as real and agree with them when they describe a common opponent (i.e., the so-called mainstream media) as an enemy of the people. What matters here is not truth but how beliefs unite us, give us an identity, and inflame our emotions. Our tendency to fall for this is moronic: we like violence and amusement, and we like to have our egos stroked. It is fun to be with the "in-crowd," with those who are denouncing fake news and rallying against the enemy of the people. Truth is irrelevant in this carnival atmosphere.

Let's conclude this chapter with a word from Julius Caesar, since it was Caesar who famously explained why fools accept fake news. In a passing remark in his account of the Gallic Wars, Caesar writes: "Men willingly believe what they want to believe" (*libenter homines id quod volunt*).[44] A similar idea is expressed by John Locke, who writes that we most easily believe what we want to believe (*quod volumus, facile credimus*).[45] Locke uses this idea to explain why a lover will refuse to believe that his mistress is unfaithful despite evidence to the contrary. In general, the idea helps explain how tyrants are able to manipulate the moronic masses. All we need is the appearance of truth to satisfy our desire to believe. The desire to believe is not about truth at all. Rather, it is about identity, emotion, and power. We want to believe in the cause, in our leader, and in ourselves. We also want to experience some fun, some anger, and maybe even some violence. Above all, we want to be amused.

(7)

THE SYCOPHANT'S COMPLICITY

On Cunning, Flattery, and the Trojan Horse

Everyone hates thieves and sycophants.

—Aristotle, *Rhetoric*[1]

Aristotle assumed that everyone hates a sycophant—and that this hatred was justified. Dante placed flatterers, hypocrites, and liars in one of the deepest corners of Hell, along with those who dabble in magic. Dante says, "Fraud is man's peculiar vice."[2] And yet each of us plays the sycophant from time to time, telling white lies, exaggerating, and flattering others. Children suck up to their parents. Students polish their teachers' apples. Employees brown-nose their bosses. Social climbers play an elaborate game of gossip, flattery, gift giving, and insinuation. Sometimes this is innocent enough. But the flattery and gifts of full-fledged sycophants are Trojan Horses. They conceal something selfish, dangerous, violent, and corrupt. Sycophants beguile and deceive us in order to take advantage. This is a serious problem in ordinary life. It is even more dangerous when the sycophant sucks up to a tyrant and helps him gain power by turning his forked tongue toward the masses, who are happy to fall for his lies and seductions.

DEFINING SYCOPHANCY

As with the other concepts discussed in this book, *sycophant* is a polarizing and insulting term that can be used subjectively to lambast an opponent. In this chapter, I will mostly focus on sycophancy in the Trump era. But let's begin with a note about President Obama to show why this is a problem for all players of the political game. At his final press conference as president, Obama said to the press:

> You're not supposed to be sycophants, you're supposed to be skeptics, you're supposed to ask me tough questions, you're not supposed to be complimentary, but you're supposed to cast a critical eye on folks who hold enormous power and make sure that we are accountable to the people who sent us here and you have done that.[3]

This is an important statement that reminds us that the free press is an important player in democracy. As soon as Obama uttered these words, conservatives howled, claiming that the press had in fact been sycophantic toward Obama. The headline for one op-ed piece put it this way: "Obama Tells Sycophantic Press Not to be Sycophants Anymore."[4] You get the point. As I have shown in previous chapters, the terms we are employing here are often used in a tit-for-tat and accusatory fashion. This makes it seem as though what one person calls a truth teller is what another person deems a sycophant. And so on. In order to solve this problem, we need an objective account of truth telling—and an objective way of distinguishing flattery from honesty, sincerity from guile. We also need an objective definition of a sycophant. So let's begin there. A sycophant is a person:

1. who *uses words in devious ways*;
2. in order *to gain advantage and access to power*;
3. while *understanding the difference* between truth and falsehood.

This definition leaves out stupid people who do not understand the difference between truth and falsehood or who, like the morons we discussed above, simply ignore that distinction. Sycophants are acutely aware of truth and falsehood and the rules of the social and political game. They manipulate truth and falsehood deliberately, in order to serve their own self-interest. It is the sycophants' awareness of the rules and the truth that makes them complicit. To say that a sycophant is devious implies that he deviates from the norm of truth telling and that he does this with malicious intent. Sycophants do not tell "white lies" or accidentally misspeak or exaggerate. Sycophants are not innocent bystanders or ignorant hangers-on. They know what's going on with the tyrant and knowingly fly his flag. This serves as a reminder that while children play at sycophancy when they suck up to their parents, this is only a pale reflection of genuine sycophancy. Full-blown sycophants give poisoned gifts, knowing both that the gift is poison and that they are seeking to manipulate the appearances of things. The sycophant is clever, cunning, and complicit.

Sycophants can be found throughout history. When the history of the Trump years is written, a number of sycophants will be identified, including those who helped him rise to power, consolidate power, and attempt to cling to power during the ignominious events of January 6. Among the many stories that could be told, let's begin by considering Michael Cohen, one of Trump's attorneys. Cohen was eventually prosecuted and imprisoned. Cohen was interviewed on CNN on September 15, 2020. The host reminded Cohen that he was once an "ardent" Trump supporter who was "seduced" by him. Cohen said, "Let's call me what I was. I was a sycophant."[5] While Cohen admits this, others do not. Consider, for example, Rudy Giuliani, who, like the sycophants of ancient Greece, led the charge in filing frivolous lawsuits to overturn the 2020 election. It was Giuliani who said, at the January 6 rally preceding the insurrection, that there ought to be trial by combat. His own daughter, Caroline Rose Giuliani, warned about this in October 2020. She wrote:

> If being the daughter of a polarizing mayor who became the president's personal bulldog has taught me anything, it is that corruption starts with "yes-men" and women, the cronies who create an echo chamber of lies and subservience to maintain their proximity to power. We've seen this ad nauseam with Trump and his cadre of high-level sycophants (the ones who weren't convicted, anyway).[6]

Ms. Giuliani directs our attention here to a related problem, which is the role of "cronies." A crony is an old friend but not necessarily a good one. Rather, the crony is often a kind of sycophant, who tells us what we want to hear without necessarily telling us the truth. Cronyism is a problem in politics, business, and life. Plato noted in *Gorgias* that tyrants prefer to surround themselves with cronies and yes-men instead of with true friends. The same problem holds for nepotism, which involves giving favors to relatives. The problem in all of this is that the cronies, relatives, and sycophants ride the tyrant's coattails, enjoying the ride. They have no interest in speaking truth to power. Instead, they benefit from reflecting the tyrant's image back to him. As Socrates explains (*Gorgias* 510d), the tyrant's cronies and sycophants behave slavishly: they train themselves to like what the tyrant likes and hate what the tyrant hates. They put on a mask and perfect the art of sucking up. This enables the tyrant or would-be tyrant to do as much harm as he can get away with.

The problem of sycophants, cronies, and nepotism is well known, as is the cure. The remedy involves moral education focused on virtues such as honesty, integrity, and courage. It also involves a legal system that prevents frivolous lawsuits while limiting the power of tyrants and the suck-ups who abet them. Alexander Hamilton made this clear in *Federalist* 71 when he explained that good leaders should focus on reason and the public good while resisting "the wiles of parasites and sycophants." But the moral character of the leader is not enough. We also need to limit the power of would-be tyrants. And there ought to be institutional safeguards that guarantee truth, transparency, and independent oversight. We need rules against nepotism. We need to limit the power of cronies and the influence of sycophants. In general, we need a social, political, and moral situation in which cronies give way to genuine, virtuous friends, in which nepotism is limited, and in which sycophants are exposed as the frauds and flatterers that they are.

SYCOPHANTS AND FLATTERERS FROM SOCRATES TO SENECA

As we've seen, a sycophant is not a moron. In the ancient world, a sycophant knew enough about the legal system to manipulate it. Modern day suck-ups are not stupid. They understand systems of power and authority. They know how to work the media to fire up the masses.

They use clever language and coy strategies to ingratiate and aggrandize themselves. Sometimes they rant and rave. But it is mostly a clever act intended to provoke and manipulate. This is why we can say of the sycophants that they ought to know better. This is why we can blame them for their complicity. A sycophant is a clever sophist and strategic flatterer: someone who uses language in deceptive ways and who is adept at playing rhetorical games. One way of defining sophistry is to say that sophists make fallacious argument. This is a fancy way of saying that they are purveyors of "bullshit," which is, as Harry Frankfurt has explained, speech that is divorced from a concern for truth.[7] The goal of flatterers, sycophants, sophists, and bullshit artists is to manipulate and persuade.

The concept of sycophant has evolved somewhat from its original Greek meaning. The Greek term *sykophantes* indicated someone who manipulated legal and political life for selfish purposes. Unlike a tyrant who simply seizes power, the sycophant is more subtle. In the ancient Greek world, sycophants were something like those we call "ambulance chasers," people who were looking to turn a profit and raise a stink at the expense of other people. An ancient Greek sycophant brought legal accusations against others as a way of aggrandizing himself. A sycophant was not really interested in right and wrong, truth or falsehood. Instead, he manipulated the system for profit.[8]

The sycophant was a familiar character in ancient Greece. Odysseus played the part. He was known for "weaving cunning schemes," which helped him escape and find his way home and which most famously included the false gift of the Trojan Horse.[9] The sycophant showed up as a character in a number of Aristophanes's comedies—as a caricature who was laughed at and driven away by the hero.[10] Perhaps one reason that the sycophant is a laughing stock is that the word itself contains the sense of something naughty and obscene. The etymology of the Greek term links it to the word for fig (*sykos*): the sycophant, or *syko-phantes*, is a fig shower (where *phanos* is related to a kind of display or showing). This might be understood as revealing something shameful—not only a secret that could be the subject of blackmail but also the genitalia.

Sycophancy developed in ancient Athens as part of the system of justice.[11] At one point, the sycophant was a person who brought charges against someone in the name of the public good. There was no public prosecutor or district attorney. So these self-appointed defenders of law and virtue took it upon themselves to denounce others. This system was subject to abuse. Sycophants were eventually seen as legal tricksters who used their ability to manipulate public opinion in order to blackmail people. In Aristophanes's comedies, the sycophant is a stock character who was a clever and manipulative parasite on the public good. Aristophanes describes these parasites in his comedy, *Birds*: he says that there exists a race of men who "pluck figs" with their tongues.[12] This is a play on words connected to the etymology of the term. There is an obscene and sexual connotation to this: figs could be understood as testicles (take a look at an actual fig to get the point . . .). So a sycophant may be someone who played with testicles—either their own or others'—in public and with their tongue. It is, by the way, from Latin that we get the word *testis*, which can mean both a witness and a testicle. One etymology of words like testimony and testify suggests that witnesses would swear on their testicles or put their hands on the testicles of a priest, magistrate, or sacred animal as part of the act of testifying.[13] At any rate, a sycophant is shameful. We see this in English where the obscene connotation exists in terms like brown-noser and ass-kisser.

Sycophants are also flatterers. The etymology of this English term connects it to the word *flat*. This may indicate something about what the flatterer does: he makes himself flat (i.e., he bows or prostrates himself). Related terms are obsequiousness and fawning. In Greek the term *kolas* can be translated as flatterer. Aristotle says that flatterers (*kolakes*) are servile and lowly people (*Nicomachean Ethics* 1125). Plato, using the same word, says that tyrants like to associate with flatterers (*Republic* 575e)—a point that echoes what he says about the tyrant's cronies in *Gorgias*. In *Republic*, Plato further explains that tyrants have to pander to the sycophants in order to retain power and that "whatever some people may think, a real tyrant is really a slave, compelled to engage in the worst kind of fawning, slavery, and pandering to the worst kind of people" (*Republic* 579e). Earlier in *Republic*, Thrasymachus (a would-be tyrant) accuses Socrates of being a *sykophantes* (*Republic* 340–41), implying that Socrates makes bad arguments in order to ingratiate himself. It is clear that the term is related to the other insult typically thrown at Socrates, which is that he was a sophist engaged in manipulative and fallacious argumentation.

In the ancient world, sycophants were widely reviled, and the term was thrown around as an insult. At one point under the rule of the Thirty Tyrants, the sycophants of Athens were rounded up and executed.[14] Among those who were killed by the Thirty was Polemarchus, a friend of Plato and Socrates—who was one of the main characters in Plato's *Republic*. Plato appears to suggest that those who brought charges against Socrates were acting as sycophants. Although Plato does not use the term in his *Apology*, Socrates says of his accuser Meletus: "Meletus is a wrongdoer, because he jokes in earnest, lightly involving people in a lawsuit, pretending to be zealous and concerned about things or which he never cared at all" (*Apology* 24c). This is exactly what the ancient *sykophantes* did. And, as Xenophon pointed out in his *Memorabilia* (Book 2, chapter 9), Socrates discussed the problem of sycophants in other circumstances, suggesting that it was useful to have a sycophant of your own who could protect you from the false accusations of other sycophants. An explicit connection between sycophants and tyrants is made by Plato in *Republic* (line 575), where Plato points out that tyrants are served by henchmen and sycophants, who—unlike the tyrants they serve—commit "small evils." Plato explains that tyrants come to power in a variety of ways, and while some "steal, break into houses, cut purses, strip men of their garments, plunder temples, and kidnap" there are others who, "if they are fluent speakers they become sycophants and bear false witness and take bribes" (*Republic* at 575b).

This problem exists as long as there are mechanisms of power, which clever and unscrupulous people can exploit. In the era of the Roman Empire, Tacitus lamented the rise of sycophancy as part of the decadence of the empire. The Latin term translated as *sycophant* is *adulatio*, a cognate for the English term *adulation*. This term often shows up in connection with other terms such as *obsequium*, a cognate for our term *obsequious*, and words derived from *servus*, which is Latin for slave and gives us words such as *servile* and *servility*. Tacitus shows that the power dynamic within the imperial system was such that sycophancy became common—either out of a cunning attempt to advance interests and career or out of a fear of the powerful. Senators and others abased themselves before Caesar with servile flattery, slavish adulation, and fawning obsequiousness. Tacitus begins his *Annals* by casting blame upon the sycophants for making it difficult to discover the truth. There were attempts at writing the history of Rome, Tacitus said. But the sycophants scared away the truth. As Tacitus put it, "The histories of Tiberius, Caius, Claudius, and Nero, while they were in power, were falsified through terror."[15]

As Roman despots rose and fell—from Julius and Augustus to Tiberius, Caligula, and Nero, Tacitus reports, the Roman Senate became sycophantic. He lamented how this occurred under the rule of Tiberius. Tacitus portrayed Tiberius as a tyrant. But even Tiberius was embarrassed by the shameful sycophancy of his subjects: "Tradition says that Tiberius as often as he left the Senate-House used to exclaim in Greek, 'How ready these men are to be slaves.' Clearly, even he, with his dislike of public freedom, was disgusted at the abject abasement of his creatures."[16]

Tacitus describes the Emperor Nero (*Annals*, Book 16) as gullible and susceptible to the flattery of the sycophants. One day a Carthaginian came to Rome and shared a vision that he had of a cave filled with a golden treasure, which he promised would belong to Nero if Nero would support him in finding it. The credulous Emperor believed the tale. As Tacitus explained, people were able to suck up to the emperor because of his credulity: he wanted to believe the adulation. Tacitus's explanation has become an aphorism that has been widely quoted in this regard: "People flatter us because they can depend upon our credulity."

Nero sent men to find the gold and began spending money profligately in anticipation of a windfall. Sycophants in Rome began talking of the treasure as a sign that the gods were smiling upon Nero. But the gold was never found. The Carthaginian agent committed suicide. And in order to cover up the embarrassment of this whole episode, the sycophants in the Senate conspired to help Nero win a music and theatrical competition. According to Tacitus, Nero disgraced himself on the stage. But the crowd was forced to applaud the tyrant by soldiers who insisted they continue applauding even when their hands were aching. The sycophants were also watching each other, waiting for a chance to pounce and take advantage. The story goes that when one of the sycophants of the Roman establishment, Vespasian, dozed off during Nero's performance, he was called out for this by Phoebus, another sycophant and was saved from being destroyed only by a stroke of good fortune.[17]

Nero was not known for his mercy—despite the fact that his philosophy tutor, Seneca, wrote a famous essay for Nero called "On Clemency." In that essay, Seneca warns that tyrants delight in cruelty, while good kings practice mercy. In this essay, Seneca was speaking truth to power. He knew that this was risky. But he hoped to call Nero to be a good, kind, and merciful king. Seneca said, "I would rather offend by telling the truth than curry favor by flattery."[18] But Nero was not a kind and merciful king. He killed his own mother and, fearing that Seneca was engaged in a plot against him, ordered Seneca to commit suicide. Some think that Seneca was himself a sycophant to Nero. But Seneca, at least, understood the danger and the problem of sycophancy. He understood that there is a fault in human nature that makes us enjoy flattery. The worst danger is that we flatter ourselves. And here we see a double problem for the sycophant: while sucking up to the tyrant, he deludes himself into thinking that all will be well, that he is clever, and that he has not sold his soul for access to power. Perhaps Seneca succumbed to this temptation himself in his relations with Nero. But Seneca warned that there is nothing more dangerous than self-flattery. In his book *Of Peace of Mind*, Seneca has Serenus say, "Who dares to tell himself the truth? Who is there, by however large a troop of caressing courtiers he may be surrounded, who in spite of them is not his own greatest flatterer."[19]

OPPORTUNISM, CONTORTIONISM, AND POLITICAL PERFORMANCE ART

If the tyrant is proud, forceful, and indifferent to moral limitations, then the sycophant is sneaky, clever, and cunning. The sycophant has a clearer sense that right and wrong are matters of importance in social and political contexts, even though morality is not his primary concern. Like the tyrant, the sycophant's concern is his own self-interest. But unlike the tyrant, the sycophant lacks the power to force his will on the situation. Instead, he plays with power to the degree that he can in order to manipulate things to turn out well for him. The sycophant does not dominate or push. Instead, he cajoles and insinuates. He does not boast bombastically about himself as the tyrant does. Instead, he praises his master and reserves his bombast for those who oppose his master. He is adept at manipulating the appearances of things. This means that he reads the social scene carefully, crafting alliances and spreading gossip. He uses the truth when it suits his purposes, but he also uses deceit and falsehood when necessary. The sycophant is an opportunist.

In an earlier chapter, I provided a brief account of some of the examples of sycophancy we've seen in the Trump era: Senator Ted Cruz of Texas, Senator Lindsey Graham of South Carolina, and so on. Senator Graham's flip-flopping on Trump has merited extensive review in the popular media. Graham called Trump a "jackass" and voted for a third-party candidate in 2016. But Graham soon became a thoroughgoing Trumpian.[20] As Richard Bond—the former Republican National Committee chairman—said of Graham, he is a "political opportunist."[21] This is a polite way of saying that Senator Graham is an unprincipled sycophant. Opportunism means that what matters is fitting oneself to the opportunities that present themselves. Instead of remaining committed to principles, the opportunist views principles as tools to be used as instruments. Said differently, the sycophant lacks integrity. Instead of remaining steadfast and true, the sycophant is a shape-shifter who molds himself to the exigencies of the moment. This means that the career of the sycophant will be riddled with contradictions and flip-flopping.

Another example from Senator Graham is worth noting. In February 2016, Graham accused Trump of being a "kook" and an "opportunist."[22] Graham said: "I think he's a kook. I think he's crazy. I think he's unfit for office." He continued: "I'm a Republican, and he's not. He's not a conservative Republican, he's an opportunist." And: "He's not fit to be president of the United States." But a year later, Graham expressed outrage that others would call Trump a "kook" who was unfit for office. In November 2017, Graham said, "What concerns me about the American press is this endless, endless attempt to label the guy some kind of kook not fit to be president."[23] This is an obvious example of the shape-shifting nature of the sycophant.

Now, we might ask, what would cause a U.S. senator to shape-shift in this way? Perhaps one causal explanation can be found in pressure from above put upon the senator. Fear of the power of the president might help to explain some of this. It is worth noting that in response to Graham's 2016 tirade against him, then-candidate Trump turned the tables on Graham.[24] Trump said that Graham was "one of the dumbest human beings I've ever seen." Trump continued, saying of Graham, "The guy is a nut job." And: "This guy knows nothing." Trump released Senator Graham's cell phone number to the public. This kind of ad hominem and the implicit threat of somehow unleashing the mob against the senator could have had some impact on Graham. But it would be odd for a seasoned politician and a U.S. senator to be susceptible to such vague threats and invective. The conversion of Senator Graham is not merely a case of a coward who is cowed by a bully's threats. Rather, the senator's shape-shifting is the result of political calculation. The senator's change is not explained by what he is afraid of as much as by what he wants, which is power. And so, in this sense, the sycophant shares something in common with the tyrant. But while the tyrant seizes power, the sycophant cajoles and insinuates himself into the good graces of the tyrant.

To make this point clear, consider a profile of Senator Graham by Mark Leibovich published in 2019: "How Lindsey Graham Went from Trump Skeptic to Trump Sidekick."[25] Leibovich recounts the shifting loyalties of what he calls the "contortionists" of the Trump era. He notes that increased polarization helps explain some of this Trump-era shape-shifting. Republicans have come to believe that they are playing a kind of zero-sum game against the Democrats. And so they believe that they have to accommodate themselves to Trump in order to remain in power. This, I submit, is part of the problem of sycophancy that emerges under tyranny. When the leader (or his party) paints the world in black and white, demanding adulation, those at lower levels on the totem pole find themselves with a stark choice: conform or be lost. The sycophantic contortionist wants to stay in power, so they choose to conform. Leibovich reports a frank conversation with Senator Graham in which he asked the senator about his opportunistic contortionism with regard to Trump. He reports that Graham said he was trying to remain "relevant." Graham reportedly said, "I've got an opportunity up here working with the president to get some really good outcomes for the country."

In order to get things done under Trump in pursuit of a conservative agenda (such as installing conservative members on the Supreme Court), the senator had to conform himself to Trump. This puts a positive spin on the idea of opportunism. It is goal oriented; the opportunist uses the instruments available and does not worry about the compromises and complicity that are involved in getting things done and remaining relevant. A less positive interpretation would focus more on Senator Graham's interest in getting reelected. He ran for reelection in 2020. With Trump in the White House (and controlling fundraising and the political machine of the Republican party), Graham had no choice but to play along with Trump. As he said in his interview with Leibovich, "If you don't want to get re-elected, you're in the wrong business."

None of this really helps to explain what happened after the insurrection of January 6. Senator Graham eventually said "count me out" and "enough is enough," in response to Trump's effort to overturn the election of Joe Biden.[26] But Graham voted to acquit the former president during his second impeachment. The same is true of Senator Mitch McConnell, who also voted to acquit the president, while excoriating the president for his part in the January 6 riot. McConnell is another sycophantic contortionist whose words after the impeachment acquittal don't fit with his vote to acquit.[27] McConnell said: "Former President Trump's actions preceding the riot were a disgraceful dereliction of duty." And: "There is no question that President Trump is practically and morally responsible for provoking the events of that day." Senator McConnell continued:

> The leader of the free world cannot spend weeks thundering that shadowy forces are stealing our country and then feign surprise when people believe him and do reckless things. . . . The unconscionable behavior did not end when the violence began. Whatever our ex-president claims he thought might happen that day, whatever reaction he says he meant to produce, by that afternoon, he was watching the same live television as the rest of the world. A mob was assaulting the Capitol in his name. These criminals were carrying his banners, hanging his flags, and screaming their loyalty to him. It was obvious that only President Trump could end this. . . . But the president did not act swiftly. He did not do his job.

But Senator McConnell voted to acquit the former president in the second Trump impeachment. According to McConnell, his acquittal vote was based on a constitutional principle having to do with the fact that Trump was no longer in office at the time of the Senate impeachment trial. Of course, it was Senator McConnell who caused this temporal problem: as Senate majority leader, he refused to bring the impeachment to trial while Trump was still in office. By stalling and deflecting, McConnell found a way to avoid convicting Trump. In this case, we see clever parliamentary maneuvering and an attempt to have things both ways: both to be able to speak out and condemn Trump in public but without connecting this to any political sanction that could restrain him.

This is clever opportunism. After the second impeachment trial, Graham and McConnell were both once again willing to accommodate Trump. Again, perhaps there is a kind of fear and cowardice at play here. After McConnell's speech condemning Trump, Trump fired back.[28] Trump said that McConnell was a "dour, sullen and unsmiling political hack," while noting that McConnell owed his 2020 reelection to Trump. Trump said, "How quickly he forgets. Without my endorsement, McConnell would have lost, and lost badly." There is a kind of veiled threat here: that without Trump, McConnell's career is over. But again, cowardice is not the only problem. The further problem is cold political calculation. Trump remains popular among Republican voters. He can use his power to help get Republicans elected in the 2022 midterm elections. This helps explain why Graham and McConnell both remain open to supporting Trump if he were to run for president again in 2024, despite their previous expressions of moral outrage about Trump's tyrannical shenanigans on January 6.[29]

This kind of opportunism and contortionism is typical in political life, which is a game of masks and performance—a kind of theater, spectacle, and show. Political agents are good at shape-shifting. They wear masks and speak in different ways to different crowds. The rhetorical skill involved is considerable. Political actors need to understand what their audience expects and deliver it with some semblance of authenticity. When the masses require a down-home, "aw-shucks" delivery, the political actor puts on his blue jeans and dumbs down his speech. But in the halls of power or in court, the actor speaks, dresses, and appears in a different manner. Bill Clinton was good at this, as was George W. Bush.

We all do this to an extent. Scholars in the fields of sociolinguistics and discourse analysis call it "code-switching" and "style-shifting."[30] The human brain evolved to fit into social networks and to judge hierarchies of power. We morph and mingle in ways that help us fit in and negotiate very complex social and linguistic systems. People who often operate in more than one linguistic context are very good at this: bilingual people, for example, or people whose lives stretch across quite different domestic and professional contexts. Politicians are also typically very good at doing this. The ability to code-switch and style shift is an asset most of the time. The problem arises, when this skill is divorced from a deeper moral structure of integrity or set of core values—or when it is put to use in the service of tyrants.

In his political autobiography, Senator Graham provides some insight into his childhood that sheds light on all of this. His parents ran a bar, and as a child, young Lindsey would hang out and entertain the patrons. He explained:

> I was one of the main attractions at the bar when I was between the ages of four and seven. . . . Folks seemed to be amused by my antics. . . . I talked my head off to anyone who would listen to me. People apparently found the combination of my slight stature and gabby nature comical. I took a great deal of pleasure in mischief, which came as naturally to me as verbosity did. But I think I was conscious, too, that I was giving a performance, that I was expected to entertain folks. And I knew the more audacious I was the more entertaining I would be.[31]

This description of a child interested in amusing others and getting attention through mischief could describe many human beings. As children, we want to be loved. And we love attention. What matters to us at this stage in our lives is the attention we receive. It does not matter exactly how we get that attention. We've all been there, and we see this in others. We brag and boast. We tell lies and exaggerate. We seek to be entertaining and amusing. All of this is a way of keeping ourselves in the spotlight, an attempt to get some power and notoriety. It is easy to see how this could lead one to a life of politics, where those same desires and skills come in handy.

But there is a thin line dividing notoriety from notoriousness. The desire for notoriety and attention fuels sycophancy, driving the sycophant to suck up to the powerful, while pandering to the mob. Most of the time this is not a problem. When those in power are decent, this can result in honorable alliances, good friendships, and good outcomes. Opportunists who fall into good opportunities can be fine and decent. The problem develops when the desire to be relevant gets hitched to a power structure—or a person—who is not good. Sycophancy is morally problematic when it is connected to tyranny. Without a tyrant in the picture, the sycophantic personality is merely an admirer or a hanger-on, an entertaining actor, a member of the entourage whose complicity does not implicate him in crime.

COMPLICITY AND STRUCTURES OF POWER

The term *complicity* is connected to the term *accomplice*. An accomplice knows about a crime and somehow provides support for it. As an old saying goes, "He who helps the guilty shares the crime."[32] There are degrees of complicity, of course. In some cases, an accomplice helps plan the crime and drives the getaway car—also enjoying the fruits of the criminal act. But someone who merely knows about a crime beforehand, while not doing anything to prevent it, is also complicit. The same is true of someone who learns of a crime after the fact and helps the criminal escape justice. In thinking about complicity, we must think about knowledge, intention, and causal efficacy. Someone who has no causal connection to a crime but who cheers it on is not really complicit. The same is true for a bus driver or taxi driver who helps a criminal get away from a crime without knowing that the person they were transporting was a criminal.

In moral philosophy and the law, there are significant questions about responsibility, blame, and punishment. Should an arms dealer be held responsible for mass murder, for example, if someone he sells guns to shoots up a school or a shopping mall? There are lines to be drawn in the law, in political life, and in professional life. To draw these lines requires more detailed analysis than we can present here. There are related questions about sycophants, which I won't address here. We might ask, for example, how we ought to punish sycophants who facilitate a tyrant's rise to power. It is likely that there will be disagreements about punishments (such as impeachment in the case of elected officials or disbarment in the case of lawyers). These disagreements will reflect deeper disagreements about punishment in general and about structural issues involving the way we weave together legal matters, political questions, and professional ethics. We can also consider the moral, psychological, and spiritual question of complicity—not as a matter of punishment but as a matter of moral evaluation and judgment. To claim that a sycophant is complicit is not necessarily to say that the sycophant ought to be punished (in the legal, political, or professional realm). Nor is it to claim that a sycophant ought to feel guilty or apologize. Rather, it is to say that the sycophant is somehow involved in the problem of tyranny. In ordinary language, we would say that the sycophant is somehow to "blame" for the tyrant's rise. But this way of speaking is very loose. We could blame a sycophant without suggesting he be punished.

This way of considering complicity—in a neutral fashion that remains agnostic about punishment—is connected to issues such as structural injustice, institutional racism, structural violence, and other kinds of systemic and institutional maladies. These issues have come to the fore recently in public discourse, especially in the aftermath of police killings of Black men. To focus on structural issues helps us look past the specific legal responsibility of individual agents. The question, from a structural vantage point, is about the contribution of the system to the problems and challenges we are interested in. While blame may still be of interest from a legal, professional, or moral standpoint, from a larger perspective what matters is the historical, cultural, economic, and other forces that cause these problems and challenges.

One might suggest, then, that from a structural vantage point, the sycophant is not really to blame. He or she is merely a victim of circumstance who is merely playing along with the customs, norms, and traditions of a given social system. Opportunism depends, after all, on the opportunities that arise.

Such a response is, however, a cop-out for at least two reasons when it comes to sycophancy. First, the sycophant benefits from the system of power in which he operates. And indeed, the higher up the political food chain we go, the more likely it is that the sycophant knows exactly what he is doing and actually intends to benefit from the game he is playing. Furthermore, because of his position within the power structure, the sycophant has a special obligation to avoid complicity. In a tyranny, the tyrant may in fact recruit sycophants to serve him. But in a representative democracy such as the United States, elected leaders and bureaucratic officials take an oath to the Constitution that commits them to the rule of law and service of the commonwealth. In a representative democracy such as the United States, sycophancy and complicity in tyranny is dereliction of duty—a phrase that Senator McConnell himself used in relation to Trump.

It was this apparent dereliction of duty that was egregious and appalling during the Trump era and its insurrectionist aftermath. And this is what is frustrating about sycophants in general: their position and relationships seem to require a certain kind of duty; but this expectation is turned upside down. In reality the sycophant is not what he claims to be.

FLATTERING THE TYRANT AND THE MOB

In Plato's world, sycophancy is closely linked to sophistry. A sophist, as Plato explains in his *Republic*, is someone who flatters the mob—who knows how to speak to the public. In the drama of the life and death of Socrates, Socrates was accused of being both a sophist and a sycophant. But this turned things upside down. It was those who made these accusations against Socrates who were in fact the sophists and sycophants— who knew how to make persuasive speeches in the Assembly that flattered the mob. This reminds us that the political sycophant has more than one audience. He sucks up to his boss, the tyrant. But he also helps his boss suck up to and flatter the mob. Bloom explained in his account of Plato's *Republic*, "The sycophants were flatterers of tyrant public opinion."[33] Flattery in either case is divorced from truth. As we've seen, the mob is not interested in truth. They want to be amused. Nor is the tyrant interested in truth. Rather, he wants his inflated self-image to be reflected back at him.

This point about flattery connects to another significant historical and literary source: Plutarch's text "How to Tell a Flatterer from a Friend." A flatterer merely appears to be a friend. But in reality, he is not. Good friends make us better—as Plato and Aristotle both taught. They tell us the truth, honestly, sincerely, and compassionately. But friends who flatter us and make us worse are merely "cronies" in the sense discussed above. With the sycophant, we encounter all kinds of slippages and illusions. As Plutarch tells it, the flatterer is cunning and crafty. He is unstable and illusory, a dissembler and a deceiver. His lies are not bold and self-aggrandizing as in the case of the tyrant. Rather, the sycophant is a reflection of the one he flatters. As Plutarch explains:

> [He is] inconstant, and not a man of himself, taking love or hatred to this or that, joying or grieving at a thing, upon any affection of his own that leadeth him thereto, for that he receives always as a mirror the images of the passions, motions and lives of other men.[34]

Flattery is not always wrong. Sometimes with children, students, and lovers, it makes sense to praise them even when the praise is not true. This sort of thing is not an outright lie. It is more like what Frankfurt calls "bullshit."[35] Bullshit is disconnected from a concern for the truth. The goal of the flatterer and bullshitter is not to declare something to be true but, rather, to persuade someone to like them, support them, or do what they want. With regard to children and students, untrue praise is a way of building trust and self-esteem. Brutal honesty can be counter-productive in coaching, teaching, and parenting. It is also not always appropriate to be brutally honest in loving relationships. And sometimes, flattery is so hyperbolic that it is not even worth considering as a report of truth. When a lover says to his beloved, "You are the most beautiful woman in the world," this is not a report of objective truth. Rather, it is an expression of love. This is an intimate communication that goes beyond an assertion of aesthetic truth. Flattery is not quite outright and deliberate lying, even though it is likely that the flatterer would admit—if pressed—that what he is saying is not entirely true.

But—and here is the problem with sycophancy and flattery directed at the tyrant and at the masses—the sycophant knows he is lying (or ought to know) and he also knows that he is trying to manipulate his target. It is one thing for a lover to flatter his beloved—especially if the feeling is mutual and the lover is not trying to manipulate his partner into sex. It is another thing for a sycophant to kiss up to his superior in order to gain a favor or a position. And it is yet another thing for the sycophant to flatter the crowd by playing to the crowd's worst appetites.

Plutarch again provides a useful source. He says in his essay on education that "to please the masses is to displease the wise."[36] Those who speak in such a way as to capture the favor of the "vulgar herd" are a danger to the community and to themselves. They are "incontinent,"

Plutarch suggests, and unable to control their lust for pleasure. Plutarch has in mind those who speak without thinking, as well as those who speak obscenely and without content. We might picture the ranting of talking heads on television news or the unthinking tweeting of those who post compulsively on Twitter. True and proper speech requires preparation and self-control. But flatterers, cronies, and sycophants speak without thinking. They speak vulgarly, theatrically, and melodramatically.

The problem of the sycophant is that he is a performer and something of a buffoon. He huffs and he puffs. He gestures and cajoles. He whispers and insinuates. Sometimes his hair dye seeps down the side of his face. Other times he makes stupid mistakes such as holding a press conference at a landscaping business called Four Seasons instead of at the Four Seasons hotel. It is easy to understand why this happens to the sycophant. He has an impossible task. He has to fire up the base and flatter the mob. At the same time, the tyrant's shadow looms over him. Every word he speaks has at least two audiences. And he must keep speaking. To remain relevant he must continue to contort himself and play-act in a world where sycophants are routinely thrown to the wolves and devoured. Nero did it to Seneca. Trump did it to Cohen. And so it goes.

CONCLUSION: THE TROJAN HORSE

Let's return to the beginning and consider a famous example of a cunning sycophant: the hero Odysseus. Odysseus plays the sycophant when he must: when he finds himself at the mercy of someone more powerful than him. In such circumstances, Odysseus is a master of disguise and clever speech. He is repeatedly described as cunning, clever, and so on. According to one scholar, Odysseus is "the incarnation of *metis*, the ancient Greek word we translate as cunning."[37] Odysseus employs his cunning whenever he finds himself in a tricky situation that requires him to devise a scheme that will help him survive and escape. When he confronts the Cyclops, for example—a symbol of raw political power and dominance—Odysseus employs a variety of cunning schemes. He gets the Cyclops drunk and then blinds him. He hides his men among the sheep. This episode includes a clever mocking joke about Odysseus's name. As you'll recall, Odysseus tells the Cyclops that his name is "nobody." This prevents the Cyclops from calling for help (since it is "nobody" who is assaulting him). And so on. Odysseus is a master of misdirection. He jokes and mocks and manipulates his way out of many close scrapes. But in the end, when he finally has a chance to take his revenge on the men who invaded his house and threatened his wife, he is brutal and cruel. In his brutality toward the suitors, Odysseus delivers vengeance on the sycophants, flatterers, schemers, and manipulators who disrupted his home.

The story of Odysseus reminds us that sycophancy can be linked to violence. Sycophants conceal their lust for power and domination beneath a veneer of sweet words. When they have to, they lie and deceive. But when they can get away with it, they can be brutal and violent. In general, the gifts they offer are often poisonous. One of the most famous stories of a poisoned gift is the tale of the Trojan Horse. Odysseus devised the plan that delivered a phony gift to the Trojans that concealed the Greek warriors who wreaked havoc on Troy. The well-known moral of this story comes from Vergil's version of the tale: "Beware Greeks bearing gifts." The flatterers and sycophants of the world are adept at gift giving. They give the tyrant what he wants to hear. They give the mob what it wants to hear. But these gifts are not good. They don't tell us the truth. They don't make us more virtuous. They conceal avarice, self-interest, and possibly even violence.

III

REMEDIES AND SOLUTIONS

8

WISDOM, VIGILANCE, AND
THE CITIZEN-PHILOSOPHER

I know no safe depository of the ultimate powers of the society, but
the people themselves: and if we think them not enlightened enough
to exercise their control with a wholesome discretion, the remedy is,
not to take it from them, but to inform their discretion by education.
This is the true corrective of abuses of constitutional power.

—Thomas Jefferson[1]

Someone needs to stand guard to ensure that the poison gifts of the
tyrant and his sycophants do not harm us. In the concluding chapters of
this book, I offer remedies to tyranny. Here I explore the development
of *citizen-philosophers* who relate to one another as friends. One might
also speak of philosopher-citizens. But the philosopher-citizen remains
elite and aloof: the concept describes a person who pursues philosophical wisdom first and then returns to political life. Plato was a philosopher-citizen who proposed the solution to tyranny in the guardianship
of the philosopher-king. Plato's ideal risks becoming tyrannical, as the
philosopher-king is empowered to impose his ideal vision of the good
life on the world. The problem of the Platonic solution is found in the
question "Who guards the guardians?" The modern democratic answer
to this question is that "we, the people" watch the watchers and guard
the guardians. It is the people who must remain vigilant and hold those

we elect accountable. We will consider structural political issues related to this modern democratic ideal in the next chapter. Here I consider the citizen-philosopher as a more inclusive and organic ideal than that of Plato's philosopher king. We find ourselves as citizens. From within this condition we seek virtue, wisdom, and enlightenment so that we might become vigilant guardians of our own liberty.

A FEW GOOD MEN

We need wise and good men and women to guard us against tyranny, sycophancy, and the moronic mob. Let's begin with an inspiring anecdote from January 6, 2021, at the insurrection in the Capitol. Eugene Goodman is a cop with a nearly mythological name. As the mob stormed the Capitol, Officer Goodman led rioters away from parts of the Capitol where they could do the most damage. He encouraged the mob to follow him, rather than harm members of Congress. He also helped to direct Senator Mitt Romney toward safety. The quick thinking and virtue of one good man can help to prevent rioters from wreaking havoc. This quick-witted act of courage shows us the importance of individual action, ingenuity, and integrity. In order for democracy to work, more of us need to become good men and women, like Eugene Goodman.

The challenge of democratic life is that we, the people are the guardians of our own liberty and well-being. We need to pursue wisdom and virtue. And we benefit from gadflies and critics who challenge our stupidity, complacency, and complicity. Martin Luther King Jr. described himself as a nonviolent gadfly, explicitly connecting his acts of nonviolent civil disobedience to the model provided by Socrates, whose critical work involved creating tension in the mind that challenged complacency and complicity.[2] Gadflies call on us to be vigilant. But vigilance must not become violent vigilantism.

January 6 shows us how difficult this is. The mob of insurrectionists believed themselves to be vigilantly protecting the Constitution. But they took the law into their own hands, acting as vigilantes. They believed that the election was being stolen and the Constitution was being undermined. Their desire to be vigilant guardians of democracy was taken advantage of by the sycophants and tyrannical personalities who urged them on. The problem of vigilantism is that when the mob starts moving, critical thought is overcome by the appetite for violence. Vigilance must be combined with nonviolence, solidarity, and fidelity to law so that it does not become vigilantism.

Wise and virtuous citizens will reject violence and tyranny. They will refuse to become complicit and play at sycophancy. And they will resist the temptation to join the unthinking mob. This sounds negative, as an approach that rejects, refuses, and resists. But the ideal of wise and virtuous citizenship is not primarily a negative doctrine. Rather, it is grounded in an affirmative ideal of a community in which good people enjoy freedom, while treating each other with kindness, hospitality, and respect. A version of this idea is found in Kant's "kingdom of ends": an ideal community in which each person respects the autonomy of the other. In addition to respect, compassion is also needed, as well as accountability. Citizen-philosophers respect one another: they refuse to enslave, oppress, and exploit their fellows. They are also compassionate. They are actively concerned with the well-being of others, and they support one another in pursuit of virtue, wisdom, freedom, and the goods of friendship. Good friendship requires accountability, truthfulness, sincerity, and commitment to justice. Accountability is, after all, another way of speaking of vigilance: vigilant people hold themselves and others accountable.

Wise and virtuous people need to live in community with other wise and virtuous people. Virtuous friends help us become better. Our own virtue, in turn, helps our friends live well. Plato points in this direction in the heart of his discussion of tyranny. He says that the tyrannical person will surround himself with sycophants, flatterers, and morons. And while he will have a clique of obsequious hangers-on, the tyrant will not have any real friends. He says, "The tyrant lives his whole life without friends. He is always either a master or a slave. He never enjoys true freedom or genuine friendship" (*Republic* 576a). Plato's ideal of the philosopher-king is, however, also a lonely affair: the philosopher-king is a rare person who rises above his fellows and imposes his vision of the good on the world. Citizen-philosophers are less exalted, more common, and less lonely. We ought to pursue wisdom and virtue in common with our fellows: making ourselves and our community better at the same time. This requires vigilance, compassion, and accountability. And while it seems as though it might require some extraordinary effort—especially in moments of crisis when tyrants seize power—most of the time, this pursuit of virtue is a basic part of the process of living well.

The solution described in this chapter is *individualistic* and *moral*. It is focused on the virtue, good will, and vigilance of private citizens. Wise and virtuous individuals create a bulwark against tyranny. They are philosophical patriots whose love of country is intimately connected to their love of wisdom. Tyrants are narcissists who value power and self-aggrandizement. Sycophants are social climbers who seek to advance their own self-interest. And the moronic mob is gullible, ignorant, and interested in amusement. Virtuous citizens are different. They value liberty, honesty, and truth, as well as firmness, integrity, and courage. They understand the value of scientific research, free inquiry, and self-examination. They are skeptical of violence. Virtuous people say no to stupidity, power, violence, and greed. Their patriotism is moderate and restrained, grounded in respect for the rule of law and universal moral principles.

CONFLICTING PATRIOTISMS

And yet. . . . We disagree about what counts as good. On January 6 there were different stories being told about courage, patriotism, and individual action. The president accused the vice president of lacking courage prior to the insurrectionist riot.[3] Vice President Pence, to his credit, had determined that he would not overturn the Electoral College result. President Trump replied by tweeting that Pence lacked courage. Meanwhile a number of the president's sycophants objected to the January 6 vote that certified Trump's electoral defeat. One of them, Senator Josh Hawley of Missouri, raised a clenched fist in a salute to the protesters who had gathered prior to the assault on the Capitol.[4] And of course, the insurrectionists who stormed the Capitol believed that they were patriots fighting for liberty and in defense of the Constitution. Pro-Trump groups often declared themselves to be true patriots. "Patriot caravans" were organized to support Trump. At the January 6 rally preceding the insurrection, Alabama congressman Mo Brooks said, "Today is the day that American patriots start taking down names and kicking ass."[5]

As we've noted throughout this book, there is a problem of polarization. While patriotism appears to be something that should unite us, it has often been a divisive concept that seeks to unite some people in opposition to others. Patriotism itself has often been a focal point of disagreement. Philosophers have long disagreed about the value of patriotism. Socrates loved his country and refused to leave it, even when he was sentenced to death. But Diogenes, the Cynic, had no interest in patriotism, claiming instead that he was a citizen of the world, a "cosmopolitan." Cosmopolitans and patriots have disagreed ever since.

During the American Civil War, Thomas Starr King spoke of patriotism as a "sacred affection": "It is a privilege of our nature . . . that we are capable of the emotion of patriotism, that we feel a nation's life in our veins, rejoice in a nation's glory, suffer for a nation's momentary shame, throb with a nation's hope."[6] This is the same sentiment invoked by Abraham Lincoln in his first inaugural address (1861), when he spoke of "The mystic chords of memory, stretching from every battle-field, and patriot grave, to every living heart and hearthstone, all over this broad land." Lincoln, of course, ruled a nation in which those mystic chords of memory were fundamentally frayed. Southern citizens felt no allegiance to Lincoln's patriotic vision. Slaves and former slaves found patriotism to be absurd. Frederick Douglass put it this way in a speech in 1847:

> I have no patriotism. I have no country. What country have I? The institutions of this country do not know me, do not recognize me as a man. . . .
> In such a country as this, I cannot have patriotism.[7]

Patriotism often excluded foreigners and noncitizens, including slaves. Women have also been excluded from the "good" of patriotism. The term itself is masculine and patriarchal, evoking images of a paternal fatherland. Virginia Woolf made this point clear in 1938 when she said that women were treated like foreigners in their fatherland. She concluded: "As a woman, I have no country. As a woman I want no country. As a woman my country is the whole world."[8] That idea echoes the cosmopolitanism of Diogenes and others who are excluded from the goods of the fatherland.

One obvious solution to the kinds of problems indicated here is to make the sphere of patriotism more inclusive, more just, and more deserving of our allegiance. But these difficulties may not be resolvable.

This has led some contemporary scholars to echo Diogenes and the cosmopolitans, in arguing that patriotism is a mistake. George Kateb says that patriotism is a source of moral error and mental confusion since it ignores universal values in the name of love of country.[9] Others have defended reasonable or enlightened patriotism, based on the importance of values like loyalty and fidelity, linked to gratitude for the goods enjoyed within communities and nations.[10] But communities and nations are imperfect human creations. So enlightened patriotism cannot be blind allegiance. It must also include a substantial allowance for dissent, critique, and conscientious refusal.

One of the most famous quotes about patriotism is Samuel Johnson's oft-quoted claim that patriotism it is the last refuge of a scoundrel.[11] This idea points to the problem of tyrants, sycophants, and the mob, who have often wrapped themselves in the flag, declaring that they are the true patriots. This is an ancient problem. When Socrates was put on trial, he pointed out that his accuser—the sycophant Meletus—was seen as a patriot (*Apology* 24b). The Greek word used here is *philopolis*, which can be literally translated as "city lover": a patriot is one who loves his city (or country). This word was also used by the great Athenian statesman Pericles, who described himself as both a patriot (or lover of the city) and a wise and honest man.[12] Pericles encouraged his fellow Athenians to love Athens and honor the legacy of those who had sacrificed and died on her behalf.[13] But as the case of Socrates makes clear, we disagree about what it means to love our country. Socratic patriotism connects love of country with love of wisdom, truth, and virtue. The *philopolis* from Socrates's point of view must also be a *philosopher*, who acts as a vigilant gadfly, reminding his friends and countrymen to pursue virtue, justice, and wisdom.

Philosophical patriots ought to ask themselves questions such as:

"Is my country good?"
"Is my country or party worthy of my love?"
"Am I exhibiting courage, wisdom, and integrity in my patriotism?"
And: "Does my country or party stand for truth, justice, and liberty?"

Our answers to these questions are subject to the problem of polarization. Trump's supporters believed that they were working to defend the

Constitution and that they were exhibiting courage and integrity. From a different perspective, they look like an angry mob infatuated with a would-be tyrant. The problem of judgment runs deep. But one thing seems clear: it is better for people to ask themselves these questions than to avoid them. Philosophical patriotism should be imbued with the spirit of questioning, curiosity, wonder, and self-examination. This is not a panacea. Different people will come to different conclusions when they engage in self-examination. But self-examination is an important step in the right direction. The problem of the tyrant, the sycophant, and the mob is that each lacks the spirit of questioning. These anti-heroes and non-philosophers operate on the level of instinct, passion, violence, and narrow self-interest. They fail to unite their philo-political patriotism to philosophical enlightenment.

The bad news is that unenlightened patriots can get away with murder, as they did in the case of Socrates. The good news is that the critical perspective of individuals such as Frederick Douglass and Virginia Woolf can be effective in offering reasonable critique that improves the world.

NOBODY'S FREE UNTIL EVERYBODY'S FREE

Among the most important virtues to be developed in individuals and citizens who would resist tyranny is a universal love of liberty that spills over into compassionate concern for the liberation of others. This is not individualistic libertarianism that is selfishly concerned only with one's own liberty, although the individual's interest in his or her own liberty is obviously part of the story. Rather, what I have in mind here is a more expansive concern for liberty that we might call "cosmopolitan liberty." This idea is summed up in a familiar phrase from Fannie Lou Hamer, one of the icons of the American liberation movement (also attributed in various ways to Martin Luther King Jr., Maya Angelou, and others): "Nobody's free until everybody's free." As Hamer put it, "The changes we have to have in this country are going to be for the liberation of all people—because nobody's free until everybody's free."[14]

Beyond selfish libertarianism, we discover a broader, more comprehensive, and socially engaged focus on liberation. Simone de Beauvoir touched upon this in her critique of tyranny in *The Ethics of Ambiguity*. Beauvoir says that the key question for those who would resist tyranny is to ask, "Am I really working for the liberation of everyone?"[15] Tyrants are aggressive, assertive, and certain of themselves. They lack humility and self-questioning doubt. The question, "Am I really working for everyone's liberation?" is an existential probing that points in the direction of compassion, kindness, and accountability. Tyrants ignore the liberty of others, viewing other people as objects to be used rather than as human beings to be loved and respected. As Beauvoir puts it in her existentialist and Hegelian language:

> The trick of tyrants is to enclose a man in the immanence of his facticity. . . . The tyrant asserts himself as a transcendence; he considers others as pure immanences: he thus arrogates to himself the right to treat them like cattle.[16]

In other words, the tyrant views himself as a real person, while viewing others as mere things or subhuman animals who can be used and manipulated. The language here is gendered. Indeed, Beauvoir's most famous work, *The Second Sex*, shows how patriarchal marital and sexual relations are caught up in the problem of tyranny. Patriarchal families are miniature tyrannies, where men tyrannize women and children. Beauvoir suggests that liberation would overthrow this structure through a combination of love and revolt. Love opens us toward the other and the future, while revolt turns against tyranny.

It may seem like a contradiction to combine love and revolt. Revolt is negative and reactive, while love is positive and affirmative. As Beauvoir explains, love opens us toward the other and toward the future. But tyrants do not love anyone other than themselves. As a result they do not deserve to be loved. Thus, the way to deal with tyranny is "not to love it but to revolt."[17] The antidote for tyranny is to refuse to be treated like cattle and to refuse to allow any other human being to be treated that way.

From this demand for respect and recognition, compassion and solidarity quickly emerge. A wise and virtuous patriotism ought to be grounded in love, respect, compassion, and solidarity. And while it makes sense to focus this on our near neighbors, these values overflow and point in a cosmopolitan direction. We begin within families and friendships and work and business relations. Each social group has its version of tyranny, sycophancy, and mob mentality. Bullies at school play the tyrant. The bully's clique is sycophantic. And the assembled kids who cheer on fights and acts of bullying play the role of the moronic mob. The way to disrupt this tyrannical situation is to show solidarity with the victims, to refuse to play along with the bully and his cronies, and to remind the mob of the need for compassion, love, and human feeling. Something similar should happen in families, at work, and in other social organizations. This anti-tyrannical impetus spreads, ultimately, toward a liberatory patriotism and, beyond that, toward cosmopolitan compassion.

One inspiring source is Nelson Mandela. At the conclusion of his autobiography, Mandela explains how his thinking developed from individualistic concern for his own freedom toward a more universal concern for the freedom of others. Like other young people, Mandela was at first concerned primarily with his own autonomy. He wanted the liberty to pursue happiness and a career. He was prevented from doing this by the tyrannical regime of apartheid South Africa. As he came to understand that his own lack of freedom was connected to the lack of liberty of others, he started working on the liberation of all Black South Africans. Eventually, he understood that what was at stake in this struggle was not just the liberation of one person or one group of people—but the liberation of all people, including the oppressors who are oppressed by their own hate. Mandela explained:

> Freedom is indivisible; the chains on any one of my people were the chains on all of them, the chains on all of my people were the chains on me. . . . My hunger for the freedom of my own people became a hunger for the freedom of all people, white and black. . . . The oppressor must be liberated just as surely as the oppressed. . . . I am not truly free if I am taking away someone else's freedom, just as I am not free when my freedom is taken from me.[18]

PHILO-POLITICS AND PHILOSOPHICAL FRIENDSHIP

As mentioned above, the characters of ordinary social life can be tyrannical, sycophantic, and moronic: we see these characters on the school playground, in the corporate boardroom, and in families. The dysfunctional social arrangement described by our three paradigmatic characters is contrasted with a healthier, wiser, and more virtuous social relationship that can be best described as genuine or virtuous friendship. In genuine friendship, we discover compassion, solidarity, love, and respect. We might also call this "philosophical friendship," as this is the kind of friendship that was described by Plato and Aristotle. And in fact, Plato suggests that friendship is what is missing among tyrants, sycophants, and morons, as seen in the quote from *Republic* discussed above. Plato links true friendship with freedom. Friends respect each other's freedom. They love each other in a way that is uplifting and supportive of freedom, virtue, and wisdom. This is the proverbial ideal of "Platonic love." Platonic love overcomes possessive sexuality and erotic desire. This is a friendship that is oriented around respect and accountability. Tyrants lack this, as Plato suggested. Tyrants view others as cattle—as objects to be manipulated and lorded over. The tyrant views himself as a god or slave master, while viewing everyone else as his playthings or property. Sycophants also fail to develop genuine friendship. Their social world is oriented around the tyrant's power: they are busily sucking up to the tyrant and pandering to the mob, while also competing with their fellows for access and prestige. Morons fail to develop genuine friendships as well, since their interest is pleasure, amusement, and fun. The moron has drinking buddies but no genuine friends.

As with everything else we have discussed in this book, this account is a simplification that offers a generalized, schematic account of social life. We each succumb at times to the temptations of tyranny, sycophancy, and stupidity. Sometimes we need drinking buddies. Sometimes, at work or in professional life, for example, we succumb to the temptations of struggles for prestige and access to power. And in some relationships, we can become tyrannical and self-obsessed. But for most people, these failures are experienced as failures because we understand the ideal that we have failed to actualize: the ideal of genuine, virtuous friendship.

Aristotle builds on Plato's ideas in his account of philosophical friendship in *Nicomachean Ethics*. Aristotle describes three types of friendship that roughly correspond to three parts of the soul. The friendship of pleasure and appetite is the lowest type of friendship: this is where drinking buddies get together and amuse themselves. Beyond this are friendships of utility: these are the friendships of business relations, where we work together in pursuit of external goods. Finally, the highest type of friendship is virtuous friendship, in which friends join together in pursuit of virtue and wisdom, working together to actualize the highest good. All of this must be understood in connection with Aristotle's famous definition of human beings as social animals endowed with reason. As social animals, we need other human beings to help us actualize the good. There are roughly three types of good that connect to these three types of friendship. We enjoy the amusement of laughing and playing with other people. We also enjoy the good produced by business and social cooperation. And finally, our highest good is to develop virtue and wisdom: in order to do that we need the support of wise and virtuous friends. These three types of friendship also give us a clue about what is missing in the morons, sycophants, and tyrants of the world. The morons remain mired in unthinking amusement. They laugh and play without taking anything seriously—and thus are easily manipulated by the tyrant and his sycophants. The sycophants are themselves busily focused on the external goods of social life, viewing the competition for prestige as the primary good. The failure of the tyrant is that he thinks that he represents the highest good in himself. In its worst manifestation, the tyrant confuses his own personality with God. Instead of working to develop wisdom and virtue, the tyrant simply declares that he is great while expecting the rest of society to bow to him.

With this schematic account in place, it is easy to see how genuine friendship provides an antidote for these corrupt and corrupting social relations. A virtuous friend will remind his drinking buddies that amusement alone is insufficient. It is okay to laugh and play, but this must not come at the expense of truth, honor, and integrity. A virtuous friend will also remind his business friends that the pursuit of wealth and prestige is only part of a good social life and a mere means toward freedom, self-sufficiency, and the development of higher good. Finally, a virtuous friend will encourage those he is most intimate with to examine their own souls and question their fundamental values. The best friendships are philosophical: they focus on self-examination and self-limitation, actualizing key philosophical maxims such as "nothing in excess" and "know thyself." Our best friends hold us accountable while respecting our autonomy.

This account of friendship has political implications. True patriots, on this account, understand the love of country as being connected to the love of wisdom that is manifest in philosophical friendship. The philosophical patriot treats his fellow citizens with respect and friendship understood in relation to self-questioning and self-limitation. This ideal was made manifest in the life and death of Socrates. This is put into vivid relief in Plato's dialogue *Crito*. The dialogue occurs while Socrates is in prison, waiting to be executed. He is presented with an opportunity to escape. But instead of escaping, he explains that his allegiance is to the city of Athens. He refuses to betray the city by disobeying its laws. Oddly enough, he affirms his allegiance to the very legal system that resulted in his death sentence. Socrates then explains that the city is like a parent: a fatherland with a sacred right to command our loyalty. This paternalistic view of the state can be subject to substantial critique from the standpoint of modern liberal, democratic political philosophy. We no longer view the "fatherland" as a mythic parent to whom we owe allegiance. But leaving this aside, consider a further point made in *Crito*, which is that Socrates's relationship to the city remains philosophical. Socrates emphasizes the importance of argument and persuasion in relation to the city. The philosopher should make arguments and attempt to persuade the city, as Socrates did in his trial. But if the city cannot be persuaded, then it must be obeyed. Socrates rules out violence, suggesting that it is wrong to return evil for evil and to harm others (*Crito* 49a–d). The philosophical citizen exhibits his patriotism, his love of city, or *philo-politics*, by arguing with his fellow citizens, trying to persuade them to be virtuous, and encouraging them in the pursuit of wisdom. At the end of the day, he refuses to harm his city or to resort to violence.

Open questions remain as to whether Socrates was wise to remain in Athens and allow himself to be executed. Aristotle reached a different conclusion a generation later, when he fled the city of Athens rather than allow Athens to sin a second time against philosophy, as he famously put it. The question of loyalty and obedience to the state is more complicated than we can discuss here. But let's note that in the modern democratic world, we have learned the wisdom of nonviolent civil disobedience from models such as Thoreau, Gandhi, and King. Nonviolent civil disobedience operates out of fidelity to law and in a space of Platonic friendship. It acts as a gadfly, encouraging vigilance, accountability, and virtue while refusing to treat others as enemies to be destroyed.

VIGILANCE, RESISTANCE, AND COMPLICITY

Virtuous friendship depends upon honesty. When a friend does something wrong, we ought to call it out. The goal of honest critique is not to complain in order to score political points or aggrandize yourself. Rather, the ideal of virtuous solidarity aims toward an honest assessment of our faults so that we might become better. Virtuous people are vigilant and accountable. They are watchful and on guard, seeking to avoid ignorance, stupidity, and complicity.

The problem of complicity runs deep in the world of tyrants, sycophants, and morons. Tyrants need accomplices. But an accomplice is not a friend. An accomplice accommodates and accompanies the tyrant in his wrongdoing. In some cases—as in the case of the sycophant—the accomplice seems to know better. The sycophant is not ignorant; rather, he willingly chooses to affirm things that he knows to be false and dishonorable. The sycophant may feign ignorance. But that is a lame excuse. We presume that the sycophant knows in his heart of hearts that he has compromised his integrity in becoming an accomplice.

With the moronic mob, matters are different. While the sycophant should know better, the moron often has no way of knowing what the truth is. Or, at least, it is much more difficult for the masses to ferret out the truth. The masses lack access and expertise. And there are conflicting messages. This is especially true when tyrants and sycophants are busy manipulating the truth and disseminating disinformation. As noted above in our discussion of "the big lie," propaganda works because it leaves residue in the mind. This is especially true when there are conflicting narratives about very basic features of reality, as when one party says that an election was stolen. How is an ordinary citizen supposed to know whether an election was stolen or not?

At some point we make a leap of faith and choose to believe the experts and authorities. But there are various forms of the leap of faith. We could simply close our eyes and leap, which is a very stupid thing to do. Or we could choose to believe these experts and authorities who flatter our egos, which is also moronic. The better solution is to be as vigilant as possible: to sift and winnow the evidence, to seek out rival points of view, to use basic critical thinking skills, and to admit that we are in fact making a leap of faith. A key component of wisdom involves modestly acknowledging what you don't know, while remaining vigilantly on guard against self-deception.

Without modesty and vigilance, we risk complicity. But there is no panacea here. The citizen-philosopher is merely an ideal. In an uncertain and tragic world, the risk of complicity remains. As I have said repeatedly, we each have a tendency to be moron, sycophant, and tyrant. The citizen-philosopher struggles to overcome these tendencies. The citizen-philosopher should be concerned with justice, truth, courage, and self-control. These virtues should help us avoid complicity.[19] But this is a process of overcoming greed, ignorance, and other vices that is ongoing and never finished. We find ourselves thrown into a non-ideal political world. The process of cultivating virtue is limited by history and biography. It is not possible for citizen-philosophers to completely escape from complicity when they are thrown into unjust regimes. There is no utopia here, only continual amelioration.

When we remain aware of the tragic problem of historical life in the non-ideal world, the solution ends up looking something like what we find in the work of an author such as Camus. Camus offered a sober critique of tyranny and totalitarianism that culminated in a call for rebellion and human solidarity combined with a critique of violence and the hope that truth could defeat falsehood. Camus explained (in a letter to a Nazi, written during the Second World War), "man is that force which ultimately cancels all tyrants and gods."[20]

Tyranny thrives, Camus suggests, on silence and untruth. That is why the tyrant and his sycophants employ censorship and propaganda. That's why the tyrant and his sycophants are focused on accusations of "fake news" and claims about the press as "enemies of the people." That's why tyrants thrive when the mob chants and screams, effectively silencing the opposition. Camus explains that the silence of tyranny keeps us separated. He says, "tyrants indulge in monologues over millions of solitudes."[21] But this shows us part of the solution—to refuse to be silent is to create solidarity out of solitude. This is what the gadflies do. Camus connects this to the work of philosophers but also to journalists and artists. He says that art unites us, while "tyranny separates." He continues,

"It is not surprising, therefore, that art should be the enemy marked out by every form of oppression. It is not surprising that artists and intellectuals should have been the first victim of modern tyrannies. . . . Tyrants know there is in the work of art an emancipatory force."[22]

But rebellion is demanding and dangerous. And tomorrow the work of Sisyphus recommences. There will be another plague, another potential tyrant, and another generation of morons and sycophants. The reality is that very few can survive the plague of tyranny unscathed. Camus concludes his tragic and metaphorical novel *The Plague* with a call for vigilance in the face of potential complicity.

> Each of us has the plague within him; no one, no one on earth is free from it. And I know, too, that we must keep endless watch on ourselves lest in a careless moment we breathe in somebody's face and fasten the infection on him. What's natural is the microbe. All the rest—health, integrity, purity (if you like)—is a product of the human will, of a *vigilance that must never falter*. The good man, the man who infects hardly anyone, is the man who has the fewest lapses of attention (italics added for emphasis).[23]

This idea is key to what I have in mind with regard to the citizen-philosopher (and who could also be a citizen-artist, journalist, scientist, doctor, or lawyer). The point is that citizens must remain vigilant. They must refuse—as best they can—to remain silent. And when a tyrant succeeds in coming to power, they must act—as best they can—to aid the victims and avoid complicity.

Camus worked on *The Plague* in a small town on a high plateau in France, just down the road from the village of Le Chambon sur Lignon.[24] This place has become famous as a focal point of Nazi resistance. It is where Pastors André Trocmé and Edouard Theis, their wives Magda Trocmé and Mildred Theis, and their congregations worked to rescue Jews from the Holocaust. Camus most likely knew of this effort. After he returned to Paris, he sent a Jewish woman to Le Chambon for rescue. Trocmé and Theis preached a sermon on June 23, 1940, the day after France capitulated to the Nazis and agreed to deport Jews. Trocmé and Theis said:

> Tremendous pressure will be put on us to submit passively to a totalitarian ideology. If they do not succeed in subjugating our souls, at least they will want to subjugate our bodies. The duty of Christians is to use the weapons

of the Spirit to oppose the violence that they will try to put on our con-
sciences. We appeal to all our brothers in Christ to refuse to cooperate
with this violence. . . . Loving, forgiving, and doing good to our adversaries
is our duty. Yet we must do this without giving up, and without being cowardly. We shall resist whenever our adversaries demand of us obedience
contrary to the orders of the gospel. We shall do so without fear, but also
without pride and without hate.[25]

In other work, I have explained and defended the power of nonviolence. Trocmé and his colleagues give us a good example. Nonviolent
resistance vigilantly avoids complicity. Trocmé is a hero of nonviolence.
That kind of heroism is necessary in a world that has already succumbed
to tyranny and totalitarianism. Resistance to tyranny was needed even
before the 1940s in Germany, when the German mob and the German
sycophants cheered Hitler on and brought him to power. A significant
number of Germans either sympathized or were indifferent to the rise
of Hitler, thus becoming complicit in the Holocaust.[26] The German
people failed to be good guardians of liberty. They failed to be vigilant.
But some individuals remained uninfected by this plague and managed
to ameliorate things even in the face of atrocity.

CIVIC AND MORAL EDUCATION

How can we learn to be like Trocmé, King, or Socrates? They seem to
have a kind of wisdom and virtue that may be too much for ordinary
people to aspire to. But ordinary people can be heroes, too. People like
Eugene Goodman, who do their jobs and do the right thing.

The model of the citizen-philosopher is of an ordinary citizen who has
been educated and enlightened. He or she does not need to be as heroic
as Martin Luther King. But it helps to have a substantial foundation in
civic and moral education. The citizen-philosopher is produced, in part,
by a process that teaches wisdom, virtue, vigilance, and enlightenment.
This includes an understanding of basic civic institutions. But it also is
character education. And it should include a substantial dose of critical
thinking.

Some versions of civic and moral education are not very enlightened.
This sometimes amounts to little more than indoctrination. When chil-

dren recite the Pledge of Allegiance, for example, they are learning to be citizens but they are not thinking critically about the civic values of the country they are pledging allegiance to. Critical pedagogy that encourages citizens to think critically about civic rituals, monuments, and ideals is what transforms citizens into citizen-philosophers. These days, civic education must also include difficult conversations about polarization, racism, religious tension, and the challenges of media literacy, science literacy, and so on. To be an enlightened citizen requires a general all-around education that teaches us to be critical thinkers in a world that is complicated and polarized.

Enlightened citizens or citizen-philosophers need not be "citizens of the world." I admire the universalizing spirit of cosmopolitanism. But at the present moment, we belong as citizens to historically defined nation-states. Perhaps we shall someday evolve to a different system of social and political life. But for the time being, citizenship is local and delimited. Like Socrates most of us will live and die in the country of our birth. Some followers of Socrates were much more cosmopolitan. Plato traveled around the ancient world, Aristotle was an immigrant to Athens, and Diogenes deliberately declared himself a cosmopolitan "citizen of the world." There are lessons to be learned from cosmopolitanism. But there is a kind of elitism here: cosmopolitanism is an idea for those who are rich enough to travel (like Plato) or who find themselves welcomed into a foreign city because of their talent and intelligence (like Aristotle) or for those who are willing to give up the trappings of ordinary life and live in a barrel with the dogs (like Diogenes). For the rest of us, the reality is much more like that of Socrates. There is nowhere else we can go. Our friends, family, and work are here. A sense of obligation and duty keeps us rooted where we've been planted, even while we realize the need to avoid complicity in whatever is rotten here at home.

The claim that moral education and wise citizenship are essential in a democracy is well-known, as is the idea that it is proper education that could prevent tyranny in the first place. Jefferson famously said (in the quote used as the epigraph for this chapter) that education is the true corrective of abuses of power. Jefferson put this in action in his commitment to the University of Virginia. This is an ancient idea. Plato's *Republic* proposed education (of elite philosophers and guardians) as a way to prevent tyranny. Xenophon suggested something similar in his account of the education of the Persian emperor Cyrus. It was Cyrus's mother who warned him when he was a youth that education ought to teach benevolent kingship and not tyranny, respect for equality and not the desire for superiority and mastery.[27] Xenophon's work was widely influential among the American founders. Xenophon's Socrates admonishes us to be vigilant and self-aware:

> Do not be ignorant of yourself. . . . Pay heed to yourself. Don't neglect public affairs, if you can improve them. If things go well, the city will benefit, along with you and your friends.[28]

Despite these important sources, the Jeffersonian ideal of education as the guardian of liberty required long centuries to develop into the free, public, and inclusive education system we have today. Plato, Xenophon, and the ancients were focused on educating the elite: emperors, aristocrats, and philosopher-kings. Aristotle, for example, was a tutor of Alexander the Great. The ancients excluded slaves, women, and noncitizens from civic education. Aristotle makes this clear in his *Politics*, where he speaks of natural slaves and women as lacking in reason. And while Plato imagined educating men and women in common in his *Republic*, Aristotle found this to be ridiculous. Aristotle also warned against allowing free children to play with slaves.

Modern democratic theories of education have evolved to be much more inclusive. But early modern theories of education remained gendered and exclusive. Consider John Locke's treatise on education, *Some Thoughts Concerning Education*.[29] Locke was interested in educating young *gentlemen*. Locke's views were progressive for his time. But he was not concerned with educating the poor, women, or the masses. Education, from Locke's point of view, was supposed to subdue the child's tyrannical urges. Locke suggested that children were driven by the love of liberty and the desire for dominion: they wanted to be free to do what they wanted, and they also wanted to have power over others. Education was needed to restrain each impulse. This idea is obviously related to Locke's discussion of dominion, liberty, and tyranny in his *Second Treatise on Government*. It is "absolute dominion"—when one person enslaves another—that lies at the heart of tyranny and leads to the right of revolution. Jean-Jacques Rousseau's *Emile* provides another example.[30] Rousseau suggested a humane method of education that was intended to allow the innate human capacity for compassion and liberty to develop—a capacity that Rousseau thought was corrupted by a society in which there was domination. As Rousseau famously said, arguing against Aristotle's idea that there were slavish types who were "slaves by nature: "If then there are slaves by nature, it is because there have been slaves against nature."[31] With regard to public education, Rousseau argued that this is essential and that in the modern world it ought to be grounded in a principle of equality.

> Public education . . . is one of the fundamental rules of popular or legitimate government. If children are brought up in common in the bosom of equality; if they are imbued with the laws of the State and the precepts of the general will; if they are taught to respect these above all things; if they are surrounded by examples and objects which constantly remind them of the tender mother who nourishes them, of the love she bears them, of the inestimable benefits they receive from her, and of the return they owe her, we cannot doubt that they will learn to cherish one another mutually as brothers, to will nothing contrary to the will of society, to substitute the actions of men and citizens for the futile and vain babbling of sophists, and to become in time defenders and fathers of the country of which they will have been so long the children.[32]

These kinds of ideas would be taken up by even more progressive proponents of liberal education after Rousseau who argued both for the outright abolition of slavery and for the extension of liberal education to those who were formerly excluded from it: women, the poor, and those who were formerly enslaved.

Along similar lines, Immanuel Kant encouraged the development of enlightenment as necessary for his ideal of "republican" political life. Thomas Jefferson understood the importance of education, as did Benjamin Franklin, Thomas Paine, and others of the American founders. Emerson, Thoreau, and the transcendentalists emphasized the importance of education for liberty and nonconformity. This idea was part of the general democratization of life that had occurred throughout the last few centuries. It included explicit calls for the education of women and of formerly enslaved and subjugated peoples. Among important voices during the Enlightenment period, we might mention Catharine

Macaulay's *Letters on Education* (1790) and Mary Wollstonecraft's *Thoughts on the Education of Daughters* (1787).[33] Macaulay noted that education at that time tended to be limited to a concern for obedience. She condemned the cruel use of corporal punishment, which she saw as a kind of tyranny. And she suggested that male domination—what she called "tyranny over women"—had reduced the female to a state of "abject slavery."[34] A central problem was the expectation of obedience. She wrote the following (to her interlocutor, Hortensia).

> It is one thing, Hortensia, to educate a citizen, and another to educate a philosopher. The mere citizen will have learnt to obey the laws of his country, but he will never understand those principles on which all laws ought to be established; and without such an understanding, he can never be religious on rational principles, or truly moral; nor will he ever have any of that active wisdom which is necessary for cooperation in any plan of reformation.[35]

Macaulay's point is that an education in mere obedience will not be sufficient for the improvement of society. What was needed was a more philosophical education. Citizens are not merely to be obedient cogs in the social and political machine. They also ought to possess what Macaulay calls here "active wisdom," which is needed for cooperation, reform, and progress. Admittedly Macaulay only intended this for the upper classes. But she implied that education for citizens who are also philosophical was needed by women as well as by men.

Wollstonecraft offered a similar analysis of the social situation. We explained in a previous chapter how Wollstonecraft saw tyranny in the social world coming at the expense of men and women. In her reflection on education, Wollstonecraft explained that "half the miseries of life arise from peevishness, or a tyrannical domineering temper"[36] and that women were subject to tyranny in a system that teaches them to be submissive. She said, "She who submits, without conviction, to a parent or husband, will as unreasonably tyrannize over her servants; for slavish fear and tyranny go together."[37] For Wollstonecraft as for Macaulay, a better and less tyrannical system would provide for a more philosophical education. In her account of national education reform in *Vindication of the Rights of Women*, Wollstonecraft warns against an educational system that breeds vice. Instead, she calls for a gentler and more compassionate and inclusive system of education, one that allowed for greater mixing of the sexes and of the social classes. The goal of this system was to produce good citizens with "public virtue."[38]

In general, a liberal/democratic education ought to prevent the instinct of dominion from becoming inflamed in a way that leads to tyranny. A second focus of this kind of education is not so much to prevent as to resist. Wisdom and virtue are needed among the ordinary citizens so that we can see tyranny when it arises, avoid voting for sycophants, and have the capacity to resist the pull of the moronic masses. In the twentieth century, these ideas were developed further in the work of authors such as John Dewey, Paulo Freire, and Nel Noddings. Dewey's ideal of democratic education provides an important touchstone for the idea of the citizen-philosopher. Dewey notes in *Democracy and Education* that there are other models of education.[39] The Greek ideal as described by Dewey sought to create a stable social system that left the leisured gentleman with time for politics and for philosophy. Criticizing Aristotle, Dewey indicates that a tension remains between the engaged citizen and the philosopher. A philosopher-citizen is a member of the intellectual elite who remains aloof as best he can from the burden of practical life (and yes "he" is usually a male). Dewey also criticizes the nineteenth-century German model, which emphasized education as producing obedient citizens who sacrifice themselves for the nation-state in the name of "social efficiency." Dewey's conception of education for democracy is different: it involves the education of citizens who are neither philosophically aloof nor merely obedient and compliant.

Building on this model, Freire's liberatory pedagogy and his objection to education as indoctrination takes this idea further still.[40] The goal of Freire's approach is critical autonomy. As Freire explains in one of his last works, "The educator with a democratic vision or posture cannot avoid in his teaching praxis insisting on the critical capacity, curiosity, and autonomy of the learner."[41] To educate democratic citizens—to help cultivate and nurture citizen-philosophers—we need to stimulate critical thinking, curiosity, and a sense of freedom and self-determination.

We should also mention the work of Nel Noddings, whose focus on care and critical autonomy resonates with some of what we have already discussed. Like Dewey and Freire, Noddings is wary of uncritical patriotic education—the kind of education that focuses on producing conformity to political tradition. Noddings's recent work has focused on critical thinking and building the democratic skill of deliberation—especially in the context of multiculturalism and polarization. As she explains in a recent book, "We want to develop citizens who can do more than use the formal procedures of a democracy; we want citizens who respect their interdependence and can work cooperatively across groups with whom they share some values but have different central interests."[42] The important point she makes here is that formal democracy is insufficient: it is not enough to vote—we also need to nurture the fundamental habits, virtues, and dispositions of democratic citizenship. Furthermore, Noddings suggests that we need a more "feminine" approach to both education and to the idea of citizenship. Beginning with her contribution to feminist care ethics in her early book *Caring* and extending to more recent reflection on globally conscious pedagogy in her edited volume *Educating Citizens for Global Awareness*, Noddings focuses our attention on the need for an education that produces citizens who are both autonomous and connected to others, who are both locally engaged and globally aware.[43] This is, in short, a vision of education that produces critical patriotism and philosophical citizenship. What we need is education that encourages an inclusive and critical approach to vigilance, respect, and accountability.

CONCLUSION: VIGILANCE AND ACCOUNTABILITY IN AN UNTHINKING CULTURE

In the chapter on foolishness, I argued that ignorant fools lack the desire to be wise. Morons want to be entertained and amused. They embrace their own stupidity and celebrate their ignorance. They do not care to think deeply. Nor do they admit doubt or explore the difficulty of establishing certainty and discovering truth. The moron's self-satisfied embrace of ignorance is important to recall as we conclude this chapter. A similar point can be made about the tyrant: he is only interested in "facts" and "truths" that confirm his own inflated self-image. Whatever does not do that, he calls "fake news." With the sycophant, the problem is more subtle. Unlike tyrants and morons, sycophants have to think carefully. They monitor their words and speak differently to different audiences, hoping to curry favor. Nonetheless, the game played by the sycophant is divorced from truth. The sycophant plays a game of appearance.

I have suggested moral and civic education as a solution for our problem. But it is clear that tyrants, morons, and sycophants will resist this effort. The reality is that moral education cannot be forced upon people. It must be freely chosen. Of course, children are subject to some kinds of coercion. They are forced to go to school, after all. But once those years of tutelage are over, citizens are free to give up on the lifelong task of education and critical thinking. And some citizens appear to do just this. They fall for absurd conspiracy theories. They suck up to tyrants. And a few behave as tyrants in their own families, in their businesses, and so on. One significant impediment we must confront, as we conclude our thinking about education as a remedy for the problem of tyranny is that many people just don't care to be educated, virtuous, vigilant, or wise.

This problem has always existed. Plato understood that the ignorant did not desire to be wise. But there are social and technological forces that make this problem difficult to solve in the contemporary world. Among these are the ubiquity of stupidity, vulgarity, and violence in popular culture and the way that social media can be used to amplify our worst tendencies. The ancient world contained stupidity, vulgarity, and violence. But there was no equivalent of Hollywood, the porn industry, and the internet in the ancient world. Violent, racist, misogynist images race across our screens in a way that would have been impossible for Plato to imagine. This means that morons can very easily immerse themselves in stupidity. Sycophants can manipulate us through modern media. And tyrants can flood our screens and our minds with propaganda and bullshit.

We must be careful in condemning pop culture and modern communications technologies. These same forces can be used either for good or for ill. Let's consider a well-known anecdote from the Trump era that shows how this works: the case of the *Access Hollywood* video clip. This was a "hot mic" moment in which Trump talked about "phony tits," bragged about "moving on" women, and said, "I just start kissing them. It's like a magnet. Just kiss. I don't even wait. And when you're a star they let you do it. You can do anything. . . . Grab them by the pussy. You can do anything."[44] Trump here indicates a misogynistic sense of impunity that exposes a tyrannical soul: he is happy to brag about the power of his celebrity, which allows him to get away with whatever he wants.

One piece of good news with regard to this episode is the very fact that it is well-known. Our technology makes it difficult to say things in private, outside of the public eye. This is especially true with regard to public figures, politicians, and celebrities. The public finds out about all of the dirt. The bad news is that the public does not seem to care. Well, some do care: the virtuous citizens and politicians who rightfully conclude that this kind of thing ought to disqualify a person from holding office. But not enough of the public appears to care. The moronic masses do not find this kind of thing disqualifying. And once it became apparent that Trump was going to win power, the sycophants lined up to kiss his ring.

In retrospect, this episode appears as one of the watershed moments in Trump's rise: a decision point where critical patriots could have said "no thanks" to Trump. But we should learn from our mistakes. The challenge of amelioration is ongoing. There will always be a new plague, a new would-be tyrant, and a new scandal. Some people give up and give in, retreating to cynicism and despair. But the task of democratic citizenship is to resist this urge, to swim against the tides of corruption, and to make a stand. History teaches us what we've done wrong and how to improve things. We can use modern communications technologies to help encourage wisdom, virtue, and accountability. Modern technology makes it easier to be vigilant in discovering disqualifying dirt and holding bad actors accountable for their misdeeds. These technologies are not a panacea. The task of moral and civic education is ongoing. But the good news is that emerging technologies make it easier to spread civic literacy, celebrate virtue, and highlight heroes like André Trocmé and Eugene Goodman.

9

THE CONSTITUTION OF WISDOM

A nation of philosophers is as little to be expected as the philosophical race of kings wished for by Plato.

—James Madison, *Federalist* 49

The last king of America was a tyrant and a madman. That's what the American rebels said about George III. Since the American colonies gained their independence, no other tyrant has been able to consolidate power in this country. The U.S. Constitution has remained the law of the land since it was ratified in 1788, which makes it the oldest extant constitution on earth.[1] According to an optimistic narrative, the rule of law has prevailed, the Constitution has prevented tyrants from seizing power, and the United States remains stable as a land of liberty. Tyrannical personalities have grasped after power, abetted by sycophants and an adoring mob. But the U.S. Constitution has been effective at preventing full-blown tyranny from taking root. So let's give a couple of cheers for the U.S. Constitution. It works. But it is imperfect. Recent events have shown how fragile it actually is.

MONTESQUIEU, MADISON, AND MIKE PENCE

What happened at the end of the Trump presidency was dangerous and appalling. In the aftermath of the 2020 presidential election, President Trump claimed that he had actually been elected and that the election of Joe Biden was the result of voter fraud in a number of states. He sought to systematically discredit the election result, filing lawsuits in state courts and in the U.S. Supreme Court, while also encouraging state-level election officials to recount votes and find a way for him to win. This came to a head on January 6, 2021, when a joint session of the U.S. Congress met to certify the result of the Electoral College vote. President Trump urged Vice President Mike Pence (who serves as the presiding officer during this ceremony) to refuse to certify the results, while encouraging senators and representatives to contest the election as well. At a rally in front of the White House, the president and his sycophants urged the gathered masses to prevent the vote from being ratified. Congress was then invaded by a pro-Trump mob, which threatened to capture and even kill members. But law and order were restored and Congress—including the vice president—went on to certify the vote, ensuring the peaceful transfer of power. The good news in this story is that the U.S. constitutional system held firm against this attempt to subvert it: the separation of powers worked, as did federalism.

Much of this depended on the actions of key players in the drama, especially Mike Pence. The vice president was often viewed by critics as a fawning sycophant. Retired general Barry McCaffrey, for example, complained about the "revolting sycophancy" of Pence and others. He continued, "There are eerie echoes of 'supreme leader' adulation to all of this. That Trump tolerates or needs this kind of faux devotion is dangerous in a democracy."[2] Pence had routinely stood stolidly beside Trump. This is, in fact, part of the job of the vice president: to be the president's bulldog and right-hand man. But when it counted, on January 6, Vice President Pence played his proper role within the constitutional system—despite death threats by the rioters who invaded the Capitol. And while this is good news, this part of the story reminds us how fragile democracy is: a more unscrupulous person in the role of vice president could have done more lasting damage.

Let's recall how damaging the previous four years were. Sycophants spread disinformation during this time, contributing to intense polarization. Pence played a part in that. During the tumultuous Trump era, there were populist uprisings: both of the left and the right. All of this was exacerbated by the radical disruption of the COVID-19 pandemic, which was also subject to polarization and disinformation. And as described in more detail earlier, this culminated in claims about a stolen election and an uprising of Trump supporters who invaded the Capitol seeking to capture or kill the vice president as part of their effort to subvert the election. The good news is that this didn't work. The government was not overthrown by the mobs marching in the streets. The sycophants were unable to consolidate power around the would-be tyrant. And the slow work of incremental change went on and continues.

The story of the Trump presidency gives us a reason to value the wisdom of the U.S. Constitution and the structural impediments to tyranny baked into this system. Three different components of our system came into play here in limiting Trump's attempt to use the power of the executive branch to subvert democracy to keep himself in power:

1. The courts refused to undermine the election result.
2. The Congress, including the presiding officer, Mike Pence, refused to accede to the president's demand to overturn the election result.
3. And state-level officials refused to acquiesce to Trump's demand for recounts that would be favorable to him.

So far, so good. The Trump years were tumultuous. But the Constitution held firm. The future is uncertain. Tyrannical forces may adapt and learn from Trump's failure. Perhaps a more unscrupulous person would be chosen as vice president in the future. But those who oppose tyranny can also learn and adapt from the failures and near-failures of the past.

The privilege of modernity is that it grows out of reflection on the past. Indeed, modern constitutions are the result of prior failures. The U.S. Constitution grew out of the failure of the Articles of Confederation. Modern constitutionalism as a whole developed out of deep historical reflection on the problem of tyranny in the ancient world. An important source here is Montesquieu, a French philosopher whose writings on history and political structure had a profound influence on the framers of the American Constitution. In *Federalist* 47, James Madison shows how the basic premise of the Constitution is provided by Montesquieu: the need for a separation of powers in order to prevent tyranny. This demonstrates the power of ideas and how historical-informed philosophy can shape the world. We inherit a world that has already been shaped by the work of prior generations. Montesquieu understood this. He said, "In the infancy of societies, the leading men in the republic form the constitution; afterwards, the constitution forms the leading men in the republic."[3] The founding generation learns from history and creates a political structure, which thereafter influences what subsequent generations can get away with and hope for.

Montesquieu's study of Rome led him to understand how tyrants made use of legal structures to amass power. In his discussion of the tyrant Tiberius, he shows how Tiberius consolidated power using mechanisms already in place in the Roman legal system. Montesquieu concluded that the most effective tyranny is one that uses the tools of the law to put itself in place. As Montesquieu explained, "a tyrant is never destitute of instruments to accomplish his designs."[4] This is why the law must be set up in such a way that a would-be tyrant such as Trump could never possibly employ it to become a Tiberius.

Madison explained how this is supposed to work in *Federalist* 47, where he extolled the "intrinsic value" of the separation of powers. Madison calls Montesquieu "the oracle" of constitutionalism. He quotes Montesquieu: "There can be no liberty where the legislative and executive powers are united in the same person, or body of magistrates."[5] Madison's argument goes on to claim that tyranny results when powers are not separated:

> The accumulation of all powers legislative, executive and judiciary in the same hands, whether of one, a few or many, and whether hereditary, self appointed, or elective, may justly be pronounced the very definition of tyranny.

This Montesquieu-Madison nexus gives us reason to hope. Political philosophers can learn from the past and shed light on the political sphere.

Political agents such as Madison can put this wisdom into action. But as noted above, would-be-tyrants can also learn and adapt. This means that while there is wisdom in the constitutional system, we must continue to remain vigilant and open to further evolution.

THE EVOLVING CONSTITUTION

A sanguine narrative that emphasizes the longevity of the Constitution presents a sanitized and idealized version of history. The reality of the American constitutional system is more complicated and ambiguous. Let's begin by questioning the vaunted wisdom and stability of this system. A number of critics have pointed out flaws in the system.[6] One telling point is the fact that, as Robert Dahl has shown, no other nation has ever copied the American Constitution.[7] The U.S. Constitution is certainly less democratic than it could be. Sanford Levinson has compared the U.S. Constitution to the constitutions of the fifty American states. He concludes, "The U.S. Constitution is, by far measure, the most undemocratic constitution among the fifty-one constitutions that exemplify constitutionalism in America."[8] Among the many problems of the U.S. Constitution is the power and representational structure of the Senate. Citizens of small states have unequal representational power in the Senate compared to citizens of large states. California has a population of about 40 million, while Wyoming has about 600,000 people—but each state has only two senators. There are also a number of American citizens who are not represented in the Senate, such as the nearly 700,000 people living in the District of Columbia. This kind of problem will be exacerbated by changing demographics. In a recent article, Levinson points out, "By 2040, it is estimated that 70 percent of the population will live in 15 states—30 Senate votes—while the remaining 30 percent of Americans will have 70 senators."[9]

In connection to this deficit in representational equity, the Constitution also includes provisions that make it difficult to remove a would-be tyrant. Donald Trump was impeached twice by the House of Representatives. But the Senate failed to convict him in each case. This exposes an apparent structural flaw in the rules governing impeachment. Of course, this interpretation bumps into the problem of polarization. The failure to remove Trump is only a flaw if we think that a president like Trump ought to be removed. This is a matter of vehement disagreement and conflicting judgments. Some saw Trump as a would-be tyrant. Others saw him as the savior of the nation. At any rate, the constitutional point is that the U.S. Senate must convict a would-be tyrant and remove him from office—with a two-thirds supermajority. Given the representational disparities in the Senate mentioned above and growing polarization, this mechanism seems ineffective.

Trump's second impeachment exposes an apparent structural flaw if we think that a president who incites an insurrection after an election should be removed from office and barred from holding office again. One obvious structural flaw here is the lag time between the presidential election and the inauguration. Inauguration day is stipulated as January 20 in the Twentieth Amendment. One fix would be to further amend the Constitution to avoid the lame-duck problem.

One of the virtues of the Constitution may be that it does not allow for the kind of tumult that a more permissive system of impeachment would. In parliamentary systems, the prime minister is more easily deposed. And in some American states, governors can be subject to recall votes. The apparent near-impossibility of convicting and removing a president shows that the American presidency is more stable than the executive power in those other systems, even though the Twenty-second Amendment only permits a maximum of two four-year terms.

Trump's second impeachment provides something of a Rorschach test for thinking about the presidency and impeachment. For those who value stability and for those who adore Trump, Trump's acquittal will appear as wise and just limitation on the power of the Congress. The House accused Trump of inciting an insurrection against the government of the United States. The articles of impeachment explained:

> President Trump gravely endangered the security of the United States and its institutions of government, threatened the integrity of the democratic system, interfered with the peaceful transition of power, and imperiled a coequal branch of government.[10]

It is difficult to imagine a charge more serious than this. But despite the severity of these accusations, the Senate acquitted Trump. Again,

Trump's supporters see this as a just outcome. But the reality of the second Trump impeachment trial was that sycophants in the Senate gamed the system to get a more favorable result. One argument at the time was that since Trump had been voted out of office in November 2020, impeachment in 2021 was a moot point. Democrats wanted the impeachment result not only to remove Trump but also to prevent Trump from holding office again. Senator Mitch McConnell, the majority leader who controlled the Senate calendar, exacerbated this process by using stall tactics. McConnell continued to act as a Trump sycophant even while he seemed to recognize that Trump was culpable (as discussed in more detail in chapter 6). This contortionism worked to keep McConnell in power in the Republican caucus even after the Republicans lost their Senate majority. These stall tactics meant that even though the House approved the Articles of Impeachment on January 13, 2021, the Senate did not vote until February 13—after Trump had already left office and when the urgency of removing him had obviously dissipated.

There was also an effort made in January 2021 to invoke the Twenty-fifth Amendment to the Constitution and have the vice president and Cabinet remove the president with a finding that he was unfit to serve. This effort was not effective. As all of this was unfolding, Trump's sycophants continued to praise him, and the masses continued to rally. McConnell, Pence, and other Republican officials played a careful game of sycophancy: being afraid to anger Trump and his supporters as the country was suffering through a major Constitutional crisis. This has continued for months after Trump left office. There are ongoing accusations about a stolen election. Republican sycophants continue to bend a knee in Trump's direction. And morons continue to purvey conspiracy theories and other idiotic nonsense that continues to polarize the nation.

Given this, it would seem wise to consider a substantial revision to the Constitution, which might occur, for example, through constitutional amendments governing the lame-duck period, the process of impeachment, the Electoral College system, and the way that representation in the Senate is apportioned. We could also add new states to the union (or representation for the people of the District of Columbia) or change the norms of the Senate—for example, by abolishing the filibuster. But the amendment process and other changes are difficult to implement in a divided nation. Constitutional amendments require a supermajority, which is unlikely in this polarized land.

Some Americans remain wedded to the idea that the Constitution is a sacred document that is nearly perfect in its design. This is obviously not true. And the first step toward fixing a problem is to admit that you have one! Thomas Jefferson once suggested that each generation needs a new constitution, recommending a new one every nineteen years or so. Perhaps this goes too far. But it would help if we understood that the Constitution itself has changed substantially since the founding fathers created it. The Constitution of today is different in important ways from that of the founders. The amendments mentioned above make this clear. Improvements were made that resulted in a more democratic system, although the system retains some anti-democratic elements. One of the founding flaws of the Constitution is the Connecticut Compromise, which gave small and large states equal representation in the Senate and thus provides small states with disproportional power. In terms of its original flaws, the most notable is the fact that the original U.S. Constitution permitted slavery, which is a kind of tyranny. The original Constitution did not guarantee voting rights for all citizens. It left the determination of voting rights up to the states, which typically excluded more than half of the population from voting: all women and many men—including, of course, slaves. The original Constitution also set up a system in which U.S. senators were not directly elected by the voters but, rather, were chosen by state legislatures. The Constitution was also weak enough that it could be manipulated and ignored by tyrannical presidents such as Andrew Jackson in ways that permitted the genocide of native people. It was flawed enough that a Civil War threatened the unity of the nation and led to a substantial series of amendments that were only made possible by the victory of the North over the South.

THE TRAGIC TRUTH OF POLITICAL PHILOSOPHY

The point of this brief history lesson is that the U.S. Constitution evolved. This points to a more subtle and important point: there is no perfect constitution. There is no Platonic ideal of the perfect state.

This is a well-known fact. While Plato imagined a perfect constitution, Aristotle thought it was naïve to imagine perfection in political life. Political life unfolds in the middle of things: it is a result of history, geography, and circumstance. Political philosophy must consider the ideal in conjunction with non-ideal reality. As Aristotle put it, we ought to consider "practical utility": "not only what is the best constitution but also what is the one possible of achievement" (*Politics* 1288b). Aristotle's analysis of political life shows that this is a messy and complicated affair, which leads to compromises and outright disasters. The first American attempt at a constitution—the Articles of Confederation—was fatally flawed. But the Constitution itself was also flawed. The same imperfection is found in the heart of Aristotle's political philosophy. Aristotle defends ideas that today are indefensible in his discussions of slavery, the subordination of women, and war against barbarians. The study of the history of political thought shows that we are in the middle of a tragic world that does not permit perfection. The best we can do is muddle through within a history we did not create and with regard to conditions we cannot master.

When this tragic awareness is combined with a practical orientation toward what is possible, we find ourselves humbled. We are not even in agreement about the goal of political thought or about what we take to be the primary political problem. Plato thought the goal was to create justice under an ideal of organic unity. Aristotle thought this Platonic idealism was too focused on the happiness of the city, while ignoring the well-being of individuals. Hobbes thought that the main problem of political philosophy was to avoid the state of war that he saw in the state of nature. Marx was focused on overcoming class conflict. And so on.

The present book has focused on the problem of tyranny. This was a central concern for the American founders, as well as for Plato and others. If that is our primary concern, then a system like the U.S. Constitution, with its separation of powers and checks and balances, seems like a good idea. But this system is dysfunctional. This is not a good system if you value a lithe and responsive government that can pivot quickly to take care of emerging crises. It is not a good system if you value something like direct democracy. But is it a good system if you value the ability to remove a would-be tyrant from power? That remains an open question.

The question of the primary focus of political philosophy is tied to a question of human nature. Are we perfectible or corruptible? Are we rational or irrational? Do we really care about justice and the good—or are we more interested in power and self-interest? And is the biggest problem to be prevented the rise of tyranny or the dysfunction of a clunky system of government?

It is difficult to answer these questions because political life is difficult and tragic. Human beings are flawed: we each have the tendency to be become tyrannical, sycophantic, and moronic. Political life can fall apart for a variety of reasons. What I am describing here as *tragic* has been discussed in a different way by others under the heading of "realism." Richard Hofstadter explained that the U.S. Constitution emerged from what he calls "an Age of Realism." The founders were Calvinists and Hobbesians who sought to prevent human beings from actualizing sin and succumbing to the chaos of the state of nature. "They did not believe in man. But they believed in the power of a good constitution to control him."[11] At the Constitutional Convention, Hofstadter claims, the founders were motivated by cynical distrust of democracy. Hofstadter explains: "This distrust of man was first and foremost a distrust of the common man and democratic rule."[12] And yet, as Hofstadter further explains, the founders understood the democratic mood of the age of Enlightenment. And so they created a system that "checked vice with vice"—or as James Madison put it in *Federalist* 51, "Ambition should be made to counteract ambition." It was also in *Federalist* 51 that Madison famously said, "If men were angels, no government would be necessary." Madison continued:

> If angels were to govern men, neither external nor internal controls on government would be necessary. In framing a government which is to be administered by men over men, the great difficulty lies in this: you must first enable the government to control the governed; and in the next place oblige it to control itself.

Similar thinking can be found in Jefferson's writing. Jefferson thought that a constitution with a strong separation of powers was needed to prevent tyranny from arising. He said, "The time to guard against corruption and tyranny, is before they shall have gotten hold of us. It is better to keep the wolf out of the fold, than to trust to drawing his teeth and talons after he shall have entered."[13] But Jefferson also warned against what he called "elective despotism." He said that despotism can arise from a committee of despotic men as well as from a single tyrant.

The concentrating these in the same hands is precisely the definition of despotic government. It will be no alleviation that these powers will be exercised by a plurality of hands, and not by a single one. 173 despots would surely be as oppressive as one. . . . An elective despotism was not the government we fought for, but one which should not only be founded on free principles, but in which the powers of government should be so divided and balanced among several bodies of magistracy, as that no one could transcend their legal limits, without being effectually checked and restrained by the others.[14]

This was the kind of thinking that prevailed among the founding generation. The main problem of government was to preserve liberty by preventing tyranny. That is why a system of checks and balances was needed, as Jefferson put it, to keep the wolf of tyranny at bay.

Moreover, the Constitution was created by men from diverse states and divergent backgrounds. It involved compromises and negotiation. We can say, then, that the Constitution is a flawed and tragic document, created in the middle of history as an attempt to prevent greater tragedy. Its aim was to control the worst inclinations of human nature toward tyranny, sycophancy, and foolishness. The U.S. Constitution has endured, not because it is perfect or created for a world of angels or philosopher-kings. Rather, it works because it prevents us from succumbing to the temptations of tyranny, sycophancy, and foolishness. This is a non-ideal constitution for a non-ideal world. And as we have seen, it may not be sustainable or sufficient: would-be tyrants may learn from the Trump era and improve their efforts to grab power. Or the system may fall apart due to the polarization, distrust, and dysfunction that we have witnessed during this tumultuous time.

There is always room for improvement in human life and in political systems. And nothing lasts forever. There is no guarantee that this system and its Constitution will endure. Jefferson suggested that nineteen years was long enough. The Constitution has already lasted for more than two hundred years with a few substantial revisions. How much longer can it last—and what might come next? Those are questions for a different book.

This tragic conclusion should not leave us depressed or dispirited. Instead, it should inspire us to remain vigilant and open-minded as we continue to work to educate the masses, rein in the sycophants, and prevent would-be tyrants from seizing power.

REPUBLICANISM TRIUMPHS AGAINST TRUMP

Recent history supports a mixed assessment of the strength and effectiveness of the American Constitution. Such a judgment depends upon what we think the Constitution is supposed to do. If we expect the Constitution to be immediately responsive to the will of the people (or what some might call the whims of the people), then it is not very effective. This is, perhaps, why the U.S. Constitution is not best understood as a "democratic" constitution. Rather, it is a republican constitution. This does not mean that it is a constitution that serves the interest of the Republican Party. Rather, this is a constitution that is less concerned with representing the whims of the people than with keeping a stable hand on the tiller in pursuit of the long-term welfare of the people and in defense of our basic liberties.

The republican ideal has a deep lineage, which goes back to Plato and Aristotle. Plato thought of the state as an organism. Justice was not focused on the private good of each citizen but on the good of the whole. Aristotle thought this went too far. But Aristotle agreed that there is a unique purpose and function of political structures, which is to provide for goods that can only be enjoyed in political communities. Cicero appealed to a similar republican idea in the motto, "*salus populi suprema lex esto*," which means that the happiness (welfare, safety, or flourishing) of the people is the supreme law.[15] Cicero also warns against the unbridled spirit of the mob, which he likens to shifting winds and waves. Rather than succumbing to the mob, Cicero explains, "It is our duty—ours, I say, who are driven about by the winds and waves of this people, to bear the whims of the people with moderation, to strive to win over their affections when alienated from us, to retain them when we have won them, to tranquillize them when in a state of agitation."[16]

A republican government, on this model, is not mob rule. It ought to be more stable and tranquil than that. A republic is, as Rousseau explained in *The Social Contract*, a government of laws focused on the common good, in conformity with the general will, and according to the rule of law. Rousseau explained, "I therefore give the name 'Republic' to every State that is governed by laws, no matter what the form of its administration may be: for only in such a case does the public interest govern, and the *res publica* rank as a reality. Every legitimate government is republican."[17] Alexander Hamilton picked up this idea in *Federalist* 71, where he explained that republican government "does not require an unqualified complaisance to every sudden breeze of passion, or to every transient impulse which the people may receive from the arts of men, who flatter their prejudices to betray their interests." Hamilton echoes Cicero in maintaining that the government, especially the executive, should withstand the "temporary delusions" of the masses.

This kind of sentiment explains why a four-year term for the president makes sense, why the president is not popularly elected, and why it is difficult to impeach the president. The problem of the Trump impeachment is not a glitch in the system. Rather, the difficulty of removing Trump from office is a feature built into the republican ideal of the American Constitution.

We might further conclude that if we expect the Constitution to prevent tyranny, to limit the simpering of sycophants, and to resist the desires of the mob, then the Constitution appears to be doing its job— so far, so good, but with obvious warning signs made manifest during the Trump years. A would-be tyrant provoked an insurrection. The insurrection failed. Yes, the system was unable to respond and remove the would-be tyrant from office. But the peaceful transfer of power occurred anyway. There is some good news here. But there are also worries and warnings that can keep you up at night.

Critics on the right will claim that the constitutional system allowed the 2020 election to be stolen, interfering with Trump's grand plan of making America great again. Critics on the left will complain that the Constitution allowed Trump to come to office in the first place. On the right, there are complaints about the "deep state" and its investigations and "resistance" to Trump, about weak and unfriendly judges who refused to acquiesce to Trump's plans, and about legislators—both Republican and Democratic—who got in the way of Trump's plans and his reelection. On the left, there are complaints about the way the Electoral College brings unpopular presidents to power, the way the Senate stifles the will of the people, and the way minority rule in this country can end up packing the courts with conservative judges and doing significant damage. The truth is that the Constitution permitted everything that transpired during the Trump era. It allowed the election of a tyrannical personality who was impeached twice. It allowed Trump to pack the courts. It also allowed him to begin building a border wall, keep children in cages at the border, abrogate international treaties and trade agreements, create a new branch of the armed services (Space Force), and pardon his cronies. But the Constitution did not allow Trump to consolidate power. It did not allow the sycophants to create a single-party state. And it did not allow mob rule to overturn the rule of law.

Constitutional constraints prevented Trump from delivering much of what he promised to the voters who elected him.[18] He promised to abolish and replace "Obamacare" (the Affordable Care Act), which he did not. He promised to put his opponent, Hillary Clinton, in jail, which he did not. One important symbolic issue for Trump was a border wall to be built between Mexico and the United States. Trump pledged to build a wall and get Mexico to pay for it. Mexico, of course, did not offer to pay for the wall. Congress also failed to appropriate funds for the wall. President Trump employed executive orders and a declaration of emergency in order to begin building the wall. There was ongoing legislative action regarding the border wall and its funding. A number of court cases also sought to prevent the wall from being constructed, claiming that the president had illegally used funds designated for other purposes to pay for the wall. The Ninth Circuit Court had ruled against Trump (in *Sierra Club v. Trump*). By the end of the Trump presidency, there was a pending Supreme Court case (*Trump v. Sierra Club*) regarding funding of the border wall. When Joe Biden took office, he paused construction of the wall. At the end of the Trump administration, some four hundred and fifty miles of wall had been built (including refurbished fencing and a stretch built by private donors). The U.S.-Mexico border is almost two thousand miles long. While the wall was a symbol of the Trump presidency, Trump's failure to build it is a sign of the kinds of limitations on power created by the bulwarks of the republican Constitution.

This example shows how difficult it is under the U.S. Constitution to get things done. While some may complain of gridlock that is exacerbated by partisan rancor, these logjams and bottlenecks have the virtue of preventing tyrants, mobs, and sycophants from instituting radical change. And most importantly, this prevents a would-be tyrant from consolidating power, breaching those constitutional ramparts, and overturning the system itself.

HITLER, MUSSOLINI, AND REAL TYRANNY

It is worth comparing the case of Trump to what happened in Europe when Hitler and Mussolini rose to power. As I have argued throughout this book, Trump is only a would-be tyrant. Throughout the Trump era, pundits and critics suggested that Trump was as bad as Hitler or Mussolini. People accused Trumpism of being fascism. But these comparisons are hyperbolic and based upon a poor analogy. Trump is not Hitler or Mussolini. Hitler was a sociopath, a warmonger, and a murderous anti-Semite who rose to power through the overt use of violence. He wrote his hateful manifesto *Mein Kampf* while in jail for his role in the violence of the Beer Hall Putsch. Trump is a billionaire whose son-in-law and daughter are Jewish. Trump is a capitalist, not a national socialist. Trump did not come into power during a global depression or in the aftermath of a bruising defeat in a world war. And most importantly, Trump failed to manipulate the Constitution to keep himself in power, which is exactly what Hitler did. Trump took over a stable two hundred-year-old system that includes checks and balances and regular elections. The stabilizing background of the U.S. Constitution provides a crucial dis-analogy for facile Trump-Hitler or Trump-Mussolini comparisons.

Hitler and Mussolini successfully subverted the German and Italian constitutions in the same way that Tiberius did in Rome: by using the law itself. Each obtained and consolidated power from within the constitutional systems of their countries. Mussolini was appointed prime minister by Victor Emmanuel III, the king of Italy. He used quasi-legal mechanisms to consolidate power. The Nazis were elected as a minority party in the Reichstag in elections in 1932 and 1933. After the suspicious burning of the Reichstag, Hitler consolidated power under the Enabling Act of March 1933. Following Mussolini's lead, Hitler had himself appointed chancellor by President Hindenburg. After Hindenburg died in 1934, Hitler became a dictator. Hitler's rise to absolute power was swift and quasi-legal. Of course, there were black shirts (in Italy) and brown shirts (in Germany) in the streets—the moronic mobs of Italian fascism and German National Socialism. But it was the weakness of the German and Italian constitutional systems that permitted the tyrants to seize power. As Robert Paxton explains, "having achieved office quasi-legally,

Mussolini and Hitler had been entrusted only with the powers granted a head of government under the constitution. . . . Completing their grasp on the state by transforming a quasi-constitutional office into unlimited personal authority: that was the real 'seizure of power.'"[19] What is remarkable is that the so-called constitution of each country still existed even after these seizures of power. Hitler never formally abolished the Weimar Constitution in Germany; and Victor Emmanuel continued as king in Italy while Mussolini's ruled.

In both cases, the constitutional framework was not able to prevent this transformation. Nor was there a well-established system of rights and an effective court system to defend those rights. It was this lack of fundamental civil liberties and human rights that allowed the Holocaust to happen—something that is impossible to imagine in the modern United States. This is not to say that the United States is perfect when it comes to defending human rights. Slavery provides the most obvious example. And even as Hitler was rounding up Jews, the United States was dispossessing Japanese Americans and imprisoning them in concentrations camps. But under the evolved Constitution of the twentieth and twenty-first centuries, something like the Holocaust is not imaginable in the United States.

Broadly speaking, what we might call "the constitution" includes both the law and the people who live under the law and execute it. After all, a written document is inert without the people who interpret and administer it. We should not forget the importance of the real people who are involved in political life at all levels of government. It is possible to imagine a city of angels living with bad laws on the books: the angels would simply ignore the bad laws and only administer the good ones. We can also imagine a good set of laws that is poorly administered or that is taken advantage of by malign actors. In the cases of Germany and Italy, this means that it was not just Hitler and Mussolini who are to blame for the rise of tyranny in these countries. Nor is the legal structure itself entirely to blame. We must also consider the people themselves. We should consider those who administered the law, those who staffed the legal structure, those who ran the presses and propaganda ministries, those who taught in schools and universities, and those who were involved in voting and other political activity. In other words, we have to consider German and Italian citizens, statesmen, bureaucracy, and military/police forces that either actively embraced the fascistic transformation of society or allowed it to occur. As I have been arguing throughout, the tyrant's power depends on the sycophants and the mob. Nonetheless, there are structural and institutional issues worth considering. A significant problem in Germany and Italy was the inherent weakness of their constitutions themselves. Scholars have noted, for example, with regard to the Weimar Constitution of Germany, that its parliamentary system of power sharing allowed the Nazis to gain power as a minority party. But the sycophants played along as Hitler rose to power and the masses cheered it on.

THE WISE DYSFUNCTION OF MIXED GOVERNMENT

Perhaps the American constitutional system is better—including the good will and anti-tyrannical spirit of the American people. The American system worked to prevent the rise of fascism in the twentieth century. But history is complicated, and as we've seen in this book, there are sycophants and morons who willingly support tyranny, even in the United States. And the Constitution is imperfect. The U.S. Civil War indicates that the U.S. Constitution is (or was) subject to dispute and the threat of insurrection. Apart from this very important exception, the basic framework put in place by the founders (and amended after the Civil War) has worked to prevent a tyrant from seizing power and subverting the system. Two central features of the success of the U.S. Constitution in this regard is the separation of powers and explicit legal protection of basic rights. As most Americans learn in high school, there are three branches of government: legislative, executive, and judicial. The legislative branch is bicameral: there are two houses, each with its own rules and each resulting from a different kind of electoral process. There are also state-level checks on power, which is what it means to say that this is a "federal" system. And although this is not formalized in the Constitution, there is also a vast bureaucracy of civil servants, police, military, and other officials. Alongside these structures are the rights enumerated in the Bill of Rights: amendments to the constitution that explicitly state that certain rights ought not be violated. These rights include the First Amendment's "five freedoms": freedom of religion, freedom of speech, freedom of the press, the right to petition the government, and the right to assemble. This system provides a stable backdrop that has prevented tyranny. It is also dysfunctional and undemocratic by design. As Thomas Ricks put it, James Madison should be understood as "designing grid-lock into the American system."[20]

Madison understood that we are not angels. We are each tempted to become tyrannical, sycophantic, and foolish. So there is a need for a system that prevents the worst aspects of our humanity from mani-festing itself. This tragic (some would say pessimistic, others would say realistic) point of view provides the background for the American Con-stitution. There are no philosopher-kings. So, instead of constructing a system that is capable of becoming Plato's utopia, Madison and the framers aimed to produce a system that prevents tyranny. This idea—of a constitution oriented toward a tragic acceptance of humanity and its shortcomings—was common among the founders. George Washington wrote in a letter to John Jay in 1786, as the Articles of Confederation were crumbling: "We have probably had too good an opinion of human nature in forming our confederation." He continued: "We must take hu-man nature as we find it. Perfection falls not to the share of mortals."[21] John Adams said something similar in a letter from 1788:

> The great Principle which renders civil Government necessary points out the Remedy for its greatest Evils. Human Passions are all unlimited and insatiable. This renders Association and Government necessary. Without it, We are in continual Danger from each other's Passions. But association does not extinguish the Passions or limit them. They remain Still craving and insatiable. The great Maxim of a Legislature therefore, Should be, to leave no Passion in Society without a Controul; No action without a Reaction.[22]

Adams suggested—quoting both the ancient philosophers and modern scholars such as Montesquieu as his sources—that each of the pure forms of government was susceptible to the unlimited and insatiable appetite for power. Monarchy, aristocracy, and democracy could each become tyrannical in this way. His solution was an old one that followed the advice of the ancients. He quoted Diogenes Laertius's account of Zeno, the Stoic: "The best form of government is a combination of de-mocracy, monarchy, and aristocracy."[23] The ideal of mixed government was fleshed out in the U.S. Constitution in terms of a separation of powers that could serve to check and balance each other. This is not a constitution created for efficiency. Rather, it is designed with the tragic insight in mind, as a brake on the concentration of power. Madison explained in *Federalist* 51 (in 1788) that the point was to create a government that would prevent itself and its various parts from becoming too strong. This was a government built for men—and not for angels. Madison wrote (*Federalist* 51):

> The great security against a gradual concentration of the several powers in the same department, consists in giving to those who administer each department, the necessary constitutional means, and personal motives, to resist encroachments of the others. The provision for defence must in this, as in all other cases, be made commensurate to the danger of attack. Ambition must be made to counteract ambition.

THE NEAR FATAL FLAW OF SLAVERY

Before going further, let's sound a cautious note about uncritically celebrating the wisdom of the founders. What is working today to prevent tyranny is a developed Constitution including the amendments, modifications, and precedents that resulted from the U.S. Civil War and other tumultuous periods of American history (for example, the women's suffrage movement that culminated in the Nineteenth Amendment to the Constitution, which granted women the right to vote). This process of modification reminds us that in its original manifestation, the U.S. Constitution was flawed. Among its most important flaws was the fact that it actually supported tyranny in the form of slavery. American colonial conquests were also permitted under the Constitution, which reflected a tyrannical aspiration for power and domination that resulted in widespread genocide of Native Americans.

These two moral outrages—slavery and Native American genocide—were intertwined. Indigenous people were forcibly removed from their lands in order to make way for slavery. This policy was instituted by Congress in the Indian Removal Act (of 1830) and executed by presidents like Andrew Jackson and Martin Van Buren. Jackson was accused of being tyrannical at the time. His opponents suggested that Jackson's primary claim to fame as a military hero who won the Battle of New Orleans was a sign of aggressive militancy that left him unsuited for the presidency and marked him with the taint of tyranny.[24] Given this history, it is interesting to note that President Trump chose a portrait of Andrew Jackson to hang in the Oval Office. Trump was likely identifying with Jacksonian populism. But Jackson is a problematic role model.

Like other presidents of that era—Jefferson, Washington, and Madison—Jackson was a slave master. Jackson owned over one hundred slaves and was known for personally brutalizing his slaves.[25] As president he led the charge on "Indian removal," resulting in what we would today call ethnic cleansing and genocide. This policy was connected to the effort to open land across southern states for the expansion of agriculture and slavery. As is well-known, this led to the Trail of Tears and the general destruction of the Choctaw, Cherokee, Seminole, Creek, and Chickasaw peoples. This occurred in violation of the famous Supreme Court ruling *Worcester v. Georgia* (1832).[26] The U.S. Constitution recognized "Indian Tribes" as something like "foreign nations" (in Article 1) and stipulated that the United States was bound by treaties made with these entities (Article 6). This was interpreted by John Marshall and the U.S. Supreme Court in a way that held that native people had a natural right to their lands and to self-government. The majority opinion, written by John Marshall, held that, "the Indian nations had always been considered as distinct, independent political communities retaining their original natural rights as undisputed possessors of the soil, from time immemorial." And: "The Cherokee nation, then, is a distinct community, occupying its own territory, with boundaries accurately described, in which the laws of Georgia can have no force, and which the citizens of Georgia have no right to enter but with the assent of the Cherokees themselves." This ruling was ignored by Jackson and his successors. VanDevelder concludes, "President Jackson was well aware that the court had no mechanism for enforcing its will, and no army or police it could call upon to impose its mandate. So Jackson dismissed Marshall's ruling with casual indignation and advised the southern states to do the same."[27] Jackson went on to pack the court with justices who eventually issued the infamous Dred Scott decision (1857), which denied citizenship to Black people and served to solidify the claims of slaveholding states, which added fuel to the fire that caused the Civil War.

This is an indication of the fact that a constitutional system does not provide an absolute guarantee against tyranny. In this case, the court's ruling was simply ignored, and the natives were removed. Something similar and more damning occurred with the outbreak of the Civil War and the battle over slavery. When the Southern states seceded, they accused the North of tyranny and despotism. Jefferson Davis provides an example: in his second inaugural speech, he condemned the tyranny and despotism of the North.[28] It is worth pausing for a moment to note that Jefferson Davis was an "American" president—albeit one who presided over an outlaw regime. As we noted above, Abraham Lincoln was accused of tyranny by his opponents, including John Wilkes Booth, who yelled "sic temper tyrannis" (thus always to tyrants) when he killed Lincoln.

While the U.S. Constitution today seems well suited for preventing tyranny—and while the prevailing narrative about the Constitution is that it was developed as a response to the threat of tyranny, the truth is that the Constitution originally allowed for the most brutal form of tyranny, which was legal slavery. The Constitution includes the infamous three-fifths of a person stipulation about counting enslaved people (in Article 1, Section 2), which recognized the de facto existence of slavery in American states. And it wasn't until after the Civil War that the Constitution was amended to outlaw slavery in 1865, with the 13th Amendment stating that "[n]either slavery nor involuntary servitude . . . shall exist within the United States."

There is an ongoing dispute about the issue of slavery and its legacy. But there is no doubt that slavery is a form of tyranny. This point was made clear by Frederick Douglass, a former slave, in the 1850s:

> Americans! your republican politics, not less than your republican religion, are flagrantly inconsistent. You boast of your love of liberty, your superior civilization, and your pure Christianity, while the whole political power of the nation . . . is solemnly pledged to support and perpetuate the enslavement of three millions of your countrymen. You hurl your anathemas at the crowned headed tyrants of Russia and Austria, and pride yourselves on your Democratic institutions, while you yourselves consent to be the mere tools and body-guards of the tyrants of Virginia and Carolina.[29]

Douglass points out a significant contradiction in the founding ideals of this country and the tyranny that existed in the slave states. This contradiction is manifest in the fact that the founders railed against the tyranny of King George while ignoring the tyranny of slavery. This systematic injustice was corrected by the Civil War and subsequent amendments to the Constitution.

Again, this shows us that there is no perfect constitution and that there is always the possibility of violence. Each constitution has its flaws and its risks. While there are advantages to the current constitution of the United States, it is wise to remain critical and open-minded. More importantly, no constitution is viable unless the citizens are willing to abide by it. The Civil War shows that the question of "abiding by" the law devolves into a matter of force. It would be nice if people were rational and shared common values. But the reality of history is that human beings are not always nice or rational. And there remain fundamental disputes about ethics and common values.

A TRAGIC CONCLUSION

The history of political philosophy discloses deep conflicts about the nature of political power, the question of sovereignty, and the meaning of justice. In general, this results in a tragic conclusion about political power: it is never perfect, and it is often quite dangerous. Plato and Aristotle understood that human diversity and struggles for power meant that there was no such thing as a perfectly good or just state. While Plato suggested that a good city would be ruled by a philosopher-king, there are serious reasons to suspect that Plato understood that this was a pipe dream. In the heart of Plato's *Republic*, Socrates indicates that people will find this idea laughable and ridiculous. He even suggests that the philosophers themselves will find the idea ridiculous because those who have been enlightened will not want to engage in the sordid business of politics. Plato suggested that those who are eager to rule—those who aspire to possess political power—are the people we should be most suspicious of. From Plato's perspective, the desire for political power is a sign of a tyrannical personality. And the enlightened, philosophical type of person will despise ruling:

> Can you name any life that despises political rule besides that of the true
> philosopher? . . . But surely it is those who are not lovers of ruling who
> must rule, for if they don't, the lovers of ruling, who are their rivals, will
> fight over it. (*Republic* 521b)

Plato suggests that the philosopher will have to be forced to engage in
politics. And even if a wise and enlightened soul were convinced that
justice required him to take up the yoke of power, the masses will not
willingly submit to the rule of the philosopher-king. At the very least,
they will find the philosopher laughable; at worst, they will kill him—
as they did with Socrates. Furthermore, Plato tells us that even if a
philosopher-king could come to power, the perfect state would not last
long. The good state will eventually fall into decline, which will be led
through the rule of military power (timocracy), the rule of the wealthy
(oligarchy), and the rise of democracy and demagogic tyrants.

There are various interpretations of Plato's *Republic*.[30] Popper read
Plato as a proto-totalitarian, whose dream of utopia meant the end of
liberty.[31] Strauss and Bloom read Plato in a different way, suggesting
that Plato's suggestions about the philosopher-king should not be taken
seriously. Strauss said, "The coincidence of philosophy and political
power is extremely improbable: philosophy and the city tend away from
one another in opposite directions."[32] He suggested that the just city is
"against nature." Building on this sort of interpretation, Bloom said that
Plato was trying to show the "impossibility" of utopia. He said: "Regimes
can be improved but not perfected; injustice will always remain. The
proper spirit of reform, then, is moderation. Socrates constructs his
utopia to point up the dangers of what we would call utopianism; as such
it is the greatest critique of political idealism ever written."[33] My sym-
pathies are with the Strauss-Bloom interpretation. But Plato is not only
being ironic in *Republic*. He is also offering us a serious warning about
tyranny. While the ideal state may be a dream, Plato is clear about the
problem of tyranny. He is quite critical of those who rule unjustly and
with absolute power oriented only toward their own aggrandizement.
And on my interpretation of *Republic*, Plato's conclusion is tragic—even
pessimistic. A clue about this can be found in the very place where he
suggests the need for a philosopher-king. Socrates says:

> Until philosophers rule as kings or those who are now called kings and
> leading men genuinely and adequately philosophize, that is, until political

power and philosophy entirely coincide . . . cities will have no rest from evils, Glaucon, nor, I think, will the human race. And, until this happens, the constitution we've been describing in theory will never be born to the fullest extent possible or see the light of the sun. It's because I saw how very paradoxical this statement would be that I hesitated to make it for so long, for it's hard to face up to the fact that there can be no happiness, either public or private, in any other city. (*Republic* 473 b–c)

The argument that I derive from this and related passages goes something like this:

- The only way to ensure justice and happiness is for the wise to rule.
- But the wise can't rule (because they won't want to rule or won't be permitted to rule by the masses).
- Therefore, there will be no justice or happiness.

This tragic conclusion—that political life is imperfect—is developed further in the work of Aristotle. Aristotle was an attentive student of Plato's. He agreed with Plato that tyranny is the worst form of government. He also agreed with Plato that democracy was another flawed form of government. But Aristotle rejected the kind of utopian speculation and myth making that we see in Plato's *Republic*. Aristotle provides a more "scientific" analysis of the different kinds of constitutions that is linked to a broad conception of human flourishing. And although he ultimately advocates aristocracy (defined as rule of the best) in a way that is reminiscent of Plato's *Kallipolis*, he is also aware of the importance of so-called mixed constitutions that involve various elements. Modern ideas about the separation of powers can be traced back to this insight in Aristotle's account.

This is useful and informative. But what I want to emphasize in Aristotle is the idea that even though political life (and human life in general) is messy and muddled, it can also be ameliorated through the work of practical wisdom. Aristotle's account of political life and of ethics (in *Politics* and in *Nicomachean Ethics*) can appear to be convoluted and inconclusive. This can be confusing for readers. But it gives us a clue about what we ought to learn from Aristotle. Aristotle implies that there is no simple schema or final solution to the problem of political life. Instead, there are various attempts at amelioration from within a diverse range of forms of life. The reality of human history and diversity is that there are different ways that people have organized themselves politically. Nonetheless, Aristotle suggests that a degree of happiness results from the right conjunction of three elements: nature, habit, and reason. A different way of expressing this is to say that happiness depends upon the right conjunction of external goods, goods of the soul, and goods of the body. This in turn depends upon several factors: being born into a good country; having a moderate amount of wealth, leisure, and education; and having good friends and family. It also helps to have the good fortune to live a long and healthy life. But health and longevity also depend upon natural predispositions, external goods, and practical wisdom.

Aristotle's own life provides an example. He was born in Macedonia and studied with Plato at the Academy, where he was a resident alien. At the time, the Macedonian empire was growing and spreading its power across the Greek world. Aristotle ended up leaving the Athenian democracy behind as a young man because of anti-Macedonian sentiment in Athens. He spent time in the court of the tyrannical regime of Hermias of Atarneus. He ended up back in Macedonia, where he tutored Alexander. He returned to Athens. While there, his nephew and student, Callisthenes, was murdered by Alexander. Finally, Aristotle fled Athens again as anti-Macedonian sentiment flared up with the death of Alexander. He reportedly said, as he left Athens, "I will not allow Athens to sin twice against philosophy." Aristotle was a wanderer and an exile. He experienced firsthand a variety of regimes. No one of them appeared to be perfect. Each one had its flaws. Rather than seeking a revolutionary ideal, Aristotle emphasized gradual reform. He thought that through education (of Alexander) and political advising (of Hermias), he could do some limited good in a tragic world.

When we understand Aristotle's approach, we begin to see why the question of the best form of constitution is only one question among many. The constitutional question is obviously an important one. We could be happy, presumably, within a variety of different constitutions, provided we were fortunate enough to live at a time of peace, lucky enough not to be a slave or a woman, and fortunate enough to have sufficient wealth, adequate education, and good friends. And when things get rough, it may be time to move on.

The U.S. Constitution is wise in its schematic separation of power. Of course, this system can also appear to be undemocratic and dysfunctional. These apparent vices can be viewed as virtues when it comes to preventing tyranny. An open question here is whether the prevention of tyranny is the main desideratum of a government. Defenders of democracy will want a more responsive system. Advocates of wisdom and virtue will follow Plato in calling for the rule of philosopher-kings. There are virtues of each kind of government, and there is no final answer to the question of how we should best organize ourselves politically. But if we view tyranny as one of the main problems of political life, then a dysfunctional republican system such as that of the U.S. Constitution makes good sense.

10

CONCLUSION

The truth is that all men having power ought to be mistrusted.

—James Madison[1]

In this book, I have explored tyranny, would-be-tyranny, and accusations of tyranny from a variety of perspectives. We have considered a broad cast of characters: Alcibiades, Alexander, Julius Caesar, Tiberius, and Nero as well as King George III, Andrew Jackson, Abraham Lincoln, and even Barack Obama and Donald Trump. I have shown how the tyrant is accompanied by sycophants and the mob. I have also proposed two remedies. One remedy focuses on the soul, emphasizing virtue and wisdom, along with vigilance and accountability. The other focuses on the structure of political life and the need for a constitution that limits the ability of a would-be tyrant to consolidate power. We have seen that the U.S. Constitution is informed by a basic desire to thwart tyranny. This system has its flaws, including the fact that at one point it allowed the outright tyranny of slavery to exist. But after evolving to eliminate this defect and others, the Constitution has worked to prevent tyranny.

I wrote this book while the Trump tragedy was playing out and the COVID-19 pandemic was also unfolding. The pandemic introduced a concern for a different kind of tyranny. Critics of pandemic restrictions condemned the supposed tyranny of masking, closed schools, and shuttered businesses. The point of this critique was that government becomes tyrannical when, in the name of a public health emergency, it prevents businesses from operating, restricts access to education, and requires people to wear masks. As I mentioned in the conclusion to chapter 1, critics such as Senator Rand Paul suggested that public health officials were advocating a kind of tyranny. Those public health officials, of course, disagreed.

And here we return to the fundamental problem of tragedy and polarization that we've seen throughout this book. Human beings will disagree about almost anything. This is among the things that make human beings so frustratingly wonderful, uncanny, and terrifying—to return to the problem indicated by the chorus in *Antigone* (line 322). We disagree about who is a tyrant and what is tyrannical. Alcibiades believed he was a hero worthy of adulation. Alexander the Great believed something similar. Tyrants and would-be tyrants have inflated self-esteem. This is encouraged by the sycophants and the adoring mob. This is why tyrants do not back down or apologize or admit they are wrong. They are convinced they are right. From this it follows that those who oppose them are wrong, evil, treasonous, and enemies of the people. The sycophants foster and support this polarizing judgment. The moronic mob cheers and jeers accordingly.

This brings me, in conclusion, to the value of philosophical modesty and self-examination. We avoid the terror of tragedy by looking in the mirror. This was what Tiresias suggested to Oedipus. It is also what we learn from Plato and the philosophers. Tyrants and their critics engage in ideological warfare that polarizes and confuses. Philosophers are more circumspect and restrained. The mirror of philosophy shows that our judgments are partial, occurring as they do within the flow of history. Philosophical reflection discloses our limitations and our flaws. It shows us that we can each be tempted to play the part of tyrant, sycophant, and fool. Understanding this can lead us to cultivate reason, wisdom, and self-restraint. The Oracle at Delphi said, "Know thyself." Socrates taught Alcibiades that this meant "see thyself," which is what we do when we look in the mirror (*Alcibiades* 132–33). But it is not external beauty, glory, and greatness that we ought to look at. Rather, we must examine our souls.

The greatest tyrants only see themselves in an external mirror. They measure their value in terms of greatness and glory. They measure their bank accounts and the size of the crowds they attract. They do not look within and understand the smallness of their souls in comparison with the good of the nation, the vastness of history, and the immeasurable power of virtue and the moral law.

Self-examination requires that we look carefully at our friends, whose eyes provide mirrors of our souls. If our friends are morons and syco-phants, we ought to be careful so that we are not playing the role of the tyrant in our relationships. And if our friends are tyrants, we should make sure that we are not sucking up to them or chuckling in amuse-ment at their bullying.

Finally, the process of self-reflection requires that we understand that wisdom actually applies to each of us. Human beings have a tendency to view themselves as special and unique. The tyrant does this more than anyone else. But history and philosophy show us that no one is special and unique. There are no saviors, messiahs, or God-anointed leaders. We are each merely human beings playing a part in a much larger story. The truth that James Madison articulated in his reflection on tyranny contains profound wisdom that puts each of us into our place. Madison said, "The truth is that all men having power ought to be mistrusted." When this truth is read before a mirror, we discover that it applies to each of us. No human being should be treated as a god, not even the person in the mirror.

APPENDIX A

Trump's View of Morality in Context

There is a moral malfunction in the thinking of tyrants and would-be tyrants. The main flaw is hubris. Hubris grows when there is a lack of moral education and a basic moral vocabulary. In this appendix, I demonstrate the moral problem as it manifests itself in Trump's worldview by using an empirical method of analysis.

A content analysis of Donald Trump's speeches and other writings indicates that Trump is morally inarticulate. I analyzed a number of Trump's speeches and communications to reach this conclusion. I read some of Trump's books and some of his most important speeches, including his two Republican Party nomination acceptance speeches (July 21, 2017, and August 27, 2020), his inauguration speech (January 21, 2017), each of his State of the Union speeches (February 28, 2017, January 30, 2018, February 5, 2019, February 4, 2020), and others. I also analyzed Trump's Twitter feed using a web archive of all of his tweets, which was updated through January 8, 2021, when Trump was suspended from Twitter for inciting violence.[1] Some of these speeches are (or were) available on the White House website; transcripts of many of his other speeches can be found at Rev.com, an online transcription service.[2]

My analysis discloses an important feature of the tendency toward tyranny—which is the lack of a moral vocabulary. Trump's limited moral language is focused primarily on his own self-interest and self-aggrandizement and on comparative measures of value. The most important point to make is that in these documents and communications, President Trump rarely used the words *moral*, *morality*, *ethics*, or *ethical*. *Value* shows up more frequently in Trump's words. But it is usually used to refer to the value of real estate. In some cases, it refers to the notion of "American values" or "traditional values," which are not really defined or defended. This is a remarkable fact, given that the rhetoric of most American presidents is infused with moral language. Trump's lack of moral vocabulary is anomalous in the American tradition and helps to explain how his presidency devolved.

Trump is not stupid. He knows how to use moral language intelligibly in speech. Some moral language does appear in Trump's discourse. But when it appears, it is often used in a way that is self-serving. Trump occasionally uses the word *right*, for example. But the word is often used to assert his own rights or to praise others for doing the right thing, which usually means helping Trump himself. A typical sentence comes from the notorious January 6, 2021, speech in which Trump incited the riot in the Capitol, where he said the following: "If Mike Pence does the right thing, we win the election." Further speaking of Pence, Trump said, "He has the absolute right to do it."[3] This claim about Pence's right to overturn the Electoral College vote was false, as was the claim that for Pence to do the right thing, he should break the law. But Trump said that Pence had the absolute right to break the law. Often, when Trump uses *right*, it is to praise himself. In his Twitter feed, for example, he often says things like "I was right" or, speaking of himself in the third person, "The President is right"—similarly, he retweets others saying things like "Trump was right" or that he was "absolutely right."

That phrase, "absolutely right," returns us to a theme discussed above in relation to paganism, where we discussed the way that absolutist language functions. Consider this example, from January 9, 2020, when Trump retweeted journalist Piers Morgan saying that Trump was "absolutely right" to kill Iranian General Qasem Soleimani in Iraq. This was a morally and legally problematic use of lethal force: the preemptive killing of an Iranian leader who was visiting a third country. This killing was far from being absolutely justified. But the language of the "absolute" is for Trump a kind of verbal tic that seems to foreclose critical thinking. The word *absolutely* shows up in over two hundred of Trump's tweets. One typical example comes from before his presidency on March 20, 2014. Trump tweeted, "I don't hate Obama at all, I just think he is an absolutely terrible president, maybe the worst in our history." This kind of hyperbole is false and infuriating.

When moral language is employed in Trump's discourse, it is often used in a divisive fashion. In some cases, there is an appeal to God and religion that seems to resonate with Jefferson's appeal to the Creator and Lincoln's appeal to God. As is typical for U.S. presidents, Trump repeats the phrase "God bless America." But Trump's appeal to religion is often linked to a divisive America First ideology. In 2019 in the State of the Union, Trump concluded by saying:

> We must keep America first in our hearts. We must keep freedom alive in our souls. And we must always keep faith in America's destiny that one nation, under God, must be the hope and the promise, and the light and the glory, among all the nations of the world.[4]

This vision of keeping "America first in our hearts" has some inspirational and moral appeal. But in a cosmopolitan world, it seems to fall short of Lincoln's more comprehensive vision of charity for all and malice toward none.

In Trump's State of the Union messages, there is no mention of *ethics*; but *moral* is employed in a couple of cases (in 2018 and 2019) in relation to foreigners and immigrants. In 2019, the president said that only those "who meet education and work requirements, and show good moral character, will be able to become full citizens of the United States."[5] This may or may not be a good idea. But "good moral character" is left unexplained. Instead of offering deeper insight into morality, Trump more typically focuses on greatness and exceptionality, glory and magnificence. In his 2020 State of the Union, he concluded:

> Ladies and gentlemen, our ancestors built the most exceptional republic ever to exist in all of human history, and we are making it greater than ever before. This is our glorious and magnificent inheritance.

Now this may be forgiven as the kind of rhetorical flourish typical of speeches such as the State of the Union. But a similar focus on glory and greatness divorced from morality can be found in an analysis of Trump's books *The Art of the Deal* and *Great Again: How to Fix Our Crippled America*. The *Art of the Deal* does not speak of "ethics" or "values" in the moral sense. There are a couple of references to value—but in the sense of market value. There is an interesting discussion of morality in the book, where Trump (or his ghostwriter) argues that gambling should not be viewed as a moral issue and basically argues in favor of legalizing gambling in Atlantic City, where he went on to open a casino. The second book was Trump's campaign book, which is probably a better indication of his more current worldview and his view on governing. The book does not use *moral* or *morality*. The word *ethic* or *ethics* shows up five times, where it is primarily used in the phrase "work ethic." In several places, Trump explains his own work ethic. The word *value* does show up, but it usually refers to monetary value. One chapter in the book is titled "Values." There is a discussion of religion there—but without moral content. Trump declares, "The Bible is the most important book ever written." But he does not indicate any moral lessons learned from his reading of the Bible.

But books are not Trump's preferred medium—and his are usually ghostwritten. So let's look at Trump's Twitter feed. I searched for mentions of "morality," "moral," "ethics," "ethical," and "values." The results were similarly disheartening. In the archive of his tweets, we find *morality* used once, *moral* 9 times, *ethics* or *ethic* 13 times each, *ethical* one time, and *values* 55 times. As in the other texts, *values* is often associated with property values and is also used in a divisive way. This divisive use of moral language shows up in many places. One typical example comes from Trump's speech at the Republican National Convention on August 27, 2020, when he formally accepted the party's nomination. He used the word *moral* twice in that speech in a short paragraph that was fallacious and intentionally divisive. He said, referring to members of the Democratic Party,

Democrat leaders talk about moral decency, but they have no problem with stopping a baby's beating heart in the ninth month of pregnancy. Democrat politicians refuse to protect innocent life, and then they lecture

us about morality and saving America's soul. Tonight, we proudly declare
that all children, born and unborn, have a God-given right to life.

The issue of abortion is indeed a moral issue—and Trump has also
uttered opinions about other moral issues, such as the death penalty
(which he is strongly in favor of). But it is simply false that Democrats
do not have a problem with stopping a baby's heart at nine months. And
Trump's use of this issue is merely a kind of virtue signaling. Nowhere
have I seen Trump attempt to really wrestle with the complex moral
issues related to abortion. The closest he comes to this, as far as I can
tell, is in his 2000 book, *The America We Deserve*, where he says, "I
support a woman's right to choose . . . but I am uncomfortable with the
procedures."[6]

But usually Trump is not so subtle. And the subtlety has clearly
faded over the years, as Trump became more extreme. A typical more
recent example of his use of a word such as *value* comes from June
25, 2016, where Trump wrote, "We only want to admit those who love
our people and support our values. #AmericaFirst."[7] It was also telling
that there was only one use of *morality* in Trump's Twitter feed—and
this was in a boast about his own greatness. In a tweet from March 23,
2016, Trump wrote (apparently quoting from some anonymous other
Twitter account), "Donald Trump will be greater president than Ragan
[*sic*]. Trump will set the button for morality, Christianity."[8] This shows
us a lot about Donald Trump's view of morality. He is bragging about
himself here as resetting morality while also misspelling the name of
President Ronald Reagan. Trump's view of morality is both careless and
self-serving.

This is different from Barack Obama and George W. Bush. Bush, for
example, eagerly discussed the moral dimension of life. He viewed the
war on terrorism as a struggle of good against evil. In his Texas guber-
natorial inauguration speech, which he recounted in his campaign book,
A Charge to Keep, Bush spoke of improving people's moral and spiritual lives. He refers to the need for moral courage and a sense of being
called to the ethical task of leadership. In his first inauguration address,
he spoke of the need for civic duty, responsibility, and conscience.

President Obama's first inaugural speech discussed virtues such as
honesty, courage, fair play, tolerance, curiosity, loyalty, and patriotism.

He said, "We have duties to ourselves, our nation and the world, duties that we do not grudgingly accept but rather seize gladly." In Obama's campaign book, *The Audacity of Hope, moral* shows up 24 times. There are 7 results for *ethic* and 46 hits for value. Obama explains that "empathy" is the heart of his moral code. He says, "It is how I understand the Golden Rule—not simply as a call to sympathy or charity, but as something more demanding, a call to stand in somebody else's shoes and see through their eyes."

Unlike Obama, when Trump speaks of the Golden Rule, he does not mean a principle of altruism. Instead, for Trump, the Golden Rule is the punch line for a joke. In his Twitter feed, the term *Golden Rule* occurs nine times (all from before he was president). In each case it is a version of a joke (from a Trump tweet on February 7, 2013): "The golden rule of negotiation = He who has the gold makes the rules."[9] And with regard to empathy and altruism, Donald Trump is silent. These terms do not show up in the texts I've analyzed except in a few telling cases. On the last page of *The Art of the Deal*, Trump talks about "giving back." He explains, "I've never been terribly interested in why people give, because their motivation is rarely what it seems to be, and it's almost never pure altruism."[10] This parting comment tells us a lot: Trump simply does not believe in altruism and thinks that most people are lying when they claim to be altruistic.

Let's conclude this brief discussion by focusing on a different set of terms that seems to better manifest Trump's values. These are words such as "greatest" and concepts and words that focus on winning. The most obvious point to make here is that Trump's campaign slogan— "Make American Great Again"—is a slogan focused on greatness. The same is true of the slogan "America First." The focus on greatness is an indication of a pagan and tyrannical vision of power. When we look for terms such as *great, greatness*, and associated ideas, we find them throughout Trump's oeuvre. "Greatest" shows up in 361 tweets. "Huge" shows up in 169 tweets. And "win" shows up in over 1,000 tweets. In Trump's RNC speech of August 27, 2020, "great" shows up 32 times. The word is used both as a superlative to compliment Trump's accomplishments (with regard to South Korea and the Trans-Pacific Partnership, for example, Trump says he made a "great deal" for our country) and as a pejorative to denigrate his opponent (Joe Biden, he says, "will be the destroyer of America's greatness"). And in the notorious January 6, 2021, speech, Trump uses "great" 31 times. One typical example shows up in his praise of Rudy Giuliani. Rudy, Trump says, is "great" and has done "a great job" because he has "guts" and "he fights." This has nothing to do with morality or integrity or dignity or ethics. Instead, Trump praises his sycophant as a great man because the man supports his fallacious claim to have been elected. Trump also praised his followers, using the language of greatness. He said that this is "the greatest political movement in the history of our country." And then, just before calling on the crowd to march on the Capitol, Trump said the following:

> As this enormous crowd shows, we have truth and justice on our side. We have a deep and enduring love for America in our hearts. We love our country. We have overwhelming pride in this great country, and we have it deep in our souls.

These sentences contain some inspiring rhetoric, including an appeal to justice and truth. Trump says that pride and love are involved in the movement that assaulted the U.S. Capitol. But the argument is fallacious and based upon an appeal to emotion. The size of the crowd is not an indication that "truth and justice" are on your side. For that you actually need moral arguments.

APPENDIX B

The Cast of Characters and Key Events

This book includes frequent historical references. Here is a quick summary of the players in this historical drama—listed in alphabetical order by era.

THE ANCIENTS

- Alcibiades (450–404 BCE): Athenian aristocrat, accused of tyranny and betraying the city, associated with Socrates, murdered in Persia
- Alexander (356–323 BCE): Macedonian emperor known as "Alexander the Great," associated with Aristotle, murdered Aristotle's nephew Callisthenes, died in Persia
- Antigone (legendary): Daughter of Oedipus the tyrant of Thebes, niece of Creon, commits suicide
- Aristophanes (446–386 BCE): Athenian comic poet, mocks Socrates, author of *Clouds*, *Wasps*, *Birds*
- Aristotle (384–322 BCE): Philosopher from Macedonia, student of Plato, tutor of Alexander, escapes Athens to avoid being murdered, author of *Politics*, *Nicomachean Ethics*

- Callisthenes (360–327 BCE): Nephew of Aristotle, accompanies Alexander but refuses to grovel to him, killed by Alexander
- Cicero (106–43 BCE): Roman philosopher and statesman, implicated in assassination of Julius Caesar, murdered by Mark Antony, author of *Republic*
- Creon (legendary): Brother-in-law of Oedipus, becomes tyrant of Thebes, implicated in the death of Antigone
- Julius Caesar (100–44 BCE): Roman general who consolidates power and brings Roman Republic to an end, wrote *The Gallic Wars*, murdered in the Roman Senate on the Ides of March
- Nero (37–69 CE): Roman emperor, tutored by Seneca, declared a public enemy by the Roman Senate, commits suicide
- Oedipus (legendary): tyrant of Thebes, murders his father and marries his mother, cause of the plague at Thebes, blinds himself and abdicates the throne
- Plato (427–347 BCE): Athenian student of Socrates, tutor of the tyrant of Syracuse, author of *Apology of Socrates*, *Republic*, *Laws*, *Alcibiades*, *Theages*, died peacefully (unlike Socrates)
- Plutarch (46–119 CE): Roman historian and philosopher, author of *Parallel Lives* (including lives of Alexander and Caesar) and *Moralia* (including "How to Tell a Flatterer from a Friend")
- Seneca (4 BCE–65 CE): Roman philosopher and statesman, tutor of Nero, author of *On Mercy*, *Of Peace of Mind*, ordered by Nero to commit suicide
- Socrates (470–399 BCE): Athenian philosophy teacher of Plato and Alcibiades, main character in Plato's *Republic*, accused of impiety and executed by the city of Athens
- Sophocles (496–405 BCE): Athenian tragic poet, author of *Oedipus the Tyrant* and *Antigone*
- Tacitus (56–120 CE): Roman statesman and historian, author of *Annals*, *Histories*
- Thucydides (460–400 BCE): Athenian general and historian, author of *History of the Peloponnesian War*
- Tiberius (42 BCE–37 CE): Roman emperor, helped consolidate imperial power

- Tiresias (legendary): Blind prophet of Thebes who speaks wisdom in Sophocles's plays
- Xenophon (430–354 BCE): Athenian general and philosopher, student of Socrates, author of *The Education of Cyrus* (or *Cyropaedia*), *Memorabilia*

MODERN PHILOSOPHERS AND HISTORICAL FIGURES

- Adams, John (1735–1826): Second president of the United States, assisted in drafting the American Declaration of Independence
- Arendt, Hannah (1906–1975): Jewish-German philosopher, emigrates to the United States, author of *The Origin of Totalitarianism*
- Beauvoir, Simone de (1908–1986): French existentialist philosopher and feminist author, author of *The Ethics of Ambiguity*, *The Second Sex*
- Camus, Albert (1913–1960): French-Algerian novelist and philosopher, involved in the French resistance to Nazism, author of *The Plague*; *Resistance, Rebellion, and Death*; *The Rebel*
- Dewey, John (1859–1952): American philosopher of democracy and education, author of *Democracy and Education*
- Douglass, Frederick (1817–1895): Escaped from slavery and went on to advocate for the abolition of slavery, author of *Narrative of the Life of Frederick Douglass, An American Slave*
- Emerson, Ralph Waldo (1803–1882): American transcendentalist philosopher and essayist, abolitionist
- Freire, Paulo (1921–1997): Brazilian philosopher of education, author of *Pedagogy of the Oppressed*
- Garrison, William Lloyd (1805–1879): American abolitionist and journalist
- Hamer, Fannie Lou (1917–1977): American civil rights activist
- Hobbes, Thomas (1588–1679): English philosopher, associated with the social contract tradition, author of *Leviathan*
- Holbach (Baron d'Holbach) (1723–1789): French enlightenment thinker, author of *De la Cruauté Religieuse* (*On Religious Cruelty*), *Good Sense without God*

- Jackson, Andrew (1767–1845): Seventh president of the United States, defeated the British at New Orleans, fought native tribes and began Indian "removal" under the Indian Removal Act
- Jefferson, Thomas (1743–1826): Third president of the United States, primary author of the Declaration of Independence
- Kant, Immanuel (1724–1804): German (Prussian) philosopher, proponent of pure reason and enlightenment, author of *The Critique of Pure Reason, What Is Enlightenment?*
- King Martin Luther Jr. (1929–1968): American minister and non-violent civil rights leader, author of *Strength to Love, Letter from Birmingham Jail*, murdered in Memphis, Tennessee
- Lincoln, Abraham (1809–1865): Sixteenth president of the United States, preserved the Union through the American Civil War, assassinated by John Wilkes Booth
- Locke, John (1632–1704): English philosopher whose writing inspired the American revolutionaries; key works: *Second Treatise on Government, Some Thoughts Concerning Education*
- Macaulay, Catharine (1731–1791): British historian, advocated for education of women, author of *Letters on Education*
- Machiavelli, Niccolò (1469–1527): Italian politician and philosopher/historian, author of *The Prince, Discourses on Livy*
- Madison, James (1751–1836): Fourth president of the United States, leading figure in drafting the U.S. Constitution, author of *The Federalist Papers* (with Alexander Hamilton and John Jay)
- Mandela, Nelson (1918–2013): President of South Africa and anti-apartheid activist, author of *Long Walk to Freedom: The Autobiography of Nelson Mandela*
- Mayhew, Jonathan (1720–1766): American minister in Boston, influenced John Adams in supporting rebellion against tyranny, author of "A Discourse Concerning Unlimited Submission and NonResistance to the Higher"
- Montesquieu (1686–1755): French philosopher who advocated separation of powers in government, author of *The Spirit of the Laws*
- Noddings, Nel (b. 1929): Philosopher of education, leading figure in care ethics, author of *Caring, Education and Democracy in the 21st Century*

- Rousseau, Jean-Jacques (1712–1788): French/Swiss philosopher, defended social contract theory and democratic education, author of *Emile*, *The Social Contract*
- Trocmé, André (1901–1971): French resistance leader, who (along with Magda Trocmé and Edouard Theis) rescued Jews from the Holocaust
- Wollstonecraft, Mary (1759–1797): Philosopher and advocate for women's equality, author of *A Vindication of the Rights of Women*
- Woolf, Virginia (1882–1941): English modernist author, author of *A Room of One's Own*, *Three Guineas*

KEY CONTEMPORARY POLITICAL FIGURES

- Biden, Joe (b. 1942): Elected forty-sixth president of the United States in November 2020
- Bush, George W. (b. 1946): forty-third president of the United States
- Clinton, Bill (b. 1946): forty-second president of the United States
- Clinton, Hillary (b. 1947): defeated in presidential election of 2016; wife of Bill Clinton
- Cruz, Ted (b. 1970): U.S. senator from Texas, Trump ally
- Giuliani, Rudy (b. 1944): Former mayor of New York City, Trump ally
- Graham, Lindsey (b. 1955): U.S. senator from South Carolina, Trump ally
- McConnell, Mitch (b. 1942): U.S. senator from Kentucky, Senate majority leader during Trump impeachments
- Obama, Barack (b. 1961): Elected forty-fourth president of the United States in November 2008
- Pelosi, Nancy (b. 1940): Speaker of the House of Representatives during Trump impeachments
- Pence, Mike (b. 1959): Vice president under Donald Trump, presiding officer at the January 6, 2021, certification of the 2020 presidential election
- Trump, Donald (b. 1946): Elected forty-fifth president of the United States in November 2016

KEY EVENTS OF THE TRUMP PRESIDENCY

- 2016: Election of Donald Trump
- 2019: First impeachment of Donald Trump—acquitted by the U.S. Senate
- 2020: Election of Joe Biden, defeat of Donald Trump
- 2021, January 6: Pro-Trump riot and assault on the U.S. Capitol
- 2021, January 13: Second impeachment of Donald Trump—acquitted by the U.S. Senate on February 23, 2021

NOTES

EPIGRAPH

Plato, *Theatetus*, 149 (my translation/interpretation of the Greek from http://www.perseus.tufts.edu).

PREFACE

1. Mary Wollstonecraft, *A Vindication of the Rights of Women*, at https://oll.libertyfund.org/title/wollstonecraft-a-vindication-of-the-rights-of-woman.

2. In this and what follows, with regard to most of the Greek sources—Plato, Aristotle, and Sophocles—I offer interpretations and translations based on original sources found at http://www.perseus.tufts.edu. I will cite texts parenthetically.

3. John Adams, Diary entry July 31, 1796, https://founders.archives.gov/documents/Adams/01-03-02-0013-0002-0020.

4. Wollstonecraft, *A Vindication of the Rights of Women*, Prefatory Letter to M. Talleyrand-Périgord, n.p., at https://oll.libertyfund.org/title/wollstochapter 6necraft-a-vindication-of-the-rights-of-woman.

5. https://www.monticello.org/site/research-and-collections/quotations-jefferson-memorial.

6. Albert Camus, *The Plague* (New York: Modern Library, 1948).

7. John Locke, *Second Treatise of Government*, chapter 18: "Of Tyranny," in *The Enhanced Edition of John Locke's Two Treatises of Civil Government (1689, 1764)* (Indianapolis: Liberty Fund, 2014), https://oll.libertyfund.org/titles/2638.

8. In what follows, I will cite *The Federalist Papers* with an in-text reference. A useful source for these texts is: https://avalon.law.yale.edu/subject_menus/fed.asp.

9. Frederick Douglass, "The War and How to End It" (1862), in *Frederick Douglass: Selected Speeches and Writings*, ed. P. S. Foner (Chicago: Chicago Review Press, 2000), 490.

10. Ralph Waldo Emerson, "Considerations by the Way," in *Emerson: Complete Works* (London: Bell & Daldy, 1866), vol. 2, 413.

11. Hannah Arendt, *The Origins of Totalitarianism* (New York: Harcourt Brace Jovanovich, 1973), 107.

12. Arendt, *Origins of Totalitarianism*, 307.

13. Arendt, *Origins of Totalitarianism*, 78.

CHAPTER 1: FROM TRUMP TO PLATO AND BACK AGAIN

1. See: "Donald Trump Insists It's Entirely Possible Democrats Are Running a Satanic Pedophile Cult," *Vanity Fair*, October 16, 2020, https://www.vanityfair.com/news/2020/10/donald-trump-qanon-town-hall; and What Is QAnon?," *New York Times*, March 4, 2021, https://www.nytimes.com/article/what-is-qanon.html. The claims about the media and intelligentsia as the "enemy of the people" were routinely made by Donald Trump throughout his presidency. At his January 6, 2021, speech, he repeated the claim saying, "Our media is not free. It's not fair. It suppresses thought. It suppresses speech, and it's become the enemy of the people. It's become the enemy of the people. It's the biggest problem we have in this country." https://www.rev.com/blog/transcripts/donald-trump-speech-save-america-rally-transcript-january-6.

2. This version of the conspiracy theory was present as early as July 2020. See: "'Everyone is Lying': Trump Undercuts Public Health Officials in Fresh Attacks," *Politico*, July 13, 2020, https://www.politico.com/news/2020/07/13/trump-questions-public-health-experts-twitter-359388. Also see: "The Long-Term Consequences of Trump's Conspiracy Theory Campaign," Vox.com, November 2, 2020, xi, https://www.vox.com/recode/21546119/trump-conspiracy-theories-election-2020-coronavirus-voting-vote-by-mail; and "Covid-19 Is Feeding the GOP Addiction to Conspiracy Theories," *The Nation*, Decem-

ber 7, 2020, https://www.thenation.com/article/politics/covid-trump-republican -conspiracy/.

3. Ashli Babbitt posted this in her social media according to the *LA Times*, January 8, 2021: https://www.latimes.com/california/story/2021-01-08/san-diego -woman-ashli-babbitt-dc-capitol-riot.

4. "Shirkey Falsely Claims US Capitol Attack Was Staged, Not Carried Out by Trump Supporters," *Detroit Free Press*, February 10, 2021, https://www .freep.com/story/news/local/michigan/detroit/2021/02/09/mike-shirkey-insur rection-hoax-trump/4455506001/.

5. "Republicans Blame Democrats, Antifa and U.S. Capitol Police for Jan. 6 Mayhem, According to New UMass Amherst/WCVB Poll," UMass Amherst, April 27, 2021, https://www.umass.edu/newsoffice/article/republicans-blame -democrats-antifa-and-us.

6. For transcripts of the January 6, 2021, speeches of Rudy Giuliani and Donald Trump, see: https://www.rev.com/blog/transcripts/donald-trump -speech-save-america-rally-transcript-january-6 and https://www.rev.com/blog/ transcripts/rudy-giuliani-speech-transcript-at-trumps-washington-d-c-rally -wants-trial-by-combat.

7. "We Love You. You're Very Special," *Washington Post*, January 7, 2021, https://www.washingtonpost.com/opinions/2021/01/07/trump-we-love-you -capitol-mob/.

8. See Carl Schmitt, *Political Theology* (Cambridge, MA: MIT Press, 1985), 47; also see Carl Schmitt, *The Leviathan in the State Theory of Thomas Hobbes: Meaning and Failure of a Political Symbol* (Chicago: University of Chicago Press, 2008). I discuss this in Andrew Fiala, "Sovereignty," in Andrew Fiala, *Bloomsbury Companion to Political Philosophy* (London: Bloomsbury, 2015).

9. https://www.rev.com/blog/transcripts/donald-trump-speech-save-amer ica-rally-transcript-january-6.

10. Walter Newell, *Tyranny: A History of Power, Injustice, and Terror* (Cambridge: Cambridge University Press, 2016); Victor Parker, "Τύραννος: The Semantics of a Political Concept from Archilochus to Aristotle," *Hermes* 126, no. 2 (1998): 145–72, JSTOR, http://www.jstor.org/stable/4477243.

11. Parker, "Τύραννος," 145–72.

12. See Debora Parker and Mark Parker, *Sucking Up: A Brief Consideration of Sycophancy* (n.p.: University of Virginia Press, 2017).

13. "Donald Trump: 'I Could . . . Shoot Somebody, and I Wouldn't Lose Any Voters,'" National Public Radio, January 23, 2016, https://www.npr .org/sections/thetwo-way/2016/01/23/464129029/donald-trump-i-could-shoot -somebody-and-i-wouldnt-lose-any-voters.

14. Donald Trump, *The Art of the Deal* (New York: Ballantine Books, 1987), 48.

15. "From 'Lyin' Ted to 'Beautiful': How Trump and Cruz Found Political Love," National Public Radio, October 22, 2018, https://www.npr .org/2018/10/22/659692611/from-lyin-ted-to-beautiful-how-trump-and-cruz -found-political-love.

16. "Is the GOP's Stop Trump Campaign Too Late?" CNN, March 18, 2016, https://www.cnn.com/2016/03/18/politics/donald-trump-republican-conserva tives/index.html.

17. "How Lindsey Graham Lost His Way," *Rolling Stone*, January 6, 2020, https://www.rollingstone.com/politics/politics-features/lindsey-graham-senate -trump-928948/.

18. "GOP Sen. Susan Collins: Why I Cannot Support Donald Trump," *Washington Post*, August 8, 2016, https://www.washingtonpost.com/opinions/ gop-senator-why-i-cannot-support-trump/2016/08/08/821095be-5d7e-11e6-9 d2f-b1a3564181a1_story.html. On Collins voting with Trump, see "The Immoderate Susan Collins," *The Cut*, February 18, 2020, https://www.thecut .com/2020/02/susan-collins-moderate-legacy-trump.html.

19. "Was Donald Trump a Democrat?," ThoughtCo, June 1, 2020, https:// www.thoughtco.com/was-donald-trump-a-democrat-3367571.

20. Stuart Stevens, *It Was All a Lie: How the Republican Party Became Donald Trump* (New York: Knopf, 2020).

21. "'We Love Trump': Enthusiasm for President's Re-election Is High at Cincinnati Rally," *Here and Now*, August 2, 2019, https://www.wbur.org/here andnow/2019/08/02/president-trump-rally-cincinnati.

22. "Trump Supporters Wave Off Impeachment at President's Rally in Hershey," *The Morning Call*, December 10, 2019, https://www.mcall.com/ news/pennsylvania/mc-nws-pa-trump-2020-pennsylvania-rally-20191210-fat 3axdrtrg7thnatkjnv4awu4-story.html.

23. "Scott Baio: I Like Trump Because He Talks Like a Guy," Fox News, October 9, 2016, https://video.foxnews.com/v/5163050437001#sp=show-clips.

24. See: "'The Final Betrayal': Trump Supporters Denounce President on Reddit after He Suddenly Decries Capitol Riot Violence He Incited," *Independent*, January 8, 2021, https://www.independent.co.uk/news/world/americas/ us-politics/capitol-riots-trump-supporters-b1784318.html; and "Donald Trump Fans Cry Betrayal as He Rebukes Capitol Violence," *Guardian*, January 8, 2021, https://www.theguardian.com/us-news/2021/jan/08/trump-incites-anger -among-acolytes-let-down-by-lack-of-support.

25. The quote is from Taylor Golden, a Trump supporter who was in Washington, DC, on January 6. At: https://www.bbc.com/news/world-us -canada-55582166.

26. Rand Paul, "Coronavirus Reaction—Is Your Government Embracing Tyranny?" Fox News, May 7, 2020, https://www.foxnews.com/opinion/coronavirus-reaction-is-government-embracing-tyranny-sen-rand-paul. The C. S. Lewis quote comes from Lewis, "The Humanitarian Theory of Punishment," http://www.austlii.edu.au/au/journals/ResJud/1954/30.pdf.

27. "Former Trump Advisor Michael Flynn Claims the COVID-19 Pandemic Was Fabricated to Distract from the 2020 Election," *Yahoo News*, May 23, 2021, https://news.yahoo.com/former-trump-advisor-michael-flynn-141901883.html.

CHAPTER 2: TYRANNY AS A THEOLOGICAL PROBLEM

1. William Lloyd Garrison, "Sonnet for Liberty," in *William Lloyd Garrison: The Story of His Life*, by William Lloyd Garrison (New York: The Century, 1885), vol. 2, 432.

2. Ashli Babbitt posted this in her social media, according to the *LA Times*: https://www.latimes.com/california/story/2021-01-08/san-diego-woman-ashli-babbitt-dc-capitol-riot.

3. Thucydides, *History of the Peloponnesian War*, Book 6, available at www.perseus.tufts.edu.

4. Nicolo Machiavelli, *Discourses on Livy*, in *The Historical, Political, and Diplomatic Writings of Nicolo Machiavelli* (Boston: James Osgood and Co., 1882), vol. 2, 233.

5. Machiavelli, *Discourses*, 232.

6. Jonathan Mayhew, "A Discourse Concerning Unlimited Submission and NonResistance to the Higher Powers" (1750)—excerpts at: http://nationalhumanitiescenter.org/pds/becomingamer/american/text5/mayhewsubmission.pdf.

7. See Andrew Fiala, *Against Religions, Wars, and States* (Lanham, MD: Rowman & Littlefield, 2013).

8. Some scholars suggest that *Theages* is a spurious work written by a disciple of Plato's in the Academy.

9. Charles Harsthorne, *Omnipotence and Other Theological Mistakes* (Albany: State University of New York Press, 1984), 59.

10. Immanuel Kant, *Lectures on Ethics* (Cambridge: Cambridge University Press, 1997), 102.

11. John Adams to Thomas Jefferson, November 13, 1815, *Founders Online*, National Archives, https://founders.archives.gov/documents/Adams/99-02-02-6539.

12. John Locke, *Second Treatise of Government*, chapter 3.

13. Frederick Douglass, *Frederick Douglass: Selected Speeches and Writings* (Chicago: Chicago Review Press, 2000), 200.

14. William Godwin, *Sketches of History* (Six Sermons)—quoted in Peter Marshall, *William Godwin: Philosopher, Novelist, Revolutionary* (Oakland, CA: PM Press, 2017).

15. My translation of: *Si les hommes se figurent un Dieu tyrannique, capricieux ou méchant leur religion respirera l'esclavage, l'inconséquence, la cruauté. Mais s'ils regardent sincèrement la divinité comme un être infiniment sage et bon, l'on a droit d'en conclure que leur religion sera pleine de raison et de bienveillance*, Baron d'Holbach, *De la Cruauté Religieuse*, Introduction, http://www.gutenberg.org/files/41336/41336-h/41336-h.htm.

16. Baron d'Holbach, *Good Sense without God*, para. 155, https://www.gutenberg.org/files/7319/7319-h/7319-h.htm.

17. Jefferson wrote an essay late in his life (1830) titled, "On the Writings of the Baron D'Holbach on the Morality of Nature and that of Christian Religion," cited in Kevin J. Hayes, *The Road to Monticello: The Life and Mind of Thomas Jefferson* (Oxford: Oxford University Press, 2008), 582.

18. William Lloyd Garrison, "No Compromise with the Evil of Slavery" (1854), https://www.blackpast.org/african-american-history/1854-william-lloyd-garrison-no-compromise-evil-slavery/.

19. Garrison, "Sonnet for Liberty," 432.

20. See Samhita Mukhopadhyay and Kate Harding, eds., *Nasty Women: Feminism, Resistance, and Revolution in Trump's America* (New York: Picador, 2017); or Juan Williams, *What the Hell Do You Have to Lose? Trump's War on Civil Rights* (New York: Public Affairs Books, 2018).

21. See: Stephen Mansfield, *Choosing Donald Trump* (Grand Rapids, MI: Baker Books, 2017). Also, "How Norman Vincent Peale Taught Donald Trump to Worship Himself," *Politico*, October 6, 2015, https://www.politico.com/magazine/story/2015/10/donald-trump-2016-norman-vincent-peale-213220.

22. Norman Vincent Peale, *The Power of Positive Thinking* (New York: Simon & Schuster, 2003).

23. See: "'He Did Not Pray': Fallout Grows from Trump's Photo-op at St. John's Church," National Public Radio, June 2, 2020, https://www.npr.org/2020/06/02/867705160/he-did-not-pray-fallout-grows-from-trump-s-photo-op-at-st-john-s-church; "Autocrats Love Using the Bible as a Prop. Americans Shouldn't," *Foreign Policy*, June 2, 2020, https://foreignpolicy.com/2020/06/02/autocrats-idolatry-trump-protests-george-floyd-america/; and "Christian Leaders Condemn Trump's Exploitation of Religious Sites as Political Tool," *Center for American Progress*, June 2, 2020, https://www.american

progressaction.org/press/release/2020/06/02/177812/release-christian-leaders
-condemn-trumps-exploitation-religious-sites-political-tool/.

24. See "Donald Trump's Strange and Dangerous 'Absolute Rights' Idea," *Atlantic*, February 29, 2020, https://www.theatlantic.com/ideas/archive/2020/02/president-trump-absolute-rights/607168/.

25. Donald Trump speech, "Save America" Rally transcript, January 6, at https://www.rev.com/blog/transcripts/donald-trump-speech-save-america-rally-transcript-january-6.

26. Donald Trump Coronavirus Press Conference Transcript, April 13, 2020, https://www.rev.com/blog/transcripts/donald-trump-coronavirus-press-conference-transcript-april-13.

27. Rick Perry is quoted in "About a Third in U.S. See God's Hand in Presidential Elections, but Fewer Say God Picks Winners Based on Policies," Pew Center, March 12, 2020, https://www.pewresearch.org/fact-tank/2020/03/12/about-a-third-in-u-s-see-gods-hand-in-presidential-elections-but-fewer-say-god-picks-winners-based-on-policies/.

28. "We'll Likely 'Never See a More Godly' President than Trump, Michele Bachmann Says," *USA Today*, April 17, 2019, https://www.usatoday.com/story/news/politics/onpolitics/2019/04/17/michele-bachmann-trump-most-godly-biblical-president/3495256002/.

29. Trump Twitter archive: https://twitter.com/realDonaldTrump/status/1164138795475881986.

30. See Stephen E. Strang, *God and Donald Trump* (Lake Mary, FL: Charisma House Books, 2017); and Lance Wallnau, *God's Chaos Candidate: Donald J. Trump and the American Unraveling* (Keller, TX: Killer Sheep Media, 2016).

31. I discuss these issues in more detail in: Fiala, *Against Religions, Wars, and States*; and Fiala, *What Would Jesus Really Do?* (Lanham, MD: Rowman & Littlefield, 2007).

32. Xenophon, *Cyropaedeia* 1.13.18, in *Xenophon in Seven Volumes*, by Walter Miller (Harvard University Press, Cambridge, MA; William Heinemann, London, 1914) http://www.perseus.tufts.edu/hopper/text?doc=Perseus%3Atext%3A1999.01.0204%3Abook%3D1%3Achapter%3D3%3Asection%3D18.

33. George Washington to James Anderson (of Scotland), December 24, 1795, *Founders Online*, National Archives, https://founders.archives.gov/documents/Washington/05-19-02-0225.

34. George Washington's letter to his brother, John Augustine Washington, June 15, 1783, *Founders Online*, National Archives, https://founders.archives.gov/documents/Washington/99-01-02-11462.

35. Thomas Jefferson to Thomas Law, June 13, 1814, *Founders Online*, National Archives, https://founders.archives.gov/documents/Jefferson/03-07-02-0307.

36. Abraham Lincoln, "The Perpetuation of Our Political Institutions: Address before the Young Men's Lyceum of Springfield, Illinois," January 27, 1838, *Lincoln Online*, http://www.abrahamlincolnonline.org/lincoln/speeches/lyceum.htm.

37. Abraham Lincoln, second inaugural address (1865), Yale University Avalon Project, https://avalon.law.yale.edu/19th_century/lincoln2.asp.

38. "Donald Trump's Ghostwriter Tells All," *New Yorker*, July 18, 2016, https://www.newyorker.com/magazine/2016/07/25/donald-trumps-ghostwriter-tells-all.

39. Donald Trump, *The Art of the Deal* (New York: Ballantine Books, 1987), 48.

40. Trump, *The Art of the Deal*, 58.

41. Trump Falsehood Database, *Washington Post*: https://www.washingtonpost.com/graphics/politics/trump-claims-database/.

42. Machiavelli, *The Prince*, chapter 18, n.p., https://www.gutenberg.org/files/1232/1232-h/1232-h.htm.

43. I discuss this in Fiala, *The Philosopher's Voice* (Albany: State University of New York Press, 2002).

44. Norman Vincent Peale, "There Are Glorious Days Ahead," *Rotarian*, November 1950, 6.

45. Peale, "There Are Glorious Days Ahead," 6.

CHAPTER 3: THE TRAGIC TRIO AND THE MIDWIFE WHO ENLIGHTENS

1. See Michael Hirsch, "The Tyrannical Mr. Trump," *Foreign Policy*, October 22, 2019, https://foreignpolicy.com/2019/10/02/the-tyrannical-mr-trump-authoritarian-impeachment-constitutional-crisis/; also see: Angel Jamarillo Torres and Marc Benjamin Sable, "Leadership, Statesmanship, and Tyranny: The Character and Rhetoric of Trump," in *Trump and Political Philosophy*, ed. Angel Jamarillo Torres and Marc Benjamin Sable (New York: Palgrave Macmillan, 2018).

2. Thomas Aquinas, *On Kingship* (Toronto: The Pontifical Academy, 1949), chapter 4, para. 29, n.p., https://dhspriory.org/thomas/DeRegno.htm.

3. Dante, *De Monarchia* (New York: Houghton Mifflin, 1904), Book 3, chapter 4: http://files.libertyfund.org/files/2196/Dante_1477.pdf.

4. John Milton, *The Tenure of Kings and Magistrates*, edited with Introduction and Notes by William Talbot Allison (New York: Henry Holt, 1911), https://oll.libertyfund.org/titles/271#Milton_1292_62.

5. Adam Schiff, Impeachment Testimony, February 3, 2020, https://www.rev.com/blog/transcripts/transcript-trump-impeachment-trial-monday-february-3-2020-key-moments.

6. "Mark Levin on Impeachment: You Are Witnessing Tyranny," Fox News, November 16, 2019, https://www.realclearpolitics.com/video/2019/11/16/mark_levin_on_impeachment_you_are_witnessing_tyranny_this_is_an_outrageous_violation_of_the_constitution.html.

7. See Andrew Jackson O'Shaughnessy, *The Men Who Lost America: British Leadership, the American Revolution, and the Fate of the Empire* (New Haven, CT: Yale University Press, 2013), chapter 1.

8. Percy Bysshe Shelley, "England in 1819," https://www.poetryfoundation.org/poems/45118/england-in-1819. See: G. M. Ditchfield, *George III: An Essay in Monarchy* (New York: Palgrave Macmillan, 2002).

9. Nathan John Hollingsworth, "England's Causes for Thankfulness during the Reign of George the Third; or, Their much loved King, an example to Britons" (Durham: Geo. Walker, 1809).

10. Lincoln-Douglas debate, October 15, 1858, https://www.nps.gov/liho/learn/historyculture/debate7.htm.

11. In Andrew S. Coopersmith, *Fighting Words: An Illustrated History of Newspaper Accounts of the Civil War* (New York: The New Press, 2004), 279. Also see John McKee Barr, *Loathing Lincoln* (Baton Rouge: Louisiana State University Press, 2014).

12. See Andrew Fiala, *The Philosopher's Voice* (Albany: SUNY Press, 2002).

13. Donald Trump speech of June 16, 2015, https://time.com/3923128/donald-trump-announcement-speech/.

14. Trump Falsehood Database, *Washington Post*: https://www.washingtonpost.com/graphics/politics/trump-claims-database/.

15. Sophia Rosenfeld, *Democracy and Truth: A Short History* (Philadelphia: Pennsylvania State University Press, 2019), 1. Also see Michiko Kakutani, *The Death of Truth* (New York: Penguin Random House, 2018).

16. Hannah Arendt, *The Origins of Totalitarianism* (New York: Harcourt, 1976), 474.

17. Christopher H. Achen and Larry M. Bartels, *Democracy for Realists: Why Elections Do Not Produce Responsive Government* (Princeton, NJ: Princeton University Press, 2017), 7.

18. Achen and Bartels, *Democracy for Realists*, 14.

19. Jason Brennan, *Against Democracy* (Princeton, NJ: Princeton University Press, 2017), viii.

20. John Locke, *Letter Concerning Toleration*, in *Classics of Modern Political Theory*, ed. Steven M. Cahn (New York: Oxford University Press, 1997), 310.

21. Thomas Jefferson, "Notes on Religion," in *The Writings of Thomas Jefferson: 1776–1781* (New York: G.P. Putnam's Sons, 1893), 102.

22. Quotations on the Jefferson Memorial, https://www.monticello.org/site/research-and-collections/quotations-jefferson-memorial.

23. Joseph Butler, "Sermon on Accession Day," June 11, 1741, in *The Works of Bishop Butler* (New York: Macmillan, 1900), vol. 1, 262.

CHAPTER 4: POLITICAL TRAGEDY AND HISTORICAL WISDOM

1. Abraham Lincoln, "Lincoln on the 1864 Election," National Park Service, Lincoln Home, https://www.nps.gov/liho/learn/historyculture/1864election.htm.

2. The following quotes are from Book V of Aristotle, *Politics* in *Aristotle: 23 Volumes*, vol. 21 (trans. H. Rackham (Cambridge, MA: Harvard University Press; London: William Heinemann, 1944), with Greek text at http://www.perseus.tufts.edu/hopper/text?doc=Perseus%3Atext%3A1999.01.0058%3Abook%3D5.

3. That last translation is from J. E. C. Weldon's translation of Aristotle, *Politics* (London: Macmillan, 1912), 395. The Greek word here is *kolas*. Aristotle uses this term in *Nicomachean Ethics* to describe the opposite of the "great-souled" person who is strong, proud, and free-spirited. Unlike the great-souled person, flatterers lack greatness—they are servile and weak and "small-souled" (*Nicomachean Ethics* 1125a).

4. There is an extensive literature on the difference between Socrates, Plato's literary re-creation of Socrates, and Plato's own thinking. I tend to agree with those who argue that the original Socrates was not an advocate of the philosopher-king and that Plato recognized that this was a strange and almost comical idea. In what follows, we will not be able to attend to the subtleties of the scholarship on Plato and Socrates. See (among others) Thomas Brickhouse, *Socrates on Trial* (Princeton, NJ: Princeton University Press, 1989); Thomas Brickhouse, *Plato's Socrates* (Oxford: Oxford University Press, 1994); Gregory Vlastos, *Socrates: Ironist and Moral Philosopher* (Cambridge: Cambridge University Press, 1991); Kojin Karatani, *Isonomia and the Origins of Philosophy*

(Raleigh, NC: Duke University Press, 2017); Robert Metcalf, *Philosophy as Agon* (Evanston, IL: Northwestern University Press, 2018).

5. Jon Herbert, Trevor McCrisken, and Andrew Wroe, *The Ordinary Presidency of Donald J. Trump* (New York: Palgrave Macmillan, 2019).

6. See: Madeline Albright, *Fascism: A Warning* (New York: HarperCollins, 2019); Jason Stanley, *Fascism: The Politics of Us and Them* (New York: Random House, 2018); and essays collected in Cass R. Sunstein, ed., *Can It Happen Here? Authoritarianism in America* (New York: HarperCollins, 2018).

7. Stephen E. Strang, *God and Donald Trump* (Lake Mary, FL: Charisma House Books, 2017), xv.

8. "Rick Perry's Belief That Trump Was Chosen by God Is Shared by Many in a Fast-Growing Christian Movement," *The Conversation*, December 1, 2019, https://theconversation.com/rick-perrys-belief-that-trump-was-chosen -by-god-is-shared-by-many-in-a-fast-growing-christian-movement-127781.

9. Joseph Parker, "In the Lion's Den," *American Family Association*, December 16, 2019, https://www.afa.net/the-stand/faith/2019/12/in-the-lion-s -den/.

10. Joseph Parker, "Spiritual Warfare: Lifting Up the President in Prayer," *American Family Association*, October 1, 2019, https://www.afa.net/the-stand/ faith/2019/10/spiritual-warfare-lifting-up-the-president-in-prayer/.

11. "Trump May Not Be Crazy, but the Rest of Us Are Getting There Fast," *Politico*, October 12, 2018, https://www.politico.com/magazine/ story/2018/10/12/donald-trump-anxiety-disorder-pscyhologists-221305.

12. President's Remarks of February 7, 2020, https://trumpwhitehouse .archives.gov/briefings-statements/remarks-president-trump-marine-one-depar ture-82/.

13. See: "How a Difficult, Racist, Stubborn President Was Removed from Power—If Not from Office," *Politico*, November 13, 2018, https://www .politico.com/magazine/story/2018/11/13/andrew-johnson-undermined-con gress-cabinet-david-priess-book-222413.

14. See for example, essays collected in Angel Jaramillo Torres and Marc Benjamin Sable, eds., *Trump and Political Philosophy: Leadership, Statesman-ship, and Tyranny* (New York: Palgrave Macmillan, 2018).

CHAPTER 5: THE TYRANT'S PRIDE: ON AMBITION, POWER, AND GREATNESS

1. See: "Donald Trump: Thin-Skinned Tyrant," *National Review*, Jan-uary 28, 2016, https://www.nationalreview.com/2016/01/donald-trump-thin

-skinned-tyrant/; "This Is What the Greeks Would Have Called Donald Trump," *Time*, March 18, 2016, https://time.com/4261816/trump-ancient-greeks/; "Is Trump a Tyrant? What His Tweets Say: 30 Days of Trump Tweets Provide Systematic Evidence about Trump and Tyranny," *Psychology Today*, June 12, 2016, https://www.psychologytoday.com/us/blog/caveman-politics/201606/is -trump-tyrant-what-his-tweets-say.

2. See: Bruce S. Thorton, *Democracy's Dangers & Discontents: The Tyranny of the Majority from the Greeks to Obama* (Stanford, CA: Hoover Institution Press, 2014); or Michael Savage, *Trickle Down Tyranny: Crushing Obama's Dream of the Socialist States of America* (HarperCollins, 2012).

3. "Lauren Boebert Brands Joe Biden 'Tyrant' after President's Gun Re-strictions Call," *Newsweek*, April 29, 2021, https://www.newsweek.com/lauren -boebert-joe-biden-gun-restrictions-tyrant-1587405.

4. CNN, January 24, 2020, https://www.cnn.com/politics/live-news/trump -impeachment-trial-01-24-20/h_f29afa42b56f592ca1ea8a6022fb5270.

5. Fox News, December 23, 2019, https://www.youtube.com/ watch?v=KHbAnMNoAJo.

6. "Impeachment Vote Shows Sharp Party-Line Split for Minnesota Del-egation," *Minnesota Star Tribune*, January 14, 2021, https://www.startribune .com/rep-ilhan-omar-in-house-speech-says-tyrant-trump-must-be-impeached/ 600010038/.

7. "House Introduces Articles of Impeachment," *Insight News*, January 11, 2021, https://www.insightnews.com/news/national/house-introduces-articles -of-impeachment/article_05b1a450-5436-11eb-acc0-036f11446dc3.html.

8. Thomas Hobbes, *Leviathan* (New York: Penguin, 1985), 722.

9. Shakespeare, *Macbeth*—Malcolm speaking in act 4, scene 3.

10. Stephen Greenblatt, *Tyrant: Shakespeare on Tyranny* (New York: W. W. Norton, 2018), 2. Greenblatt cites the Treasons Act of 1534, http://fs2 .american.edu/dfagel/www/1534treasons.htm.

11. Quoted in George M. Logan, "Thomas More on Tyranny," *Thomas More Studies* 2 (2007): 19–32—the sources are in Latin, *Epigrams* 109 and 115.

12. Shakespeare, *Julius Caesar*, act 2, scene 1.

13. Adapted from William Shakespeare, *Hamlet*, act 2, scene 2. The scene is between Hamlet and Rosencrantz and Guildenstern.

14. John Locke, *Second Treatise of Government*, chapter 18: "Of Tyranny," from *The Enhanced Edition of John Locke's Two Treatises of Civil Govern-ment (1689, 1764)* (Indianapolis: Liberty Fund, 2014), https://oll.libertyfund .org/titles/2638.

15. Locke, *Second Treatise of Government*, chapter 18.

16. Locke, *Second Treatise of Government*, chapter 18.

17. Roger Boesche, *Theories of Tyranny from Plato to Arendt* (University Park: University of Pennsylvania Press, 1996), 86 and 167.

18. John Locke, *Second Treatise of Government*, chapter 15: "Of Paternal, Political and Despotical Power," in *The Enhanced Edition of John Locke's Two Treatises of Civil Government (1689, 1764)* (Indianapolis: Liberty Fund, 2014), https://oll.libertyfund.org/titles/2638.

19. Jean-Jacques Rousseau, *The Social Contract*, Book X, conclusion, n.p., in *The Social Contract and Discourses by Jean-Jacques Rousseau* (London and Toronto: J.M. Dent and Sons, 1923), https://oll.libertyfund.org/title/cole-the-social-contract-and-discourses#Rousseau_0132_894.

20. See Fiala, *The Philosopher's Voice*.

21. Quoted in Jack Random, "The Stench of Hypocrisy: Ted Cruz & the Right to Rebellion," *CounterPunch*, January 8, 2016, https://www.counterpunch.org/2016/01/08/the-stench-of-hypocrisy-ted-cruz-the-right-to-rebellion/.

22. Ted Cruz, foreword to *Lawless: The Obama Administration's Unprecedented Assault on the Constitution and the Rule of Law*, by David E. Bernstein (New York: Encounter Books, 2015), xii.

23. Cruz, foreword, xvi.

24. Bernstein, *Lawless*, 8.

25. A list of executive orders from the Federal Register indicates that Clinton, G. W. Bush, Obama, and Trump have liberally employed the power of the executive order; see https://www.federalregister.gov/presidential-documents/executive-orders.

26. Jeffrey Sachs, "Trump Is Taking US down the Path to Tyranny," CNN, July 24, 2018, https://www.cnn.com/2018/07/23/opinions/trump-is-taking-us-down-the-path-to-tyranny-sachs/index.html.

27. Jason Stanley, "Yes, 'Send Her Back' Is the Face of Evil—I Know Fascism When I See It," *Newsweek*, July 19, 2019, https://www.newsweek.com/yes-send-her-back-face-evili-know-fascism-when-i-see-it-opinion-1450243.

28. Angel Jaramillo Torres and Marc Benjamin Sable, eds., *Trump and Political Philosophy: Leadership, Statesmanship, and Tyranny* (New York: Palgrave Macmillan, 2018), 13.

29. Leo Strauss, *On Tyranny* (corrected and expanded edition) (Chicago: University of Chicago Press, 2013), 104.

30. Trump Tweet August 21, 2019, at Trump Twitter Archive: https://www.thetrumparchive.com/.

31. Thomas Aquinas, *Summa Theologica*, II-II, Q. 162 http://www.newadvent.org/summa/3162.htm.

32. http://www.perseus.tufts.edu/hopper/morph?l=tu%2Frannos&la=greek&can=tu%2Frannos0#lexicon.

33. See Andrew Fiala, "Sovereignty," in *The Bloomsbury Companion to Political Philosophy*, ed. Andrew Fiala (London: Bloomsbury, 2015).

34. See Jean Bethke Elsthtain, *Sovereignty: God, State, and Self* (New York: Basic Books, 2008).

35. Carl Schmitt, *Political Theology* (Chicago: University of Chicago Press, 2005), 5.

36. This is the Jebb translation at: http://www.perseus.tufts.edu/hopper/text ?doc=Perseus%3Atext%3A1999.01.0191%3Acard%3D873.

37. See Paul Ricoeur here, in *Oneself as Another* (Chicago: University of Chicago Press, 1992), Seventh Study.

38. The Online Liddell-Scott-Jones Greek-English Lexicon, http://stepha nus.tlg.uci.edu/lsj/#eid=109126&context=lsj&action=from-search.

39. Mark E. Button, "'Hubris Breeds the Tyrant': The Anti-Politics of Hubris: From Thebes to Abu Ghraib," *Law, Culture and the Humanities* 8, no. 2 (2012): 305–32, https://doi.org/10.1177/1743872110383106.

40. Donald Trump, *The Art of the Deal* (New York: Ballantine Books, 1987), 48.

41. Rick Reilly, *Commander in Cheat: How Golf Explains Trump* (New York: Hachette, 2019).

42. Determining Trump's real height is more difficult than it should be, given the misinformation surrounding the question. One useful piece of evidence is a photo of Trump at a G7 meeting, where he stands near Justin Trudeau, who is 6'2": Trump is shorter than Trudeau in the picture. See MacLeans: https://www.macleans.ca/news/world/the-g7-group-shot-where-don ald-trump-cant-hide-from-his-height/.

CHAPTER 6: THE FOOL'S STUPIDITY: ON WILLFUL AND VICIOUS IGNORANCE

1. Martin Luther King Jr., *Strength to Love* (Augsburg Fortress Press, 2010), 39.

2. King, *Strength to Love*, 39.

3. "Springfield Man Charged in Jan. 6 Attack on US Capitol," *State Journal Register*, April 14, 2021, https://www.sj-r.com/story/news/2021/04/14/u-s -capitol-attack-investigators-charge-springfield-man/7230243002/. This story is quoted and linked to *USA Today*'s evolving list of arrests and charges related to January 6, at https://www.usatoday.com/storytelling/capitol-riot-mob-arrests/.

4. "U.S. Capitol Riots: How the Mystery Man in the Carhartt Cap Was Identified as a Kentuckian," *Courier Journal*, April 20, 2021, https://www

.courier-journal.com/story/news/crime/2021/04/20/kentucky-capitol-riot-arrest -stephen-chase-randolph-arrest/7302622002/. This story is quoted and linked to *USA Today*'s evolving list of arrests and charges related to January 6, at https://www.usatoday.com/storytelling/capitol-riot-mob-arrests/.

5. Quoted in Anthony Read, *The Devil's Disciples: Hitler's Inner Circle* (New York: Norton, 2003), 514.

6. "Don't Call Rioters Protesters," *Wall Street Journal*, June 4, 2020, https://www.wsj.com/articles/dont-call-rioters-protesters-11591293310.

7. Quoted in *The Guardian*: https://www.theguardian.com/books/2005/ feb/21/huntersthompson#:~:text=%22He%20that%20is%20taught%20 only,Riots%20are%20fun.%22.

8. "Tarantino Is Aiming for More Gore," *The Times*, May 17, 2004, https:// www.thetimes.co.uk/article/tarantino-is-aiming-for-more-gore-6x3nd6npxld.

9. See Andrew Fiala, *Transformative Pacifism* (London: Bloomsbury, 2018).

10. In Diogenes Laertius, *Lives of Eminent Philosophers*, Book 6: 24, trans. Pamela Mensch (Oxford: Oxford University Press, 2020), 200.

11. See James Miller, "Carnivals of Atrocity: Foucault, Nietzsche, Cruelty," *Political Theory* 18, no. 3 (August 1990): 470–91.

12. "Trump: Joe Biden Is a Dummy," *Reuters*, June 11, 2019, https://www .reuters.com/video/watch/idOVAIWI2FZ.

13. One can discover this at the Trump Twitter Archive by searching for "dummy" https://www.thetrumparchive.com/?searchbox=%22dummy%22.

14. Trump tweet May 22, 2020, at https://www.thetrumparchive.com/?search box=%22AOC+is+such+an+embarrassing%2C+barely+literate+moron%22z

15. "Chuck Schumer Says Americans Are Dying of COVID Because Trump Is a 'Moron,'" *Newsweek*, October 29, 2020, https://www.newsweek.com/chuck -schumer-says-americans-are-dying-covid-because-trump-moron-1543392.

16. This is found in an excerpt from John Boehner, *On the House* (New York: St. Martin's, 2021)—at: https://www.politico.com/news/magazine/2021/04/02/ john-boehner-book-memoir-excerpt-478506.

17. "Tillerson's Fury at Trump Required an Intervention from Pence," *NBC News*, October 4, 2017, https://www.nbcnews.com/politics/white-house/ tillerson-s-fury-trump-required-intervention-pence-n806451.

18. Trump tweet, December 7, 2018, at Trump Twitter Archive: https:// www.thetrumparchive.com/?searchbox=%22tillerson+%22.

19. "'Dumb Son of a Bitch': Trump Rips McConnell at Mar-a-Lago," *Politico*, April 11, 2021, https://www.politico.com/news/2021/04/11/trump-mcco nnell-dumb-son-of-a-bitch-rnc-480748.

20. Hillary Clinton speech of September 9, 2016—at *Time*: https://time .com/4486502/hillary-clinton-basket-of-deplorables-transcript/.

21. Newt Gingrich, *Understanding Trump* (New York: Hachette, 2017), no page numbers (chapter 1).

22. See discussion in Merriam-Webster: https://www.merriam-webster .com/words-at-play/moron-idiot-imbecile-offensive-history.

23. Edmund Burke Huey, "Backward and Feeble-Minded Children, 1912"—quoted at: https://www.merriam-webster.com/words-at-play/moron -idiot-imbecile-offensive-history.

24. See Gerald V. O'Brien, *Framing the Moron: The Social Construction of Feeble-Mindedness in the American Eugenic Era* (Manchester: Manchester University Press, 2013).

25. For comparison, French Bibles translate the word *moros* in these passages as *folie* and as *fou*—words that can be translated as *crazy* and *mad*. German translations use the word *Narr* and *Torrheit*, which can be translated as *fool* and *folly*.

26. The Greek word used to translate the Hebrew is *aphron*, which means "without reason" (as in the alpha privative applied to the word for reason— especially practical reason, as in the idea of the wise man as a *phronimos* who applies *phronesis*).

27. Hobbes, *Leviathan*, chapter XV.

28. Friedrich Nietzsche, *Twilight of the Idols*, paragraph 52: https://www .gutenberg.org/files/52263/52263-h/52263-h.htm.

29. Jean Bethke Elshtain, *Public Man, Private Woman: Women in Social and Political Thought* (Princeton, NJ: Princeton University Press, 1981), 22.

30. Cf. Matthew Landauer, "The '*Idiōtēs*' and the Tyrant: Two Faces of Unaccountability in Democratic Athens," *Political Theory* 42, no. 2 (April 2014): 139–66.

31. See Shankar Vedantam, *The Hidden Brain: How Our Unconscious Minds Elect Presidents, Control Markets, Wage Wars, and Save Our Lives* (New York: Random House, 2010).

32. Francis Bacon, *Novum Organum*, in *The Works of Francis Bacon* (London: Longman, 1858), vol. 4, para. XLVI, p. 56.

33. Jonathan Haidt, *The Righteous Mind: Why Good People Are Divided by Politics and Religion* (New York Vintage, 2013), 105.

34. See Stacy Clifford, "Indispensable Idiocy: Cognitive Disability and the Social Contract" (dissertation, Vanderbilt University, 2011)—at https://etd .library.vanderbilt.edu/available/etd-12022011-135421/unrestricted/Clifford_ Dissertation113011.pdf.

35. John Locke, *Second Treatise of Government*, chapter 6: "Of Paternal Power" from *The Enhanced Edition of John Locke's Two Treatises of Civil Government (1689, 1764)* (Indianapolis: Liberty Fund, 2014), https://oll.libertyf und.org/titles/2638, para. 60.

36. Kant, *Anthropology from a Pragmatic Point of View* (Cambridge: Cambridge University Press, 2006), 106.

37. Kant, *Anthropology*, 96–97.

38. Adolf Hitler, *Mein Kampf* (New York: Reynal and Hitchcock, 1941), 313.

39. "Whose 'Big Lie'? Trump's Proclamation a New GOP Litmus Test," *AP News*, May 3, 2021, https://apnews.com/article/politics-campaign-2016-election-2020-government-and-politics-f3428d42d4d3fdfe59c560b6fadbbc70.

40. "Whose 'Big Lie'?," *AP News*."

41. See "Here's What the 'Blue Shift' in Pennsylvania Looks Like as Trump's Lead over Biden Narrows," *Philadelphia Inquirer*, November 4, 2020, https://www.inquirer.com/politics/election/pennsylvania-2020-election-results-trump-biden-blue-shift-chart-20201104.html. Also: "Why Do Election Results Change after Election Day? The 'Blue Shift' in California Elections," *American Political Science Association*, March 25, 2020, https://preprints.apsanet.org/engage/api-gateway/apsa/assets/orp/resource/item/5e7bce380e55c30019685cca/original/why-do-election-results-change-after-election-day-the-blue-shift-in-california-elections.pdf. Also see: "Fact-Checking False Claims about Pennsylvania's Presidential Election by Trump and His Allies," *Philadelphia Inquirer*, December 7, 2020, https://www.inquirer.com/politics/election/pennsylvania-election-results-trump-fraud-fact-check-20201206.html.

42. "Why Fact-Checking Doesn't Faze Trump Supporters," *The Atlantic*, July 5, 2017, https://www.theatlantic.com/politics/archive/2017/07/the-strange-effect-fact-checking-has-on-trump-supporters/532701/.

43. Trump, *The Art of the Deal, 58*.

44. Julius Caesar, *The Gallic Wars* (New York. Harper & Brothers, 1869), Book 3, chapter 18. At Perseus.Tufts: https://www.perseus.tufts.edu/hopper/text?doc=Perseus%3Atext%3A1999.02.0001%3Abook%3D3%3Achapter%3D18.

45. John Locke, *An Essay Concerning Human Understanding*, Book 4, chapter 20 in *The Works of John Locke in Nine Volumes*, 12th ed. (London: Rivington, 1824), vol. 2, at: https://oll.libertyfund.org/title/locke-the-works-vol-2-an-essay-concerning-human-understanding-part-2-and-other-writings.

CHAPTER 7: THE SYCOPHANT'S COMPLICITY: ON CUNNING, FLATTERY, AND THE TROJAN HORSE

1. Aristotle, *Rhetoric*, 2.4.31, at Perseus.Tufts.edu—my translation.

2. Dante, *Inferno*, Canto 11: https://digitaldante.columbia.edu/dante/divine-comedy/inferno/inferno-11/.

3. "President Obama's Final Message to the Press: You Can't Be Sycophants for Those in Power," Media Matters January 18, 2017, https://www.media matters.org/barack-obama/president-obamas-final-message-press-you-cant-be -sycophants-those-power.

4. "Obama Tells Sycophantic Press Not To Be Sycophants Anymore," *Investor's Business Daily*, January 19, 2017, https://www.investors.com/politics/com mentary/obama-tells-sycophantic-press-not-to-be-sycophants-anymore/.

5. CNN transcript, January 16, 2020, http://transcripts.cnn.com/TRAN-SCRIPTS/2009/16/nday.04.html.

6. "Rudy Giuliani Is My Father. Please, Everyone, Vote for Joe Biden and Kamala Harris," *Vanity Fair*, October 15, 2020, https://www.vanityfair.com/style/2020/10/rudy-giulianis-daughter-on-voting-for-biden.

7. Harry Frankfurt, *On Bullshit* (Princeton, NJ: Princeton University Press, 2005).

8. Sanders explains a sycophant was "a busybody who sought to prosecute (frequently innocent) people on a regular basis, possibly in order to receive money from the fine, more likely as a bribe from the opponent to drop the case, or even for payment to act as another's front-man." Ed Sanders, "The Arousal of Hostile Emotions in Attic Forensic Oratory," in *Unveiling Emotions: Sources and Methods for the Study of Emotions in the Greek World*, ed. A. Chaniotis (Stuttgart: Franz Steiner Verlag, 2012), 370. Christ explains, "Sycophancy tends to connote malicious and devious legal behavior for personal advantage, including monetary profit. A sycophant brings false charges; blackmails individuals with the threat of litigation; and generally subverts democratic legal process for his own ends." Matthew R. Christ, "Sycophancy and Attitudes to Litigation," in "Athenian Law in Its Democratic Context," ed. Adriaan Lanni (Center for Hellenic Studies On-Line Discussion Series). Republished in C. W. Blackwell, ed., *Dēmos: Classical Athenian Democracy* (A. Mahoney and R. Scaife, eds., The Stoa: a consortium for electronic publication in the humanities [www.stoa .org]), edition of March 26, 2003, n.p., http://www.stoa.org/demos/article_syco phancy@page=all&greekEncoding=UnicodeC.html. As LeCaire explains, "The sycophant was known to exploit the system by using his legal right to prosecute without justification and for personal gain. This was a common avenue for young, up-and coming politicians in Athens." Lucas D. LeCaire, *Tyranny and Terror: the Failure of Athenian Democracy and the Reign of the Thirty Tyrants* (master's thesis, Eastern Washington University, 2013), 35 https://dc.ewu.edu/theses/179.

9. The quote is from Robert Fagles's translation of Homer's *Odyssey* (New York: Penguin, 1999), p. 224, line 470.

10. See Debora Parker and Mark Parker, *Sucking Up: A Brief Consideration of Sycophancy* (n.p.: University of Virginia Press, 2017).

11. See John Oscar Lofberg, *Sycophancy in Athens* (Chicago: University of Chicago, 1917) and J. O. Lofberg, "The Sycophant-Parasite," *Classical Philology* 15: 1 (January 1920): 61–72.

12. Aristophanes, *Birds*, lines 1695–1700 at http://www.perseus.tufts.edu/hopper/text?doc=Perseus%3Atext%3A1999.01.0026%3Acard%3D1694. See interpretation in Scott Porter Consigny, *Gorgias, Sophist and Artist* (Columbia: University of South Carolina Press, 2001).

13. See Joshua T. Katz, "Testimonia Ritus Italici: Male Genitalia, Solemn Declarations, and a New Latin Sound Law," *Harvard Studies in Classical Philology* 98 (1998): 183–217.

14. Xenophon, *Hellenica*, 2.3.13, at Perseus.Tufts.edu.

15. Tacitus, *Annals*, 1.1 (from *Complete Works of Tacitus* with Latin text (New York: Random House, reprinted 1942) at Perseus.Tufts.edu: http://www.perseus.tufts.edu/hopper/text?doc=Perseus%3Atext%3A1999.02.0078.

16. Tacitus, *Annals*, Book 3.

17. Tacitus, *Annals*, Book 16. For discussion see: Karen Actonm, "Vespasian and the Social World of the Roman Court," *American Journal of Philology* 132, no. 1 (2011): 103–24.

18. Seneca, *On Clemency* (*De Clementia*), Book 2, chapter 2, https://en.wikisource.org/wiki/Of_Clemency/Book_II).

19. Seneca, *Of Peace of Mind*, chapter 1, https://en.wikisource.org/wiki/Of_Peace_of_Mind.

20. "How Lindsey Graham Lost His Way," *Rolling Stone*, January 6, 2020, https://www.rollingstone.com/politics/politics-features/lindsey-graham-senate-trump-928948/.

21. Richard Bond, "The Mysterious Case of Lindsey Graham's Political Transformation," CNN, February 22, 2021, https://www.cnn.com/2021/02/22/opinions/lindsey-graham-political-transformation-bond/index.html.

22. "Graham Accuses Media of Painting Trump as a 'Kook,' But Once Used Same Attack Himself," *The Hill*, November 30, 2017, https://thehill.com/homenews/senate/362611-graham-accuses-media-of-same-trump-criticisms-he-once-offered.

23. "Graham Accuses Media."

24. "Graham Calls Trump 'a Kook,' Trump Says Senator 'Knows Nothing,'" *The State*, February 17, 2016, https://www.thestate.com/news/politics-government/politics-columns-blogs/the-buzz/article60894047.html.

25. "How Lindsey Graham Went from Trump Skeptic to Trump Sidekick," *New York Times Magazine*, February 25, 2019, https://www.nytimes.com/2019/02/25/magazine/lindsey-graham-what-happened-trump.html.

26. "Lindsey Graham Says 'Enough Is Enough' on Trump Bid to Overturn the Election: 'Count Me Out,'" *The Hill*, January 6, 2021, https://thehill

.com/homenews/senate/533055-lindsey-graham-says-enough-is-enough-on
-trumps-bid-to-overturn-the-election-count-me.

27. "McConnell Speech after Trump's Impeachment Trial Acquittal," *US News and World Report*, February 14, 2021, https://www.usnews.com/news/politics/articles/2021-02-14/read-mcconnell-speech-after-trumps-impeachment-trial-acquittal.

28. "McConnell Says He Could 'Absolutely' Support Trump if He's the 2024 GOP Nominee," CBS News, February 26, 2021, https://www.cbsnews.com/news/mcconnell-support-trump-2024-republican-nominee/.

29. "Graham: Trump Will 'Be Helpful' to All Senate GOP Incumbents," *The Hill*, February 26, 2021. https://thehill.com/homenews/senate/540720-graham-trump-will-be-helpful-to-all-senate-gop-incumbents.

30. See: Peter Stockwell, *Sociolinguistics: A Resource Book for Students* (London: Routledge, 2002); or Barbara Johnstone, *Discourse Analysis*, 3rd ed. (Wiley Blackwell, 2018).

31. Lindsey Graham, *My Story*, https://www.lindseygraham.com/ebook/mystory_lindseygraham.pdf, p. 14.

32. Attributed to Publius Syrus—quoted in Peter French, "Complicity: That Moral Monster, Troubling Matters," *Criminal Law and Philosophy* 10 (2016): 575–89. Also see Chiara Lepora and Robert E. Goodin, *On Complicity and Compromise* (Oxford: Oxford University Press, 2013); and Lepora and Goodin's response to French: "On Complicity and Compromise: A Reply to Peter French and Steven Ratner," *Criminal Law and Philosophy* 10, no. 3 (2016): 591–602.

33. Allan Bloom, *The Republic of Plato* (New York: Basic Books, 2016), 445, n. 34.

34. Plutarch, "How a Man May Discern a Flatterer from a Friend," 47, at: https://en.wikisource.org/wiki/Plutarch%27s_Moralia_(Holland)/Essay_4).

35. Harry Frankfurt, *On Bullshit* (Princeton, NJ: Princeton University Press, 2005).

36. Plutarch, *De Liberis Educandis*, sec. 9: http://www.perseus.tufts.edu/hopper/text?doc=Perseus%3Atext%3A2008.01.0137%3Asection%3D9.

37. Don Herzog, *Cunning* (Princeton, NJ: Princeton University Press, 2006), 15.

CHAPTER 8: WISDOM, VIGILANCE, AND THE CITIZEN-PHILOSOPHER

1. Thomas Jefferson to William Charles Jarvis, September 28, 1820, at Founders Archive: https://founders.archives.gov/documents/Jefferson/98-01-02-1540.

2. See King, "Letter from Birmingham Jail" (1963): https://kinginstitute
.stanford.edu/sites/mlk/files/letterfrombirmingham_wwcw_0.pdf.

3. "Trump Says Pence 'Didn't Have the Courage' after VP Says He Can't
Change Electoral Vote," *McClatchy*, January 6, 2021, https://www.mcclatchydc
.com/news/nation-world/national/article248313445.html.

4. "Hawley Defends Decision to Object to Electoral Votes," National Public Radio, January 13, 2021, https://www.npr.org/sections/trump-impeachment
-effort-live-updates/2021/01/13/956497657/hawley-defends-decision-to-object
-to-electoral-votes.

5. "Brooks: No Apology for Remarks ahead of Riot," AP News, January
9, 2021, https://apnews.com/article/joe-biden-donald-trump-alabama-violence
-6d532cc05f7f6c58e2f7f4142652e9fc.

6. Thomas Starr King, "The Privilege and Duties of Patriotism," in *The
Book of Patriotism*, ed. George Frisbie Hoar (Boston: Hall and Locke, 1902),
58.

7. Frederick Douglass, "The Right to Criticize American Institutions," in
Frederick Douglass, *Selected Speeches and Writings* (Chicago: Chicago Review
Press, 1975), 77.

8. Virginia Woolf, *Three Guineas* (New York: Harcourt, 1938), 109.

9. George Kateb, *Patriotism and Other Mistakes* (New Haven: Yale University Press, 2006).

10. In the background here is Josiah Royce, *Philosophy of Loyalty* (Nash-
ville, TN: Vanderbilt University Press, 1995). See Alasdair MacIntyre, *Is Patriotism a Virtue?* (Lawrence: University of Kansas, 1984) at: https://mirror.ex-
plodie.org/Is%20Patriotism%20a%20Virtue-1984.pdf. See William A. Galston,
"In Defense of a Reasonable Patriotism," Brookings Institution, July 23, 2018,
https://www.brookings.edu/research/in-defense-of-a-reasonable-patriotism/.

11. James Boswell, *The Life of Samuel Johnson* (London: Baldwin/Dilly,
1791), vol. 2, 478.

12. Thucydides, *History of the Peloponnesian War*, 2.60.6, at Perseus.Tufts
.edu, http://www.perseus.tufts.edu/hopper/text?doc=Perseus%3Atext%3A1999
.01.0200%3Abook%3D2%3Achapter%3D60.

13. Thucydides, *History*, 2.43.1. See Victoria Wohl, *Love among the Ruins:
The Erotics of Democracy in Classical Athens* (Princeton: Princeton University
Press, 2002).

14. Fannie Lou Hammer, speech of July 10, 1971, in *The Speeches of Fannie Lou Hamer: To Tell It Like It Is*, ed. Maegan Parker Brooks and Davis W.
Houck (Jackson: University Press of Mississippi, 2011), 136. Hamer also put
it this way: "Until I am free, you are not free either," in a speech at Madison,
Wisconsin, January 1971.

15. Simone de Beauvoir, *The Ethics of Ambiguity* (New York: Kensington, 1976), 133.

16. Beauvoir, *The Ethics of Ambiguity*, 133.

17. Simone de Beauvoir, *The Second Sex* (New York: Vintage Books, 2011), 577.

18. Nelson Mandela, *Long Walk to Freedom: The Autobiography of Nelson Mandela* (Boston: Little Brown, 1995), 624.

19. See Eric Beerbohm, *In Our Name: The Ethics of Democracy* (Princeton, NJ: Princeton University Press, 2012).

20. Albert Camus, *Resistance, Rebellion, and Death* (New York: Vintage, 1988), 14.

21. Camus, *Resistance, Rebellion, and Death*, 104.

22. Camus, *Resistance, Rebellion, and Death*, 269.

23. Albert Camus, *The Plague* (New York: Modern Library, 1948), 229.

24. See: Patrick Henry, "Albert Camus and the Secret of Le Chambon," *Tablet Magazine*, June 21, 2020, https://www.tabletmag.com/sections/arts -letters/articles/albert-camus-le-chambon, accessed February 26, 2021; and "Albert Camus' 'The Plague' and the Art of Living during Times of Catastrophe," *Waging Nonviolence*, April 14, 2020, https://wagingnonviolence.org/pod cast/albert-camus-the-plague-nonviolent-resistance-rescue-wwii-coronavirus/, accessed February 26, 2021.

25. Quoted in André Trocmé, *Jesus and the Nonviolent Revolution* (Rifton, NY: Plough Publishing House, 2011), vi.

26. One famous account of this is Daniel Goldhagen, *Hitler's Willing Executioners* (New York: Vintage, 1997).

27. Xenophon *Cyropaedia*, Book 1, para. 13, https://www.gutenberg.org/files/2085/2085-h/2085-h.htm.

28. Xenophon, *Memorabilia*, 3.7.9. This my translation, modified from *Xenophon in Seven Volumes*, trans. E. C. Marchant (Cambridge, MA: Harvard University Press; London: William Heinemann, 1923), http://www.perseus .tufts.edu/. Also compare with Thomas L. Pangle, *The Socratic Way of Life* (University of Chicago Press, 2018), 137. Pangle refers to Socrates as a "citizen philosopher."

29. John Locke, *Some Thoughts Concerning Education* in *The Works of John Locke in Nine Volumes*, 12th ed. (London: Rivington, 1824), vol. 8.

30. Jean-Jacques Rousseau, *Emile* (New York: Basic Books, 1979); See: Jonathan Marks, "Rousseau's Critique of Locke's Education for Liberty," *Journal of Politics* 74, no. 3 (2012): 694–706.

31. Jean-Jacques Rousseau, *The Social Contract*, in Rousseau, *The Social Contract and Discourses by Jean-Jacques Rousseau* (London and Toronto: J.M.

Dent and Sons, 1923), chapter 2, n.p., https://oll.libertyfund.org/title/cole-the-social-contract-and-discourses#Rousseau_0132_894.

32. Rousseau, "A Discourse on Political Economy," in Rousseau, *The Social Contract and Discourses*, n.p.

33. See: Catharine Macaulay, *Letters on Education. With observations on Religious and Metaphysical Subjects* (London: C. Dilly, 1790); Mary Wollstonecraft, *Thoughts on the Education of Daughters* (London: J. Johnson, 1787); Elizabeth Frazer (2011), "Mary Wollstonecraft and Catharine Macaulay on Education," *Oxford Review of Education* 37, no. 5, 603–17.

34. Macaulay, *Letters on Education*, 206–7.

35. Macaulay, *Letters on Education*, 192.

36. Wollstonecraft, *Thoughts on the Education of Daughters*, 61.

37. Wollstonecraft, *Thoughts on the Education of Daughters*, 63.

38. Mary Wollstonecraft, *A Vindication of the Rights of Woman with Strictures on Political and Moral Subjects* (London: J. Johnson, 1792), chapter 12, n.p., at Online Library of Liberty: https://oll.libertyfund.org/title/wollstonecraft-a-vindication-of-the-rights-of-woman.

39. John Dewey, *Democracy and Education* (New York: Macmillan, 1916).

40. Paulo Freire, *Pedagogy of the Oppressed* (London: Continuum, 2005).

41. Paulo Freire, *Pedagogy of Freedom: Ethics, Democracy, and Civic Courage* (Lanham, MD: Rowman & Littlefield, 1998), 13.

42. Nel Noddings, *Education and Democracy in the 21st Century* (New York: Teachers College, 2013), 23.

43. Nel Noddings, *Caring: A Feminine Approach to Ethics and Moral Education*, 2nd ed. (Berkeley: University of California Press, 2003). Also: Nel Noddings, ed., *Educating Citizens for Global Awareness* (New York: Teachers College, 2005).

44. "Transcript of Trump's Obscene Videotape," BBC News, October 9, 2016, https://www.bbc.com/news/election-us-2016-37595321.

CHAPTER 9: THE CONSTITUTION OF WISDOM

1. See Zachary Elkins, Tom Ginsburg, and James Melton, *The Endurance of National Constitutions* (Cambridge: Cambridge University Press, 2009).

2. "Retired Four-Star Military General Rips Mike Pence's 'Revolting Sycophancy' and 'Devotion' to Trump," *Salon*, March 15, 2020, https://www.salon.com/2020/03/14/retired-four-star-military-general-rips-mike-pences-revolting-sycophancy-and-devotion-to-trump_partner/.

3. Montesquieu, *Considerations on the Causes of the Grandeur and De-clension of the Roman Empire* in *The Complete Works of M. de Montesquieu* (London: T. Evans, 1777), vol. 3, chapter 1, n.p. https://oll.libertyfund.org/title/montesquieu-complete-works-vol-3#Montesquieu_0171-03_9.

4. Montesquieu, *Considerations on the Causes*, vol. 3, chapter 14, n.p. https://oll.libertyfund.org/title/montesquieu-complete-works-vol-3#Montesquieu_0171-03_371

5. A note to *Federalist* 47 explains the source of this quote from Montesquieu, which is traced to Montesquieu, *The Spirit of the Laws*, Book XI, chapter VI, ed. Neumann, I, 151–52. The editor explains, "James Madison may have been translating from a French edition of the work, for his quotations vary slightly from the standard English translation by Thomas Nugent," https://founders.archives.gov/documents/Madison/01-10-02-0266.

6. I have discussed some of this in Andrew Fiala, *Against Religions, Wars, and States* (Lanham, MD: Rowman & Littlefield, 2013), chapter 10. Among the sources consulted are: Robert A. Dahl, *How Democratic Is the American Constitution?* (New Haven, CT: Yale University Press, 2003); Robert A. Dahl, *Democracy and Its Critics* (New Haven, CT: Yale University Press, 1989); Sanford Levinson, *Our Undemocratic Constitution: Where the Constitutions Goes Wrong* (Oxford: Oxford University Press, 2006).

7. See Dahl, *How Democratic Is the American Constitution?*, chapter 3.

8. Sanford Levinson, *Framed: America's Fifty-One Constitutions and the Crisis of Governance* (Oxford: Oxford University Press, 2012), 389.

9. Sanford Levinson, "The Constitution is the Crisis," *The Atlantic*, October 1, 2019, https://www.theatlantic.com/ideas/archive/2019/10/the-constitution-is-the-crisis/598435/.

10. House Resolution 24 at https://www.congress.gov/bill/117th-congress/house-resolution/24.

11. Richard Hofstadter, *The American Political Tradition and the Men Who Made It* (New York: Vintage, 1948), 3.

12. Hofstadter, *The American Political Tradition*, 4.

13. Thomas Jefferson, *Notes on Virginia II, Correspondence 1782–1786*, in *The Works of Thomas Jefferson*, Federal Edition (New York and London, G.P. Putnam's Sons, 1904–1905), vol. 4, https://oll.libertyfund.org/title/jefferson-the-works-vol-4-notes-on-virginia-ii-correspondence-1782-1786 (n.p).

14. Jefferson, *Notes on Virginia II, Correspondence 1782–1786*, vol. 4, n.p.

15. Cicero, *Treatise on the Laws (De Legibus)*, Book III, https://oll.libertyfund.org/title/cicero-treatise-on-the-laws.

16. Cicero, "For C. Plancius" in Cicero, *Orations* (London: George Bell and Sons, 1886), vol. 3, 105–6.

17. Jean-Jacques Rousseau, *The Social Contract* in Rousseau, *The Social Contract and Discourses by Jean-Jacques Rousseau* (London and Toronto: J.M. Dent and Sons, 1923), chapter 2, n.p., https://oll.libertyfund.org/title/cole-the -social-contract-and-discourses#Rousseau_0132_894.

18. See "Trump and the Trapped Country," *New Yorker*, March 13, 2021, https://www.newyorker.com/news/our-columnists/trump-and-the-trapped -country.

19. Robert O. Paxton, *The Anatomy of Fascism* (New York: Vintage Books, 2005), 106.

20. Thomas Ricks, *First Principles: What America's Founders Learned from the Greeks and Romans and How That Shaped Our County* (New York: HarperCollins, 2020), xix.

21. George Washington to John Jay, August 15, 1786, https://founders.ar chives.gov/documents/Washington/04-04-02-0199.

22. John Adams to Louis Alexandre, Duc de La Rochefoucauld d'Anville, 1788, https://founders.archives.gov/documents/Adams/99-02-02-0449.

23. Diogenes Laertius, *The Lives of Eminent Philosophers* (Oxford: Oxford University Press, 2020), 261.

24. Newton Cannon—a Tennessee opponent of Jackson—reportedly said that Jackson was "a tyrant in every situation in which he has been placed," quoted in David Heidler and Jeanne Heidler, *The Rise of Andrew Jackson* (New York: Basic Books, 2018).

25. See "Why Andrew Jackson's Legacy Is So Controversial," History.com, August 29, 2018, https://www.history.com/news/andrew-jackson-presidency -controversial-legacy.

26. *Worcester v. Georgia*, 31 U.S. 515 (1832), https://supreme.justia.com/ cases/federal/us/31/515/.

27. Paul VanDevelder, *Savages and Scoundrels: The Untold Story of America's Road to Empire through Indian Territory* (New Haven CT: Yale University Press, 2009), 123.

28. Jefferson Davis, second inaugural address, February 22, 1862, https:// jeffersondavis.rice.edu/archives/documents/jefferson-davis-second-inaugural -address.

29. Frederick Douglass, "The Meaning of July Fourth for the Negro" (1852), in Frederick Douglass, *Selected Speeches and Writings* (Chicago: Chicago Review Press, 1975), 202,

30. See Malcolm Schofield, *Saving the City: Philosopher-Kings and Other Classical Paradigms* (London: Routledge, 1999).

31. Karl Popper, *The Open Society and Its Enemies*, vol. 1 (Princeton, NJ: Princeton University Press, first published 1945).

32. Leo Strauss, *City and Man* (Chicago: University of Chicago Press, 1964).

33. Allan Bloom, "Interpretive Essay," in Bloom's translation of Plato's *Republic* (New York: Basic Books, 1968), 410.

CHAPTER 10: CONCLUSION

1. This quote is traced to notes of what Madison said during the debates at the Constitutional Convention, July 11, 1787, https://avalon.law.yale.edu/18th_century/debates_711.asp.

APPENDIX A: TRUMP'S VIEW OF MORALITY IN CONTEXT

1. Originally at: http://www.trumptwitterarchive.com/; the archive has since migrated to: https://www.thetrumparchive.com/.

2. https://www.rev.com/blog/transcript-category/donald-trump-transcripts.

3. https://www.rev.com/blog/transcripts/donald-trump-speech-save-america-rally-transcript-january-6.

4. Originally at: https://www.whitehouse.gov/briefings-statements/president-donald-j-trumps-state-union-address/; now at archive: https://trumpwhitehouse.archives.gov/briefings-statements/president-donald-j-trumps-state-union-address-2/.

5. Originally at: https://www.whitehouse.gov/briefings-statements/president-donald-j-trumps-state-union-address/; now at archive: https://trumpwhitehouse.archives.gov/briefings-statements/president-donald-j-trumps-state-union-address-2/.

6. Donald Trump, *The America We Deserve* (New York: St. Martin's Press, 2000), chapter 1.

7. https://www.thetrumparchive.com/?searchbox=%22%23AmericaFirst%22.

8. https://www.thetrumparchive.com/?searchbox=%22ragan%22&results=1.

9. https://www.thetrumparchive.com/?searchbox=%22The+golden+rule+of+negotiation+%22&results=1.

10. Trump, *The Art of the Deal*, 367.

INDEX